Basic Home Repairs
Illustrated

By the Editors of Sunset Books and Sunset Magazine

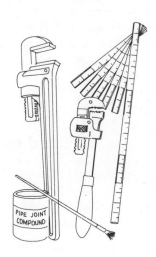

Lane Books · Menlo Park, California

Acknowledgments

Basic Home Repairs Illustrated focuses on the type of repair that demands fixing right now—leaks in plumbing, leaks in roofs, locks that will not work. It also deals extensively with repairs of long-term annoyances—squeaking floors or stairs, stuck windows, peeling wallpaper.

In every case the text assumes that you have never attempted such a repair in your life. As a result, the instructions will seem kindergartenish in those cases where you have some practical experience. We beg your indulgence in remembering that everybody faces each problem for a first time, so, somewhere, someone else will bless the thing you find too simple and grumble about one that makes you glad.

With that in mind, the following organizations deserve your thanks and ours for supplying much of the information presented here:

A&B Veteran Locksmith Shop; Agalite Bronson Company, Inc.; Armstrong Cork Company; Atlas Heating and Ventilating Company; Bickell Bros. Lumber & Building Supplies; Bud's Electric, Inc.; California Redwood Association; Devcon Corporation; Doors, Incorporated; Fraser-Johnston Furnaces; General Electric Company; Hardware Products Company; Heise's Plumbing and Heating; W. W. Henry Company; Hubbard & Johnson Lumber Company; Imperial Paper Company; Kirhill, Inc.; Kirsch Company; Macklanburg-Duncan Company; Naganuma Plumbing; Owens-Corning Fiberglas Company; Overhead Door Company of San Francisco; Pacific Gas & Electric Company; Edward J. Panky Distributors; Parker Weather Strip Company; Pemko Manufacturing Company; Peninsula Building Materials; R. L. Reaves Roofing Company; Richmond Glass Company; Robertshaw Controls Company, Grayson Controls Division; Roof Drainage Manufacturers' Institute; Schlage Lock Company; Sylvania/General Telephone and Electronics; Tuff-Kote Company; Westinghouse Electric Corporation; Wilhold Glues, Inc.; Window Shade Manufacturer's Association.

Special editorial research and writing by: Lee Klein, Bart Benedict, Richard Osborne, Wallace Tennyson, Esther Hornik, and Carol Blitzer.

Art direction (and unfailing source of information and advice): E. D. Bills. Drawings executed by Joseph Seney, Lawrence Laukhuf, and Dale Rusch. Cover design consultant was John Flack.

Edited by Bob Thompson

Executive Editor, Sunset Books: David E. Clark

Fifth Printing February 1973

Contents

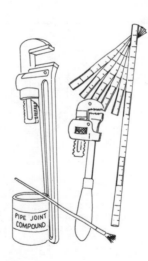

Plumbing systems

Short of fire, water is the most destructive force in a home when it gets out of control. Few plumbing failures turn into calamities, however, if met with prompt remedial steps.

There are two sides to a plumbing system. One is the fresh water supply; the other is waste disposal. The waste drains are often unpleasant to deal with, but they are simple in principle since water moves through them solely by the force of gravity. The fresh water system holds more pitfalls for the novice handyman because it is pressurized to about 50 pounds per square inch. Under this circumstance, fixing an old problem sometimes causes a new one. This is especially true in systems with galvanized iron pipes that are 25 years old, or older. These can become extremely fragile when corrosion has pitted the pipes deeply and frozen fittings rigid.

A home handyman of limited experience can successfully cure noisy toilets, a wide variety of small leaks in faucets, pipes and drains, and can free most sluggish drains. Extending a length of pipe is also within reach of even a novice. Complications begin to arise when a length of pipe in the middle of the fresh water system requires replacement, or when a main drain becomes blocked. A man with some experience can succeed if he approaches his problem cautiously. However, these types of difficulties may require a professional plumber.

This section provides basic remedies for the irritating small failures of plumbing, and also tells how to keep major breakdowns under control until a plumber arrives.

The sketch below explains a typical plumbing system and serves as an index for this section on plumbing.

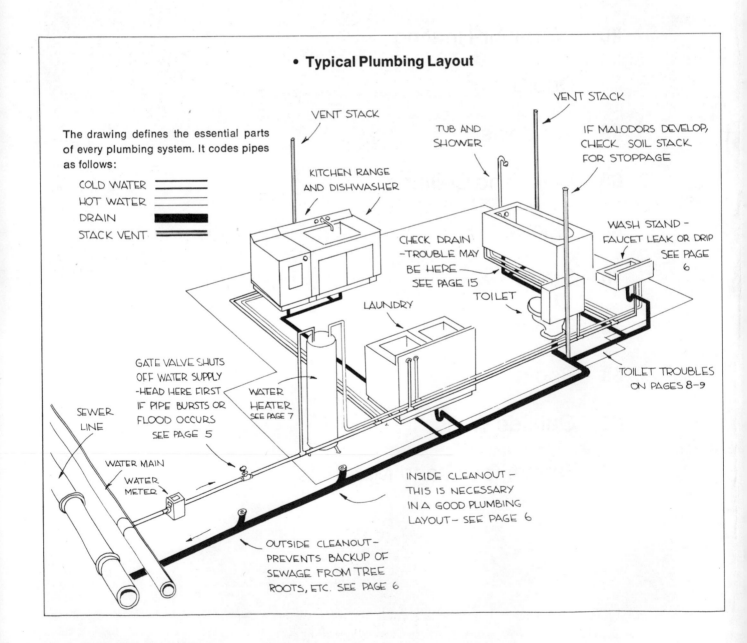

• Typical Plumbing Layout

The drawing defines the essential parts of every plumbing system. It codes pipes as follows:

COLD WATER
HOT WATER
DRAIN
STACK VENT

VENT STACK

KITCHEN RANGE AND DISHWASHER

TUB AND SHOWER

VENT STACK

IF MALODORS DEVELOP, CHECK SOIL STACK FOR STOPPAGE

CHECK DRAIN -TROUBLE MAY BE HERE - SEE PAGE 15

WASH STAND - FAUCET LEAK OR DRIP SEE PAGE 6

LAUNDRY

TOILET

GATE VALVE SHUTS OFF WATER SUPPLY -HEAD HERE FIRST IF PIPE BURSTS OR FLOOD OCCURS SEE PAGE 5

WATER HEATER SEE PAGE 7

TOILET TROUBLES ON PAGES 8-9

SEWER LINE

WATER MAIN

WATER METER

INSIDE CLEANOUT - THIS IS NECESSARY IN A GOOD PLUMBING LAYOUT - SEE PAGE 6

OUTSIDE CLEANOUT - PREVENTS BACKUP OF SEWAGE FROM TREE ROOTS, ETC. SEE PAGE 6

• First, Stop the Flood

When water breaks loose, the first thing to do is shut it off at the source. If you have time to think, pick the valve nearest the leak. But if things are moving too fast, head first for the gate valve and shut down the whole system while you plot the rest of your attack.

These are typical valves. Know where to find the ones in your house.

Gate valve, on the line from your water meter into the house, is the quickest, easiest way to shut down all water in the system for repairs.

Meter valve, requiring a wrench, does the same job as a gate valve, but more slowly. Since some homes do not have gate valves, it may be the choice.

Water heater inlet valve shuts off the flow into the tank and all hot water lines. The pressure relief valve (at left) does not shut off water.

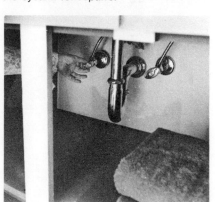

Sink shutoff valves affect only the connected faucet. Both hot and cold lines must be shut off before working on single valve faucets.

Stop toilet flooding by pushing tank ball down so it seats in outlet, then raising float ball to close inlet. Next, close inlet valve below tank.

• Patching a Leaky Pipe

Once a pipe begins to spring leaks, it probably is corroded enough to require replacement. But clamps can stop most leaks for a period of months.

All clamps should be used with a solid rubber blanket. For this, buy a sheet of rubber at a hardware store, or cut up an old inner tube.

Make pencil marks on the pipe so you can center the clamp over the leak.

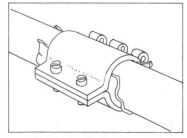

Sleeve clamp works best. It must fit pipe diameter exactly. Rubber blanket over leak seals the hole when pressure is exerted by the clamp.

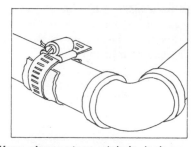

Hose clamp stops pinhole leak on any size pipe, so is handier to keep in stock than sleeve. Best sizes for fresh-water pipes: Nos. 16 and 12.

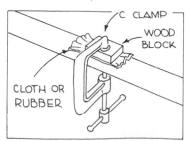

C-clamp coupled with rigid block (to spread pressure) and rubber blanket is a modestly successful temporary solution if no other clamp is at hand.

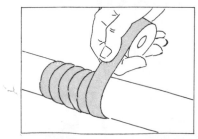

Plastic electrical tape stops pinhole leaks on copper or PVC pipe. Wrap three layers three inches on either side of leak. Overlap each turn.

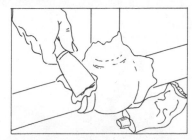

Epoxy putty can be used to halt leaks around pipe fittings where clamps will not work. Pipe must be dry. Each packet has specific instructions.

• Fixing Leaky Faucets

The exact point where a leak appears on a faucet is the best clue to finding the cause.

A spout drip is caused by a worn faucet washer or a corroded valve seat. A leak at the stem suggests a loose cap nut or worn cone bonnet packing. Water oozing below the cap nut indicates a worn bib washer. Water coming from the base of the faucet body seeps through a worn washer there.

To dismantle a faucet: (1) Shut off water at valve below sink, then open tap to drain the faucet. (2) Remove handle screw and handle. (3) Unscrew cap nut, covering jaws of wrench with adhesive or friction tape to avoid marring the chrome finish. (4) Unscrew stem with finger pressure and lift it out.

These steps give access to all points except the washer at the base of the faucet body. It is reached by loosening the slip nut that connects the faucet body to the pipe. Raise the faucet body away from the pipe rather than trying to bend the pipe if the fit is too close to remove the washer.

In replacing a faucet washer, check the seat to be sure it is not pitted or otherwise rough. If the seat is rough an inexpensive "reseater kit" can be purchased to grind it smooth again.

On reassembling the faucet, tighten the cap nut just enough so it does not leak. Screwing the nut down hard can cause rapid wear on the stem.

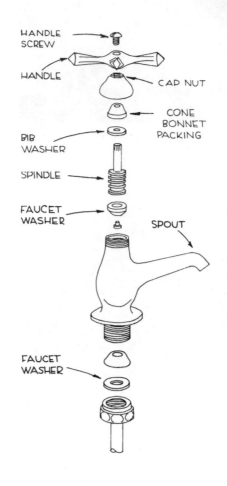

HANDLE SCREW
HANDLE
CAP NUT
CONE BONNET PACKING
BIB WASHER
SPINDLE
FAUCET WASHER
SPOUT
FAUCET WASHER

SINGLE VALVE FAUCETS

Many single valve faucets cannot be repaired except by the manufacturer. Some now come with a removable, replaceable cartridge like the one shown. Shut off both hot and cold water valves below the sink before exploring the inner workings of these faucets.

WASHER SIZES

This chart shows washers at exact size, with their trade designations as well as actual measurements. It can be used to match sizes of washers too worn to be read for size.

The code size embossed on the washer should be turned toward the seat when the washer is installed.

Before buying replacements, check also to see whether you want a flat washer or a conical one. Make sure it's like the old one.

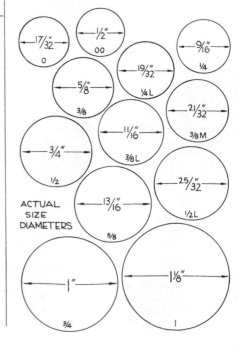

LEAKING VALVES

Valves sometimes spring leaks at their stems or bases because of failed washers. Techniques for replacing washers are much the same as those used for faucets, except that some valves do not have cap nuts and must be wrenched off their pipes for access to the washers.

In the latter case, use one wrench on the flattened flange at the base of the valve, and a second wrench on the pipe to exert counterpressure. Failure to use the second wrench risks splitting the pipe by twisting it.

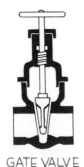

GATE VALVE

GLOBE VALVE

ANGLE VALVE

• Water Heaters

Water heaters, whether electric or gas-fired, are the least troublesome of all appliances according to utility company service records. That is to say, they suffer very few mechanical failures. But there are a few nuisance factors to deal with.

Two of the most common nuisances are leaking pressure relief valves and drain valves. These problems are described separately on this page. Otherwise, the problems center on how much hot water you can get, and how hot it comes from the tap. The following are variables to think about if you are dissatisfied with the temperatures of your hot water supply.

No hot water. In a gas-fired heater: (a) Pilot light is extinguished. *Relight according to instructions on tank.* (b) Gas supply valve on supply pipe inadvertently has been closed—turned so handle is at right angles to direction of the pipe. *Open it—turn handle so it is parallel to the pipe. Then relight pilot according to instructions on tank.* (c) Thermostat has been shut off. Some models have exposed thermostat switch. *Turn switch to full "on" position.*

In an electric heater: (a) Heater switch has been shut off. *Turn it to "on."* (b) Fuse has blown in circuit supplying the heater. *Restore circuit (see method on page 21).*

Not enough hot water, or not hot enough. In a gas-fired heater: (a) Thermostat dial set too low. *If thermostat is in view, adjust upward.* Normal is 140°; a range of 10° on either side will compensate for temperature of water delivered from the mains. If you cannot find a thermostat it is probably buried in the insulating layer around the tank, and will require a visit by a utility company serviceman. (b) Valve on supply line partially closed. *Open full—so the handle parallels the pipe exactly.*

In an electric heater: Any difficulty with a thermostat will require a visit by your utility company's serviceman. The thermostats must be buried in the insulation to work properly, so are out of reach. Disturbing the insulation is almost certain to make a thermostat function less accurately than before. A second cause of too little hot water in an electric water heater is failure of one heating element—this requires a repairman. Utility company servicemen do not make repairs, only adjustments.

Either type of heater may not hold enough water to meet your needs. A full bath or big wash may take 30 gallons of water. Small heaters need as much as half an hour to recover from the use of this large a volume.

Water too hot. In a gas-fired heater: Thermostat set too high. *Adjust lower—140° is normal.* If steam or boiling water comes from a tap, the thermostat has failed and must be replaced. Should this happen, do *not* shut off the inlet valve. Its being open allows the water to flow back into the main system, thus keeping pressure below the explosion point. If possible, shut the heater off until a repairman can be called. If you must continue to have hot water, the heater will operate, although furiously. (A heater with a pressure relief valve will not emit steam, except through the safety valve.)

In an electric heater: (a) Thermostat set too high. *Many are purposely set high to cover peak use periods.* (b) Heating element not grounded. Symptom is excessively hot water only after long idle periods, such as early in the morning. *A utility*

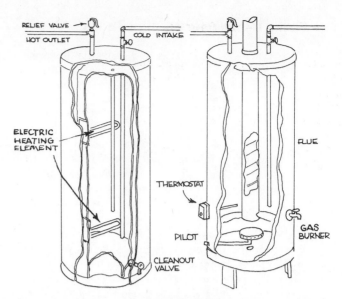

company serviceman will adjust the thermostat; you will need a repairman to ground the heating element.

PRESSURE RELIEF VALVES

In many communities hot water heaters are required by law to have a pressure relief valve. Where a home system is "closed" by other plumbing devices so that pressure cannot escape back into the mains, such a valve is also required.

These valves allow steam to escape safely in case of malfunction in the hot water heater's thermostat. They are invaluable for safety purposes, but also pose something of a nuisance because they tend to leak with every slight surge in pressure.

There is no way to prevent the valve from leaking since that is its specific purpose. The recourse, therefore, is to catch the leaking water.

One way is to attach a hose to the valve, and run it outdoors, or into a drain. The location of a heater may make this impractical or unsightly.

A second approach to collecting the water is with a waterproof pan under the heater. Ideally, the pan will have a drain hole that lets water escape through the floor to earth or to a drain.

If a pressure relief valve leaks constantly, it is out of adjustment. A utility company serviceman can adjust it to withstand higher pressure.

DRAIN VALVES

Nearly all recently-made hot water heaters carry a drain valve at the bottom—it looks like a regular hose bib—so owners can keep the tank free of accumulated sediments.

The valve should be opened every two to six months on a new tank, depending on the amount of dirt and rust in your water pipes.

The valve is fine if used regularly from the start. But, some experts warn, suddenly opening one of these valves after a tank has been in service for more than two years is an invitation to a chronic leak. The valve freezes in position if unused; opening one literally breaks a seal. The only repair is to take a tank out of service and replace the entire valve, a costly job requiring a plumber. The reduction in service life of the heater is likely to be less costly than replacing the valve.

•Troubles with Toilet Tanks

The mechanisms within toilet tanks vary somewhat from one manufacturer to another, but most are designed to produce enough water for thorough flushing of the bowl through the following sequence of steps:

1. Handle causes the tank ball to lift, opening the outlet so water can flow from tank to bowl.

2. Tank ball sinks slowly back into place, closing the outlet.

3. Float ball drops with water level, opening the ballcock assembly, through which fresh water flows into the tank.

4. Rising water pushes the float ball up until it closes the ballcock assembly, shutting off the supply of fresh water when the tank is full.

The problems a homeowner can remedy in these mechanisms are listed with their symptoms, causes, and cures.

Before attempting any repair, shut off the water intake valve (usually just below the tank on its left side), then flush the toilet to empty the tank. If you have to work at the bottom of the tank, sponge it dry.

Singing toilet. Water continually enters tank through slightly open ballcock assembly (then is drained into bowl through overflow tube). The valve makes a continuous high-pitched sound. The water level is at the top of the overflow tube. Either the float ball or the ballcock assembly is at fault.

If the float ball is partially filled with water, it will not rise to the proper level. Replace a leaky ball with a new one. Plastic ones will not corrode as old copper ones did.

If the float ball is simply riding too high, bend the arm downward to cause the ball to close the ballcock assembly sooner. If the tank does not have a water level mark, set the float to shut off the water supply when the tank has filled to within 1½ inches of the top of the overflow tube.

If the float ball is working properly, the trouble is in the ballcock assembly. In most cases the washers will have failed. It is much simpler to replace the whole unit than to replace the washers, but costs more.

To replace the whole unit, shut off the water, drain and dry the tank, and then begin the mechanical steps: (1) Unclip fill tube from overflow tube. (2) Unscrew the float ball arm from the ballcock (and save both pieces if they are sound). (3) Working on the underside of the tank, loosen the coupling nut and remove the lock nut and washer. The unit will be free to move.

A new unit is installed as follows: (1) Remove coupling and lock nuts, and washer from shank. (2) Place unit in tank. (3) Secure unit loosely with washer, lock and coupling nuts. (4) Position unit so that refill tube can be clipped in place with its mouth over overflow tube, and so float ball can rise and fall freely. (5) Clip refill tube in place. (6) Attach float ball arm to ballcock. (7) Tighten lock and coupling nuts fully. (8) Turn water on at valve and allow tank to fill. Adjust the float ball arm if necessary to obtain proper water level in full tank.

To replace a washer in an old ballcock assembly: (1) Shut off the water and flush the tank to empty it. (2) Remove float ball and its arm. (3) Unscrew the ballcock lever and lift it

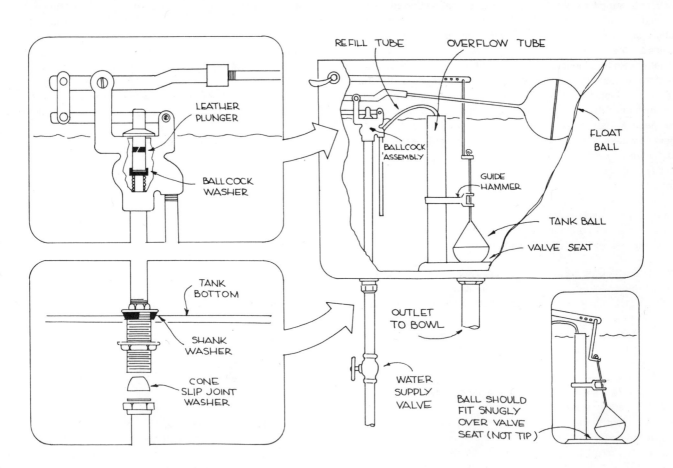

away from the brass cap of the assembly. (4) Unscrew the cap from the tube and pull it up to reveal the washer. You may have to pull the split leather piston plunger packing from its groove to get at the washer. Be sure the leather is firmly in place after replacing the washer.

Reverse the steps to reassemble the unit.

Running toilet. The tank ball does not seat properly in the outlet. Water can be seen flowing as ripples into the bowl. The tank ball itself may be worn and in need of replacement. The tank ball seat may need cleaning. Or the tank ball guide may be bent, mis-aligned or corroded (especially in the older style shown on the facing page).

If the tank ball is to be replaced, unscrew it from the bottom end of the guide and replace with a new one.

If the tank ball seat needs cleaning, empty the tank of water and dry it, then sand the dried seat with emery paper until it is smooth to the touch. Remove the tank ball for easier access to the seat.

If the guide is corroded, sand the wire smooth with emery paper. If the guide does not drop freely, be sure it is not bent or out of alignment. The old wire guides can corrode beyond saving, in which case they can be replaced. A guide out of alignment is repositioned by loosening the screws holding its hammers to the overflow tube, then tightening them again. The sketch below shows some more recently developed tank ball assemblies. Both are attempts to overcome the shaky guide system shown in the main sketch and described in the paragraphs above.

These assemblies succeed as guides. But, like the older model, they are subject to wear of the tank ball itself. To replace the type shown on the right, disconnect the vertical rod from the handle rod, and lift the rod and ball out together. The ball is of the conventional type. The type shown on the left is more complex, using the overflow tube as the guide. When the ball

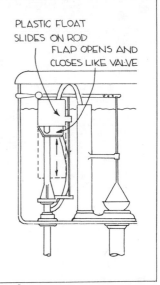

NEW TYPE OF BALLCOCK

If you are in need of a new ballcock assembly, you may wish to look into a certain new type. The new development operates with a positive action valve that allows the water to run at full force until the tank is full, when it shuts off crisply. There is no float ball or arm, hence no protracted filling process with all its whistling or singing. The units are priced at about the same level as conventional ones in most major hardware and plumbing supply shops.

PLASTIC FLOAT SLIDES ON ROD

FLAP OPENS AND CLOSES LIKE VALVE

Leak at base of tank. There are three potential sources of leaks at the base of the tank. One is at the outlet. The second is where the outlet pipe joins the bowl. The third is at the intake pipe (the same one that leads to the ballcock assembly). Only the third is easy to deal with. The first two require removing the tank from the wall, and are best done by a plumber.

To replace a leaking washer on the intake pipe, loosen the lock and coupling nuts. Lift the ballcock assembly just enough to free the washer if it does not slip out easily. Replace the washer and resecure the unit.

Toilets sometimes leak at the base of the bowl when a large gasket there fails. Replacing the gasket requires dismantling the tank and the bowl, and is almost always a job best done by a professional plumber.

Inadequate flush. If not enough water flows into the bowl for proper flushing, it is most likely because the tank ball is seating too soon because its guide is set too low in an old-model toilet. Newer units do not have to be adjusted. To adjust an old unit, loosen the screws that secure the guide hammers to the overflow tube, and raise the hammers about ½-inch, allowing the tank ball to float longer before it drops into its seat again.

Once in a while an inadequate flush can be caused by the float ball being adjusted too low to allow a full tank of water. Bend the float ball arm upward.

An inadequate flush may also be caused by clogged outlet ports around the underside of the rim. This is a fairly common source of trouble in communities with "hard" water. Watching the water action during a flush will reveal this as a cause if little water washes down the surface of the bowl, or if there are sizeable gaps between streams of water. The condition is not easy to cure. Start by scrubbing the ports vigorously with a stiff brush. If this does not succeed, form a tight loop on the end of a piece of wire and use this to ream each port. The job will go better and faster if you hold a small hand mirror down in the bowl so that you can watch what is happening with the wire.

If the bowl is emptying sluggishly, the trouble is in the drain rather than the tank. See pages 15 and 16.

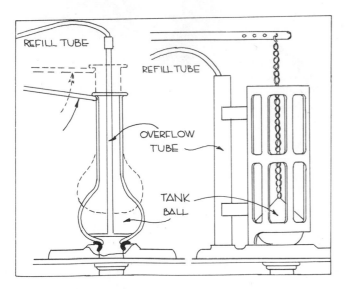

REFILL TUBE

REFILL TUBE

OVERFLOW TUBE

TANK BALL

has to be replaced, disconnect the refill tube and lock nut, then lift the plastic sleeve straight up. The replacement ball must be identical with the worn one to fit properly. This type uses a special rubber collar to adapt the outlet; wipe this collar clean before replacing the ball since sediment collected on it may be the source of the leak.

• Pipe and Pipefitting

Replacing a hose bib or a garden water line are the kinds of pipefitting tasks novice plumbers can do. All they call for are the two simple skills of plumbing: measuring and assembling a joint.

A professional plumber earns his money in plotting layouts and making substantial alterations on old ones. These fields should be left to him for diverse reasons, the main one being that you are dealing with a complicated system. Like any other system, it will transmit and even magnify mistakes.

There is no easy distinction between a job best suited for a plumber and a job a home handyman can do. Don't tackle a job that you have not helped do, or that you have not seen done enough times to allow you to think through the complete sequence of steps.

Three generalities are worth remembering:

Try to use as few fittings as possible. With fewer fittings there are fewer chances for leaks.

If you strip the thin galvanized metal coating off a length of pipe, paint it to prevent rust.

If you are connecting copper (see page 12) to galvanized iron pipe be sure to isolate the two with a 12-inch section of brass pipe, or a dielectric or insulated union. Otherwise you are likely to induce electrolysis, the rapid corrosion of pipe caused by chemical interactions between copper and iron.

TOOLS YOU NEED

For simple pipefitting using pre-cut, pre-threaded pipe, tool requirements are extremely simple:

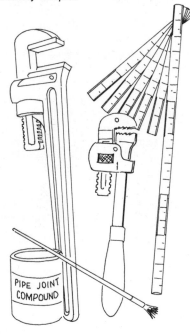

PIPE JOINT COMPOUND

• Two pipe wrenches. One must be 14 inches long for proper leverage. The other can be 10 to 14 inches long.

• Yardstick, or some other rigid rule that can be held against a pipe for measuring.

• Pipe compound and a stiff brush to apply it *or* a spool of fluorocarbon tape. The tape is less messy, but more costly.

Pre-cut, pre-threaded pipe comes in lengths up to one foot at hardware stores. Many stores will also cut and thread lengths of pipe to order. For major jobs, measuring and threading should be done as the job goes along to avoid costly mistakes. A competent amateur plumber can rent pipe-threading equipment for a complex assembling job.

TECHNIQUES TO KNOW

The two basic skills of plumbing are measuring and assembling joints.

Measuring pipe between two fittings. (1) Measure the distance between the centers of the two pipes. (2) Subtract for each fitting an amount equal to the inside diameter of the pipe. That is, for a ¾-inch pipe, subtract ¾-inch for each fitting. In the example photo there are two fittings, so the total amount subtracted is 1½ inches.

Assembling pipe. (1) With an old toothbrush, brush out the threads of both pipe and fittings so they can fit cleanly. (2) Brush a light coat of pipe compound on all outside threads, *or* wrap the outside threads with fluorocarbon tape. (3) Screw pipe and fitting together as far as they will go by hand. (4) Then, slowly and gently, tighten the joint with two wrenches. Use one to hold the already-installed pipe or fitting rigid, and the second to turn the new pipe or fitting tightly into place. (5) Turn on water and inspect for leaks. You may need an extra quarter or half turn for a complete seal.

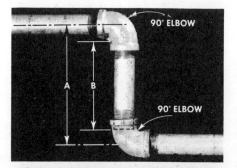

FLUSHING SEDIMENT FROM PIPES

Working on pipes almost always produces bits of foreign matter in the lines whether you do the work or the water district is working on the mains.

These solids, along with rust that forms in aging pipes, can clog the aerators on faucets, and even diminish the flow in seriously affected pipes.

There is no magic cure, but you can flush a considerable amount of material out of pipes this way: (1) Remove—and clean—aerators on faucets. (2) Close the valve that controls the line you wish to clean. This may be the inlet valve on the water heater, or the gate valve. (3) Open wide the faucet at the farthest point from the valve, and a second faucet nearer the valve. (4) With a rag, plug the faucet nearer the valve, but do not shut it off. (5) Open the gate valve and let water run through the farther faucet for as long as sediment continues to appear.

TYPES OF FITTINGS

Pipefittings are used to join sections of pipe; to change the direction in which a pipe runs; to reduce or expand the pipe so that it can be joined to a different size pipe; and to plug the end of a pipe.

The union is used to join two pipes separated by a short gap, especially when one pipe leads to an appliance. A bushing joins a pipe and fitting of unequal size. A bell reducer joins two pipes of unequal size. A coupling joins pipes of equal size. Nipples join pipes separated by wider gaps than a union can reach.

Tees allows a branch to tap into a main line. A reducing tee allows the use of a smaller pipe for the branch.

To turn corners, elbows join pipes of equal size. A Street Elbow joins pipes of differing size in combination with some other fitting.

BUSHING

BELL REDUCER

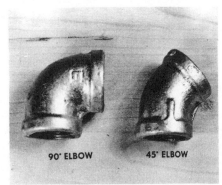

90° ELBOW   45° ELBOW

90° STREET ELBOW   COUPLING

UNION

REDUCING TEE

TEE

NIPPLES

COUPLING

PLUG

REPLACING A PIPE

Removing an old, leaking pipe from a system and installing a new length can be a touchy business. This technique is the gentlest way to get old pipe out. It also minimizes strain on remaining old pipe when a new section is installed.

(1) Shut water off at gate valve and drain the system by opening the lowest faucet in the house. (2) With a fine-toothed hacksaw, cut clear through the piece of pipe you wish to remove. Have the section braced firmly so sawing does not cause any motion in the pipes. Also, do not let a heavy stub sag down when the cut is finished. (3) Using two wrenches (see example sketch), unscrew each stub from its fitting. (4) Replace the old pipe with *two* new sections, tightening

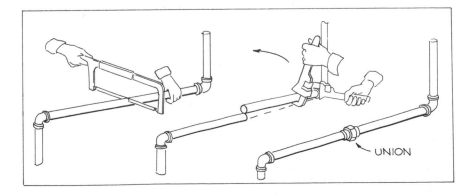

UNION

each into its fitting individually. Allow a gap equal to the inside diameter of the pipe between the two sections to receive a union. (5) Install the union, which can be tightened without exerting pressure on any other part of the system. (If you are sure of your measurement, fit the union's two halves onto the pipes before you install them in the existing fittings. Then there will be no need to use a wrench on the pipes once they have been fitted into the existing system.)

WORKING WITH COPPER PIPE

Copper pipe, used more and more, is fitted in a different way than galvanized iron pipe. Joints are soldered tight rather than turned on threads. So working with it requires a different set of tools and skills.

You need a fine-toothed hacksaw, a round file, a gas torch, solder (in the form of wire), soldering flux, and some fine steel wool.

To join a pipe to a fitting: (1) Cut the pipe to length with the hacksaw. Measure as with galvanized iron pipe. See page 10. (2) File the cut smooth and remove all burrs. (3) At the end to be fitted, clean one inch of the pipe with fine steel wool until it is shiny and bright. 4) Coat this shiny tip with a thin layer of flux. (5) Press pipe and fitting together with a slight twisting motion so the flux is spread properly. Align the fitting properly if you are turning a corner. (6) Clamp the pipe in a vise, or otherwise support it so you do not have to hold it. (7) Heat the fitting with the gas torch. Aim only at the thickest part of the fitting. Do not aim at the pipe. (8) When the fitting is properly hot, solder will melt on contact and will be drawn into the fitting by capillary action. A good joint requires about one inch of wire. Professional plumbers bend the tip of the soldering wire before they start as a ready measure of how much to use.

Trying to solder too quickly results in a poor, probably leaky joint. If the fitting is not hot enough, no capillary action takes place, and the solder itself is likely to crystallize as it cools.

A fitting that is to take two or three pieces of pipe should be attacked as one job. Reheating a fitting to add a pipe almost always damages the existing joint.

Copper pipe and galvanized iron pipe cannot be mixed without safeguarding against electrolysis. See page 10.

To dismantle an existing joint: Melt the old solder by heating the fitting with a gas torch until the solder in the joint becomes liquid. Then pull the pipe in a straight line. You may need to twist it slightly to free it from the solder.

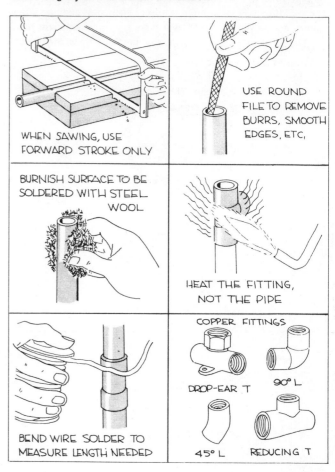

WHEN SAWING, USE FORWARD STROKE ONLY

USE ROUND FILE TO REMOVE BURRS, SMOOTH EDGES, ETC.

BURNISH SURFACE TO BE SOLDERED WITH STEEL WOOL

HEAT THE FITTING, NOT THE PIPE

BEND WIRE SOLDER TO MEASURE LENGTH NEEDED

COPPER FITTINGS

DROP-EAR T   90° L

45° L   REDUCING T

CURING WATER HAMMER

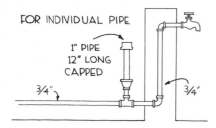

FOR INDIVIDUAL PIPE

1" PIPE 12" LONG CAPPED

3/4"   3/4"

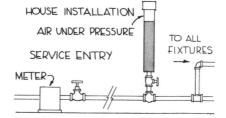

HOUSE INSTALLATION

AIR UNDER PRESSURE

SERVICE ENTRY

TO ALL FIXTURES

METER

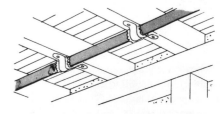

Water hammer, the sound of pipes shuddering, comes from three causes: loss of air cushion, no air cushion designed into the system, or unsupported pipes.

Loss of air cushion. Most water systems have short sections of vertical pipe rising above each faucet as the sketch shows. These sections hold air that cushions the shock when flowing water is stopped by a closing valve. To restore lost air, take these steps: (1) Check toilet tank to be sure it is full, then shut off valve just below the tank. (2) Close the gate valve, the

main valve between your meter and the house. (3) Open the highest and lowest faucets in the house to drain all water from pipes. (4) Close the two faucets and re-open the gate valve. (5) Normal water flow will re-establish itself for each faucet when you turn it on. There will be a few grumbles from the pipes before the first water arrives.

Lack of air cushion. A master air chamber can be added to a plumbing system designed without air cushions. Modestly

experienced handymen can do the installation, but it is a relatively inexpensive job for a plumber. If you plan to tackle the job, the techniques are similar to those for installing a pressure-reducing valve. See page 14.

Unsupported pipes. Pipes not anchored securely to framing members of the house may shudder when a valve is closed. U-brackets will secure the pipes. A rubber or felt blanket in the bracket adds insurance against rattle.

PATCHING A LEAKY HOSE

Hoses with pinhole leaks can be fixed by wrapping them with electrician's tape —the black, shiny-surfaced plastic type. To begin, the hose should be completely dry. It helps if both hose and tape are warm so the tape can adhere firmly.

Wrap at least two inches on each side of the leak, overlapping each turn by half the width of the tape. Three or four layers are enough.

A hose that is split but worth saving has to be cut into two sections and re-joined with a special clamp, shown in the sketch. The claws can be tapped into place with a hammer (and pried up again

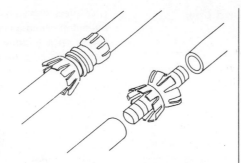

with a screwdriver for re-use). When a hose end splits, a new coupling can be installed in much the same way. Cut off old coupling and two inches of hose, then clinch the new coupling in place.

PATCHING PVC PIPE

PVC (polyvinylchloride) pipe is as common as galvanized iron in the gardens of many recent subdivisions. Easy and inexpensive to install, it is also easy and inexpensive to repair. A leaking pipe can be taped in the same way as a hose, but only if it is not buried. It is better to cut the leak out of the pipe and re-join the severed sections with a union; or, if the split is a long one, with a new length of pipe and two unions.

Plastic pipe fittings are ridged rather than threaded. It takes real force to push

joints together, and they cling firmly, but to guarantee a leakproof joint many installers use a stainless steel hose clamp at each fitting.

PVC comes in ½, ¾, and 1-inch sizes (inside diameters). Typically a lawn sprinkler system uses ¾-inch pipe for its main lines, and ½-inch for branch lines. No. 16 hose clamps fit both.

Fittings correspond to those used with galvanized pipe. Fit the pipe when it is warm—it is more pliable. Align fittings before clamping them to avoid twisting the pipe.

Fine-toothed hacksaws cut PVC cleanly if you need a replacement length.

Joints are made watertight by using hose clamps (stainless steel).

PVC pipe joints can be fit together easily using only hand pressure.

Brace PVC wherever it is above ground. It will not stand much strain.

CLEARING CLOGGED SPRINKLER HEADS

Sprinkler heads are quite simple mechanically. If they misbehave, it is usually because of dirt-clogged water jets.

The accompanying sketch shows a fairly complex type, but one that is easily cleaned.

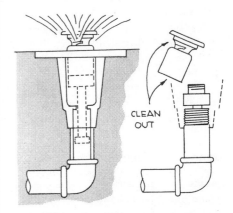

CLEAN OUT

(1) Insert a screwdriver in the notch between the core and the housing, and lift the core. This will reveal two flattened sides of the core. (2) Use a wrench to unscrew the top piece of the core. (3) With a wire or other sharp object dislodge any foreign matter in the core. Tightening and loosening the deflector will help. (5) With top part of core still off, turn on the sprinkler to flush dirt out of the pipe and lower part of the unit. (6) Replace top part or core unit after the flushing has been finished.

If your sprinkler head does not have a core that extends, the screw in the top of the head will usually loosen several turns so that cap fits loosely atop the body of the sprinkler. Do this, then turn water on to flush dirt out of the jets. Let it run for several minutes. Tighten the cap down again, and check action of water.

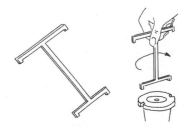

If a housing of any type is cracked, or the unit consistently malfunctions, it should be replaced. A special wrench will loosen it from the tee that secures it to the main line. The wrench is shown in the sketch. It is specially designed to avoid uneven strain on pipes or fittings.

• Water Pressure—High and Low

Most appliances and valves that use water are engineered to take 50 to 60 pounds of pressure per square inch (abbreviated as psi).

Mains deliver water at pressures as high as 150 psi, and as low as 10 psi. Excess pressure is much simpler to cure than a deficiency.

The symptoms of high pressure are dishwashers that shut off with loud clangs, or faucets that spray wildly when first turned on. High pressures usually occur in houses on the lower slopes of steep hills, or in subdivisions where high pressure is maintained as a matter of fire protection. Above-normal pressure can be cured easily and inexpensively by the installation of a reducing valve, described below.

The low pressure symptom is an extremely thin trickle of water from faucets. Chronic low pressure is usually found in homes on hills above reservoir level, or in old buildings with pipes badly clogged by scale and rust. Episodic low pressure occurs during peak service hours in many communities and is no fault of a home's location or plumbing. Whatever the cause, cures are either very expensive or mechanically infeasible—ranging from complete replacement of the plumbing to building your own reservoir in a tank on a tower above the house.

Some modest improvements can be made. Systems with the beginnings of clogged pipes can regain some lost pressure by flushing the system (see page 10). Low pressure can also be alleviated in some cases by installing a larger meter and larger supply line from the street. The pressure does not actually rise, but larger volume compensates.

MEASURING PRESSURE

To measure pressure, you will need a gauge of the type shown. One costs less than the fee a plumber would charge to come to your house with his gauge.

Pressure gauge fits on hose bib.

The gauge will attach to any regular hose bib. Measure pressure at mid-morning of a weekday, when it is most likely to be at its average level. For an accurate reading, turn the bib open full with no other water running anywhere in the house.

Ask your water district for its pressure reading for your area in order to have a comparison figure.

The maximum workable pressure in a house is about 60 psi. Most appliances will operate with as little as 15 psi, but a 50-foot garden hose requires 30 psi to deliver a decent stream.

INSTALLING A REDUCING VALVE

A reducing valve on the supply line leading from the main in the street to your house can diminish pressure to suit your exact needs without appreciably lowering the volume of water you can draw.

The valve must go between the meter and the gate valve. The most convenient place is usually where the supply pipe comes out of the ground to go into the house.

Once the valve is in place and adjusted, it keeps water in the house at a selected pressure. Most are factory-set at 50 psi, but nearly all models have adjusting screws so the homeowner can get whatever pressure works best for him—or can change pressure as water supply changes with the seasons.

Two makes are shown in the photos. Both have filters on their inlet sides, which help keep out sand or metal filings that sometimes follow work on the mains. Filters should be cleaned twice a year.

If possible, reducing valves should be installed on a horizontal length of pipe. If you must use a vertical pipe be sure the valve you buy will function in that position. Some types do not.

The top photo shows an ideal installation. The valve is horizontal and does not govern water lines to the garden. (If you cannot keep high pressure in garden lines you may need to replace some sprinkler heads with low-pressure types, or else have fewer heads on each line.)

Any time you adjust the valve—for higher pressure during dry summer months, for example—use a gauge of the type shown at left and in the installa-

tion photo. For this measure, one faucet should be running in the house since the pressure reducing valve needs water flowing through it to get an accurate adjustment.

A reducing valve closes the water system in your house—makes it impossible for water to flow back out into the mains. If you install such a valve you will also be required to have a pressure relief valve on your hot-water heater. (See page 7.)

Ideal installation is horizontal.

Some models can be placed vertically.

• Clearing Blocked Drains

The best defense against blocked drains is a good offense—regular cleaning with a caustic drain-pipe cleaner. But if one of your drains has become sluggish or completely stopped, several remedies offer themselves.

The first is a plumber's friend which uses alternating pressure and suction to loosen a block. It can work only on blocks close to the affected fixture. To increase its effectiveness, plug the overflow drain of a sink or tub with a wet rag. A dozen rapid push-pulls should be enough if the device is going to work at all.

Second, try a caustic drain cleaner. Any of these should be used in strict accordance with the manufacturer's instructions. None should be poured into standing water in an enamelled or porcelain fixture. Two consecutive doses are the maximum.

If these approaches do not work, the blockage is probably hard, or deep in the system, and will yield only to a snake or a jet of water from a hose. The approach points are through waste vents, or cleanouts in the drains, or a trap.

First, locate the block. This requires some knowledge of your plumbing layout. The accompanying sketch shows how to analyze a typical problem. Should a block occur between the sink and Point A, only the sink will drain poorly. A block at or near Point B will cause water to back up into the bathtub as well as impeding the drains of sink, tub and toilet. If the block is at Point C, no drain will flow properly.

Once you have a clear idea of where the blockage rests, attack it through whichever access gives you the straightest angle of approach. In the example, Point A would be reached best from the sink trap. Point B would be most accessible through the waste vent. Point C would be approached through the cleanout.

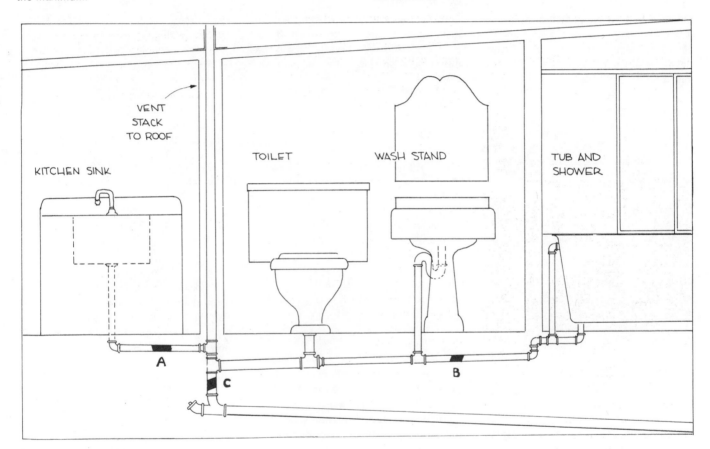

VENT STACK TO ROOF

KITCHEN SINK

TOILET

WASH STAND

TUB AND SHOWER

A   C   B

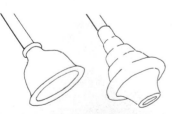

Plumber's friend breaks up blockages close to a fixture by alternately exerting pressure, then suction. The molded model is generally the more efficient, particularly in toilet bowl.

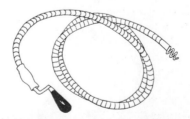

Plumber's snakes come in lengths from 10 to 50 feet. A good one has a cable that turns inside an armored sheath. Rotating the inner cable causes the tip to burrow through the drain blockage.

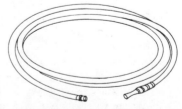

Garden hose can substitute for a snake in attempting to free a block deep in the drains. Hose is fed slowly into the drain, then turned on to force a powerful blast of water against the block.

GETTING AT DEEP BLOCKS IN PLUMBING

There are two ways to get at blocks deep in drains: through the vents on the roof or through cleanouts on the drain lines themselves.

Choose the method that provides the straightest approach to the blockage.

The only tool needed is either a plumber's snake or a garden hose with plenty of water pressure. Neither tool is automatically better than the other. Since few homes have a 50-foot snake to get to the deepest parts of a drain, most home handymen try a hose first. Feeding a hose into a drain demands patience. It must go an inch at a time or it will kink and bind. The nozzle should be set to yield its most forcible stream. Several short blasts are better than one long one.

Snakes, which can be rented in most communities, are easier to use.

Through the vent. If the blockage is complete, it may be better to use a snake from the beginning. Water backs up from the hose rapidly, and can flood through fixtures. If you do use a hose, post scouts at the fixtures.

Through a cleanout. The plugs have square nuts on them which almost always are hard to loosen. Stiff plugs can be freed by clamping a pipe wrench on the nut and tapping the wrench handle with a hammer.

Do not be too hasty to open a cleanout at the bottom of a vertical drain. If the pipe is packed full of waste, it will run out of the open cleanout faster than you want it to.

CLEANING TRAPS

Traps, the U-shaped pipes beneath sinks, are designed to keep sewer gasses from seeping into your home. They do that but become plugged from time to time. Also, old traps can spring leaks at the bottom of the U if corroded.

Most blocked traps will yield to a plumber's friend or a caustic drain pipe cleaner. But occasionally one must be opened to be cleared or replaced.

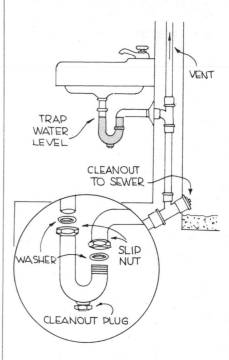

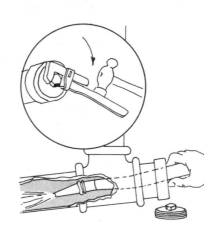

To dismantle a trap: (1) Place a good-sized pan beneath the trap to catch spilling water. (2) Loosen slip nuts at the tops of both legs of the "U". Tape the jaws of your wrench to avoid marring chrome. (3) Ease the washers away from the joints so they do not split. (4) Pull the trap downward to free it, spilling its contents into the pan.

Sometimes the blockage turns out to be beyond the trap. Even if this is so, the effort of dismantling the trap is not wasted since this provides a freer access to the pipe farther along, and makes an 8 or 10-foot snake quite effective.

Once the blockage is cleared, replace the trap by reversing the four steps outlined above.

If it is a question of installing a new trap in place of a leaky one, be sure the replacement has exactly the same dimensions as the original. The sketch shows a type with a small cleanout plug, an improvement worth considering if your old trap did not have such a plug.

FREEING A TOILET DRAIN

The toilet bowl has its own built-in trap within the porcelain part of the fixture. A snake is about the only tool you can use since caustic cleaners cannot be

effective in the bowl. It is rather difficult to force the snake into the trap. One useful technique is to pull a plastic garbage pail liner onto your arm, and guide the tip of the snake into the trap, or beyond.

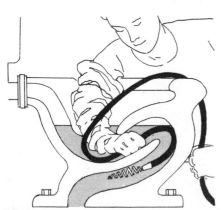

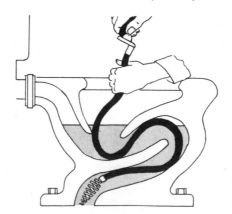

• Drain Leaks in Sinks and Tubs

Any sink or tub is subject to leaks around the drain, but the ones that use rubber gaskets are more prone than ones which have their drains cemented in place.

Laundry tubs: A laundry tub drain may leak because the gasket has failed, or because the screws that hold it in place have been loosened.

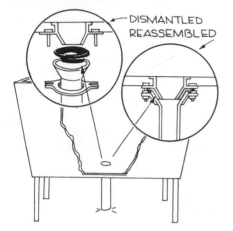

DISMANTLED
REASSEMBLED

The assembly, shown in the sketch, is mechanically simple. However, rust frequently makes disassembling this type drain difficult. If you have a leak and rusted screws, treat the screws with a solvent. Give the solvent a full day to work if possible, but no less than an hour.

Once the drain is dismantled, you may want to use the old gasket as a model in buying a replacement.

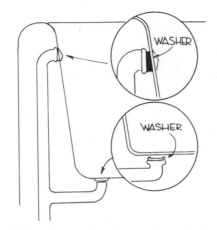

WASHER

WASHER

Sink and tub drains: Most sinks and bathtubs of recent manufacture have their drains cemented in place, but fixtures that date back many years may still have their drains sealed by a rubber gasket.

The latter are easy to recognize. A screw is visible in the middle of the small bar that crosses the drain to catch solid objects before they slip down into the trap.

Loosen the screw, and the chrome ring will lift up, exposing a gasket. If the drain leaks, a worn gasket is almost surely the cause.

If there is no screw in the crossbar, the drain is cemented in place and should not be forced. Leaks are highly unlikely from this source.

Other possibilities to check: A pinhole leak in a sink trap (see facing page), or the cast part of a bathtub drain pipe (you will need a plumber).

• Patching a Laundry Tub

Laundry tubs made of cast cement become porous and fragile with age.

If a tub begins to seep water through decomposing cement, there is nothing to do but replace the tub. Paint cannot bond to the soap-saturated surface, nor can any other sealing compound.

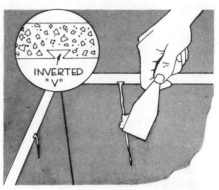

INVERTED "V"

But cracks can be patched to prolong the life of a tub. Regular cement mixed in finish proportions (1 part cement, 3 parts sand—or a bit leaner on sand) is adequate, but not as good as one of the special patching cements.

One of these uses a liquid latex binding agent in place of water. Another has a plastic (vinyl) binding agent mixed in with the cement powder. This type uses water. These special cements are advertised to have superior binding properties that do away with the need to undercut the crack. In the case of these tubs, the undercut is worth making even so.

GARBAGE DISPOSERS

Some disposers are equipped with an automatic shutoff that prevents the motor from operating when overloading occurs. This safety feature protects both the house wiring and the appliance.

With another type of cut-out switch, the grinding mechanism stops when overloaded, but the motor keeps running.

In either case, you must turn the switch off, wait three to five minutes for the motor to cool, then press the reset button at the bottom of the motor.

Overloading generally is caused by forcing waste material into the unit, or by putting in a material it cannot digest. (Styrene foam, plastic, string, aluminum foil, wire and other metal will jam any disposer. Glass, seafood shells, paper and fibrous vegetable are not advisable.)

The most general method of unjamming a disposer is by applying pressure against one of the impellers (cutting blades) on the turntable. (1) Turn off the power source.

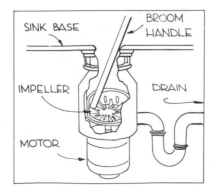

SINK BASE

BROOM HANDLE

IMPELLER

DRAIN

MOTOR

(2) Place a 1x2 (or broom handle) so it rests against one of the impellers. (3) Using the wood piece as a lever, give the turntable one full turn counterclockwise. Repeat until the jam is dislodged. (4) Push the reset button to restart motor.

Aside from avoiding the materials that jam disposers, these two additional points are worth observing:

• Always use cold water to flush a disposer, because cold congeals greases and keeps them from coating drain pipes.

• Caustic drain cleaners should not be used in disposers. They damage seals, and grinding chambers. There never should be a need for the cleaners if enough cold water is used to wash away material as it is ground up.

Natural gas systems

Natural gas is a commonly used fuel for furnaces, water heaters, and kitchen ranges. It is distributed through the house, exactly as water is, through a system of pipes.

As the diagram shows, the supply pipe leads from the street through a meter, and then into branch lines. There is a main shutoff valve on the pipe adjacent to the meter. Each appliance also has a shutoff valve nearby on the pipe that fuels it.

These valves and the pilot lights that allow ready starting of each appliance are the only working elements of a gas system that an amateur needs to deal with in the event of some failure. The valves are described in further detail below; the pilot lights are described on the facing page.

Kitchen ranges are described along with pilot lights on the facing page. Other gas-fueled appliances are described in greater detail elsewhere in the book. Water heater information is found on page 7, and furnace information on pages 29-35.

Any time you smell raw gas you should take instant action. Sometimes a burner control can be left slightly open on a range. An extinguished pilot light will also produce a faint odor of raw gas. (Although naturally odorless, gas is treated with a highly odorous substance called mercaptan. If you have any doubt, turn on a burner on your range slowly so a bit of the gas can escape without igniting. One sniff is usually memorable enough so that you will recognize the odor next time you meet it.) If you cannot isolate a simple source of raw gas, such as a burner or pilot, close the main valve at the meter and call for a serviceman from your utility. When the utility hears that you have a suspected leak, it will respond promptly.

Above all, do not light matches and run them along the pipes in an effort to find the source. The chances of explosion or fire are altogether too great to make the attempt worthwhile.

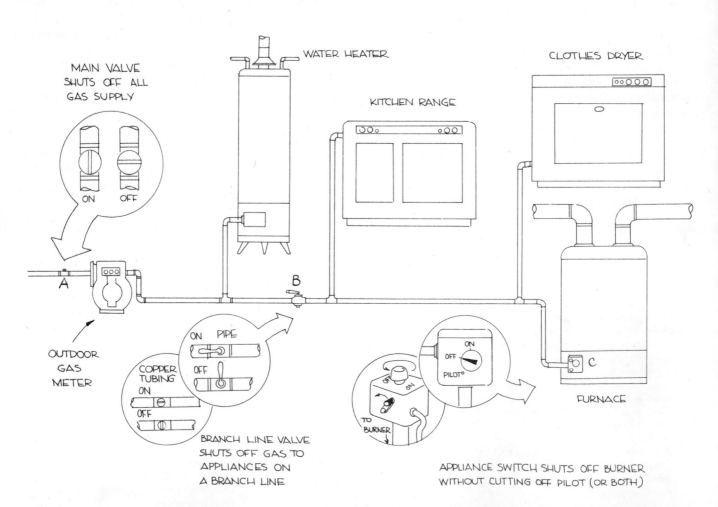

Gas valves come in these shapes: *The plug (A) is found only at the meter. It is the main valve, and can be turned only with pliers or a wrench. The sketch shows it open and closed. The handle (B) on the line leading to each appliance is an easy* means of shutting down any one outlet for the system. Finally, valves of the type labeled (C) shut off individual appliances without shutting off their pilot lights. These function as simple switches; the others require relighting pilots.

• Balky Pilot Lights

Pilot lights sometimes extinguish themselves for one of the following reasons: The orifice clogs, a gust of wind snuffs the flame, the air supply becomes exhausted, or, on a stove, liquid spills over the flame.

Only rarely is the cause a pilot that is set too low.

If strong drafts blow out a pilot light repeatedly, baffle the drafts but *not* by closing off ventilation holes in the appliance. Gas combustion depends on a free supply of air around the flame, so work on the source of the draft instead. For example, a door may need weather-stripping or a different window should be opened for fresh air.

In general, be sure that ventilation holes for the appliance are not blocked so that the pilot and burner flames are smothered. Nothing should be kept under a gas-fired appliance, and nothing should be stacked around its base (most appliances are designed to draw air in at the bottom).

Too high a pilot flame often means incomplete combustion of the fuel. Symptoms are soot on and below the pilot assembly, and a flame that is yellow for more than half its length. A flame of this type will in time clog the orifice with soot.

If you think a flame is out of adjustment—too high or too low—call your utility serviceman to have him adjust the pilot. A screw does the adjusting, but each assembly has several, and you should not experiment to find out which one does what. Once you have seen an adjustment made, you might remember how to do it.

Relighting an extinguished pilot is an easy task now. All appliances made after 1950 are required to carry a plate of instructions. There are literally dozens of variations, but these two types are basic:

On ranges or furnaces, the pilot has a heat sensor. When the sensor becomes cold, it shuts off the valve. To relight, you have to push a red button and keep it depressed until enough warmth generates to keep the sensor from closing the valve again.

On water heaters, there is seldom a red button, but only a direct action switch on the valve. It is coupled to the main on-off switch so that the pilot cannot be shut off without shutting off the main switch at the same time. The link does not work the other way—the main switch can be closed without shutting off the pilot.

• Cleaning Burners on Gas Ranges

The burners on gas ranges are designed to stay clean and to operate without adjustment. However, once in a while a burner will have something spilled on it that requires cleaning in order for it to function correctly.

The sketch shows all of the component parts of a typical burner assembly. If a burner does not light easily from its pilot, or otherwise grows balky, the following steps should help.

(1) Check the flash tubes, and wash any soot or other foreign matter out of them. (2) Check the orifice at the end of the flash tube. If it has become clogged, clean it with a needle or similar sharp object. (3) Check the ports around the gas ring. Clean as in step two. (4) If you think a considerable amount of foreign matter has been spilled into the ring through the ports, you can lift the entire assembly up and away from its main gas jets, and wash it in a sink with warm

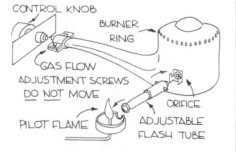

water and a regular soap or detergent. One word of caution in this regard: The inside of the unit must be absolutely dry for the gas to burn properly. The burner unit should be given considerable time to drain, and then subjected to a blast of warm air from a furnace, hair dryer, or similarly warm source before being replaced in the range.

Do not turn the screws at the end near the main gas jets during any cleaning operation. These control vanes inside the unit that are carefully set to direct the flow of gas. No screws hold the unit in place.

• Correcting Oven Controls

Oven temperature controls go haywire on occasion either because the control knob or thermostat has become misadjusted, or because the thermocouple has failed. Gas and electric ranges act identically.

The knob can account for only minor variations, and can be reset after you determine the difference between its indication and the true temperature.

Some thermostats can be adjusted. If the owner's manual for the range has instructions, the home-owner can adjust the device himself. If the manual carries no instruction, a utility serviceman should do the work.

A failed thermocouple has to be replaced by a repairman. The thermocouple is a thin, rod-shaped device inside the oven. It is filled with a gas that measures the heat. If the rod becomes pitted, the gas escapes and the thermostat and thermocouple stop working. (A common cause is corrosion induced by the use of spray oven cleaners; if you use these, cover the rod with aluminum foil before spraying.)

How ovens work: When you turn the oven to a selected temperature, the heat comes on until the temperature rises above the selected point, then shuts off. With the heat off, the oven cools to a point below the selected point. Then the heat clicks on again.

Ovens vary in this cycling pattern, but the normal range is 25° above the setting to 15° below it for porcelain-lined ovens, or 15° above and 25° below for chrome-lined ones. The first cycle requires 10 to 15 minutes; subsequent cycles are more rapid.

How to check temperatures: Place an accurate thermometer as near the center of the oven as possible, and so it can be read through the oven window if you have one, or so you can see it through the narrowest crack in a solid door.

Set the oven at 350°, and prepare to watch for half an hour. Record high and low points, and the length of two or three cycles.

If the variation is 50° or less, reset the control knob to compensate. If it is greater, check into the thermostat and thermocouple, or have them checked.

Any thermometer that can register to 400° is adequate for checking temperatures.

Electrical systems

Electricity is the most versatile source of power in the home. It heats, cools, lights, drives motors, runs televisions and radios, and even curls hair.

The way electricity moves along a wire is similar to the way water flows through a pipe. It is pushed by a pressure measured in volts. The amount of current (the flow) is measured in amperes, a word which expresses both amount and time interval—as gallons per minute measures flow of water. Pressure and current together produce power. Electrically, such power is measured in watts. The three terms form this equation:

$$Volts \times amperes = watts.$$

This formula is the basis of all design of electrical circuits in homes. On the opposite page is a description of a typical circuit with its component parts from service entry to convenience outlet. On page 26 is a primer description of wiring and wiring devices.

Circuit wiring techniques are far simpler than plumbing techniques, but circuit wiring is more complex in design because every component is rated to perform within certain minimum-maximum limits and is required to approach both limits frequently. Also, many products are designed to perform only under certain conditions—wet vs. dry for example. So choosing wiring and wiring devices has to be based on both considerations of capacity and type of insulation.

Choice of wiring is critical because an overloaded electrical circuit will become overheated if the condition persists. A poorly designed or executed system may even ignite a home fire—a thought for amateur electricians to keep in mind.

Electricity can also shock—painfully at least, fatally at worst —but only when a circuit is carrying current. De-fusing the circuit before you begin to work on it removes the possibility of such an injury.

This section deals principally with the visible parts of an electrical system: Switches, convenience outlets, light fixtures, cords, plugs, and fuses. All of these, when they fail, can be replaced easily. The only technical requirement is that the new unit must be equal to the one that it replaces. All reliable manufacturers print this information clearly on the piece. While this section outlines several aspects of circuit design to help you understand how these replacement parts fit into the system, it does not give enough information to allow a novice to make any installation of new wiring. This is purposefully done. City or county building inspectors are free sources of specific wisdom as well as building permits. They have no aversion to amateurs doing their own work as long as it ends with an inspection and approval. If a building inspector tells you that a professional will save you money and woe, take him seriously. He has seen problems like yours more than once before.

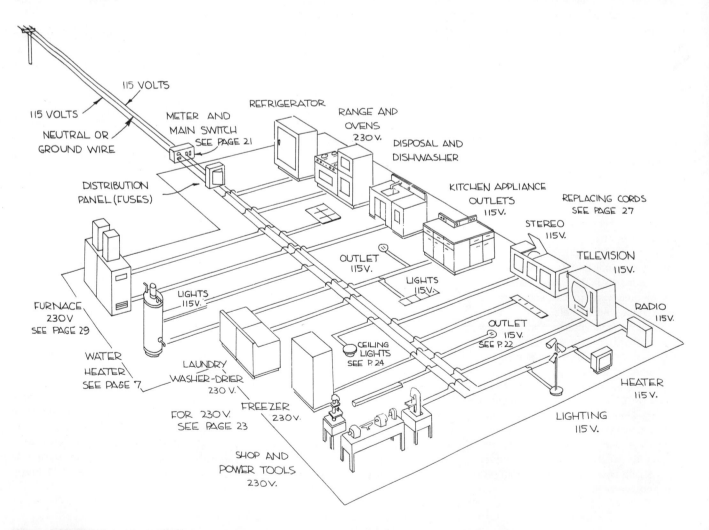

• The Service Entry

The service entry is the terminal at the house through which power delivered from the street is funneled into all of the branch electrical circuits throughout the house.

It is also called the fuse box. As such, it is the weak point of each circuit—the safety device that keeps wiring from overheating and catching fire.

In a small apartment the fuse box may hold as few as two 110-volt circuits. In a good-sized home, there will be two or more heavy-fused 220 or 230-volt circuits labeled as "range" and "main," plus as many as a dozen plug-fused 110 or 115-volt branch circuits. (Increasingly, an alternative called a circuit breaker is replacing fuses. See below.)

The range and main fuses (see sketch) protect house wiring against sudden upsurges in power from the street. The plug fuses limit to safe levels the amount of power a branch circuit can draw. Both types "blow" when stressed beyond their limits.

The "range" fuse is so-named because kitchen ranges require 215 or 230-volts of power, and such a circuit is normally provided for a range. The fuse is rated at 40 to 60 amperes, giving it a potential of 6,800 watts. The circuit may also serve power tools in a workshop.

The main fuse protects the side of the service entry that divides power among the 110 or 115-volt branch circuits. Branch circuits usually are fused at 7½, 15 or 20 amperes. Using the formula of $volts \times amperes = watts,$ these circuits have the potentials of 825, 1650, and 2200 watts. Plug fuses of all three ratings can be bought with common base sizes, or with individual base sizes. For the latter, there are adapter rings called "fusestats" that must be screwed into the fuse box.

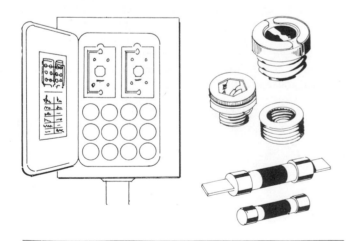

CIRCUIT BREAKERS

Circuit breakers are heavy-duty switches designed to serve the same purpose as fuses. They have two advantages: They do not blow out, but simply switch to "off," and they have a built-in delay that allows brief overloads before the switch trips.

The toggle has to be pushed to "reset" then allowed to drop to "on" after a circuit is broken.

• Testing and Replacing Fuses

It is absolutely necessary to know which circuit you will be working with in attempting any repair so you can shut it off before you begin. Knowing your circuits hastens the work when you are trying to track down the cause of a blown fuse.

The sequence of steps in tracing out a circuit, or in searching for the cause of a blown fuse, is the same.

(1) Throw the main switch to "off." This happens in any of several ways. On some service entries opening the door shuts off service. Some have throw switches. Some have blocks that pull out of the entry box panel carrying the "main" fuse with them. (2) Once the main switch is off, unscrew the burned-out plug fuse, or any plug fuse if you are about to trace an unknown

circuit. (3) Restore the main switch to "on." (4) Trace along the circuit until you find the cause of the short, or until you have pinned down exactly which appliances, fixtures and convenience outlets it serves. (5) If it is a short, cure the cause or at least unhook the offending appliance. (6) Turn the main switch to "off" again. (7) Put a new plug fuse in place, or replace the one you removed to make your test. (8) Return main switch to "on," or move to the next branch circuit if you are tracing them all.

If you have circuit breakers, all you must do to trace circuits is flip the switches to "off" one at a time, resetting them as you finish with each.

Tracing a circuit is simple. Once you have removed the fuse, circulate through the house trying each appliance or light switch and each convenience outlet. The ones that do not have power are on the circuit you are testing.

Hunting the source of a short circuit is more difficult. Most occur in appliances, or in their cords or plugs. On occasion a short will reveal itself as a blackened surface near the point of the short, which is sometimes accompanied by a large arcing flash. But almost invariably you will have to work your way through the whole circuit bit by bit. This technique works fairly quickly and should cost no more than one extra fuse. You must know the location of the circuits when using this technique. (1) Turn off every appliance and fixture on the affected circuit. (2) Turn on each appliance, one at a time. Do the same thing with each light fixture. If one is at fault, it will blow the fuse. If no single appliance or fixture was at fault the circuit most probably was overloaded. Turn on all appliances and fixtures at once. If the fuse blows when several appliances are on, total up the wattage. If the total wattage exceeds the circuit's capacity, redistribute some of the circuit's burden to other circuits.

If a fuse blows as soon as you throw the main switch to "on," the short is somewhere in the wiring. The most likely place for a short is in a light fixture, especially one that is free to swivel. Check all visible wiring to see if insulation has cracked and peeled away. If this search does not reveal a cause you probably will need a professional electrician to pinpoint and correct the trouble.

• Replacing Wall Switches

When a switch fails, it is usually because the contact points have oxidized or been worn. In almost any case a failed switch cannot be fixed as reasonably as it can be replaced.

To remove a wall switch: (1) Turn off circuit by removing fuse, following instruction on page 21. (2) Unscrew and remove face plate. (3) Unscrew top and bottom mounting screws and pull switch body out of junction box. (4) Loosen terminal screws to free switch from circuit wires.

To replace, reverse steps. The loops in the wire ends should be fitted to the terminals so the curve runs clockwise. This way the screw pulls the wire tighter as it winds.

Replacements: There are many different types of switches. Silent mercury switches do away with the "click" of the old-fashioned sort. Pressure-plate switches turn on and off with alternating touches. With these, you can switch lights on with your knuckles, elbows, or even your nose when both hands are full. There are also high-low or full-range dimmer switches that will fit into regular receptacle boxes.

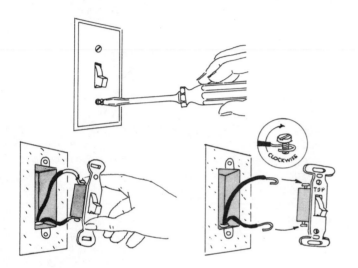

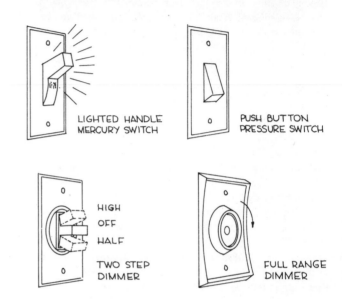

LIGHTED HANDLE MERCURY SWITCH

PUSH BUTTON PRESSURE SWITCH

HIGH
OFF
HALF
TWO STEP DIMMER

FULL RANGE DIMMER

• Replacing Convenience Outlets

Convenience outlets occasionally wear out; their contacts oxidize and loosen through use. If appliances will not work in a certain outlet, but you are not having trouble with short circuits, chances are that replacing the troublesome outlet is all you need to do.

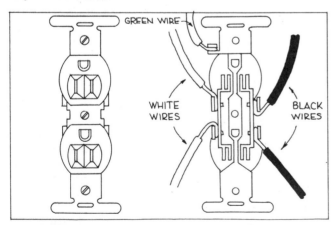

GREEN WIRE

WHITE WIRES

BLACK WIRES

The steps: (1) Shut off the circuit by removing the fuse following the instructions on page 21. (2) Unscrew and remove the outlet face plate. (3) Unscrew mounting screws at top and bottom (or either side) of the unit and pull it out of the junction box. (4) Loosen the set screws to free the wires from the terminals.

Replace with the new outlet by reversing the steps, being sure to attach the black (hot) wire to the dark (brass) terminal, and the light (neutral) wire to the silvery terminal. If there is a green wire, it is a ground wire and should be attached to the ground terminal (painted green) at one end of the outlet... if it is a grounded outlet.

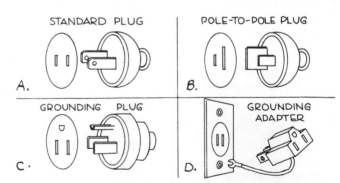

STANDARD PLUG

POLE-TO-POLE PLUG

A.

B.

GROUNDING PLUG

GROUNDING ADAPTER

C.

D.

Replacements: Worn-out outlets do not have to be replaced with exactly the same model. The advent of special appliances has given rise to several specialized models. The ordinary type (a) contrasts with pole-for-pole types (b), which use two differently shaped prongs to make sure that the plug corresponds to the wires in the circuit. Such plugs are frequently found on TV sets. The three-pronged grounded outlet is another possibility (c). If you have an appliance with such a plug, but do not wish to replace a convenience outlet, you can buy a special adapter plug (d).

• Replacing Plugs

Every cord has a male plug to connect it to a circuit. The detachable cords used with many small appliances also have a female plug connected to the appliance.

Any plug that has a cracked shell or loose contacts should be replaced with a new one. A plug that arcs when it is pushed into or pulled out of an outlet should be examined to be sure that its wires are firmly attached to the terminals. Some molded plugs cannot be checked visually, but will betray poor connections by transmitting power erratically or becoming overwarm to the touch after a period of use.

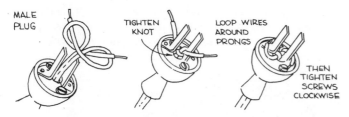

To replace a male plug: (1) Cut off the old plug plus an inch of cord to get rid of the weakened end. (2) Split the insulation on the cord two inches to separate the wires. (3) Strip the insulation from ½ inch of each tip, then scrape the wire until bright without nicking it. (4) Tie an underwriter's knot (see sketch) so contacts with terminals cannot be strained when cord is pulled during normal use. (5) Form a loop on each wire so it will curl clockwise around its terminal. (6) Loop wires so they do not touch prongs as shown in sketch, and fit loops around terminals. (7) Tighten the terminals to hold wires securely.

This type of plug should be used for most appliances. For a lamp or radio cord, you might prefer a self-connecting plug like the ones shown at right.

To replace a female plug: (1) Cut off the old plug plus an inch of cord to get rid of the weakened end. (2) Separate the halves

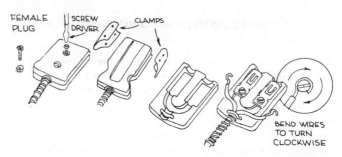

of the new plug. (3) Strip the wires clean of insulation far enough to let you make hooks to fit around the terminals. (4) Secure the contacts by tightening the terminal screws. (5) Screw or clasp the halves of the plug body together. If the plug and cord are required to endure strains, buy a plug with a spring coil built into it as shown in the sketch.

SELF-CONNECTING PLUGS

Several manufacturers now sell plugs that clamp onto wires, making automatic connection. These plugs remove all the fuss of stripping and cleaning wire and forming wire around terminals. They are, however, weak and suited only for light use with lamps, radios, or other devices that are seldom unplugged and plugged. Most limit themselves by being molded to take only lamp cord.

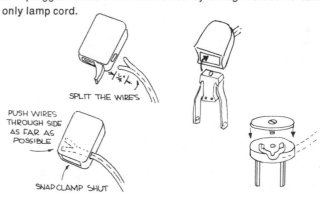

• Cords for 220-Volt Appliances

There are not many instances in which an inexperienced electrician should tinker with a 220- or 230-volt circuit. Electric ranges, clothes dryers and many of the larger shop tools use 220 or 230 volts (different communities use one or the other).

When plugs or cords on these are damaged, an amateur can do his own repair or replacement if he proceeds with an adequate amount of caution. A man with some experience can also replace a defective outlet.

Plugs and outlets are shown in detail in the sketches. **Remember to shut power off before working on any electrical wiring.** If you are working on a cord or an appliance, simply unplug it from its source. The point to be most careful about: Match terminals with wire color codes. On a plug, the white wire connects to the wide (grounding) prong, usually aluminum in color. The black wire attaches to the brass terminal. The red wire attaches to the copper terminal. If metals do not differ, daubs of paint will mark the matches. The terminals at the appliance end of the cord are similarly coded.

The outlet box may contain three wires—white, black and red—or may have only black and red, with a ground strap serving in place of a white wire.

Screw all terminals tight. Wrap all exposed wire carefully.

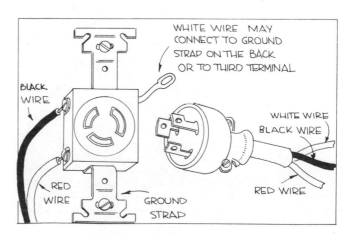

• Replacing Wall or Ceiling Fixtures

Ceiling and wall-mounted light fixtures occasionally fail. Most, however, are replaced because new uses for a room have made the fixtures unsuited to their tasks.

Light fixtures come with their own wiring, and are connected to the wires of the circuit either with a pigtail splice or a wire nut. (See page 26 for detailed drawings of each.) These connections are housed within a metal junction box recessed into the wall or ceiling and hidden by an ornamental plate that is part of the light fixture. Replacing a fixture principally involves undoing the old wiring connection and forming a new one just like it. In sequence the steps are:

(1) Shut off the circuit following the instructions on page 21. (2) Unscrew the ornamental plate that covers the junction box, and the fixture from the junction box if it has a second set of screws. The fixture will sag away from the junction. You may need an assistant to hold it while you proceed. (3) If the wires are spliced with wire nuts, unscrew them counterclockwise. If the wires are spliced with pigtails, snip them off with wire-cutter pliers *unless* the old splice is tight against the junction. In this case unwind the electrician's tape, then untwist the wires. (4) If you have snipped off the old splice, strip half an inch of insulation off the circuit wires without nicking the copper. (5) Trim the wiring in the fixture to get rid of excess (there usually is). No splice should ever be made outside a junction, nor should the junction be full of a tangle of wire. A completed installation should have about as much play in the wire as the sketch shows. (6) Strip insulation from the ends of the fixture wires to match the circuit wires. For either a wire nut or a pigtail splice, one-half inch is enough. (7) Form the splices (again having an assistant hold the fixture). Match the wires by color code. (8) Move the fixture into position and secure it with the reverse steps of the ones that loosened the original.

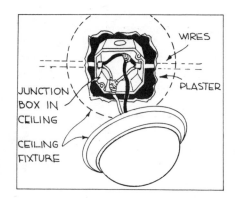

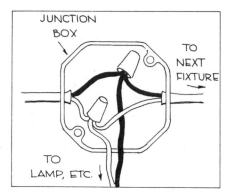

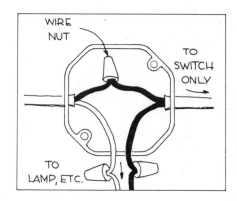

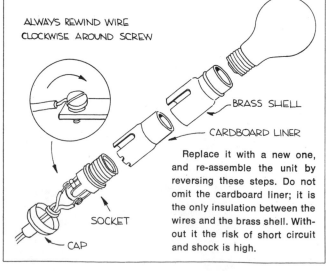

FIXING BULB SOCKETS

Table and floor lamps and some wall fixtures use simple sockets to hold light bulbs. The contact points of these sometimes wear out, requiring replacement. The job is simple:

(1) Unplug the lamp, or de-fuse the circuit of a mounted fixture. (2) Remove the bulb. (3) Find near the switch button the embossed word "press," and do so. This will separate the cap and shell. (4) Remove the cardboard liner. (5) The socket itself is now exposed. Loosen the terminal screws, free the wires, and remove the socket.

ALWAYS REWIND WIRE CLOCKWISE AROUND SCREW

BRASS SHELL

CARDBOARD LINER

Replace it with a new one, and re-assemble the unit by reversing these steps. Do not omit the cardboard liner; it is the only insulation between the wires and the brass shell. Without it the risk of short circuit and shock is high.

SOCKET

CAP

EXTRACTING SHATTERED BULBS

When light bulbs are shattered in their sockets, removing the base is a minor problem. Before attempting to remove any base, be sure the lamp is disconnected or the mounted fixture on a de-fused circuit.

Some home handymen keep an old rubber ball or tennis ball at hand. The ball is pressed firmly against the socket, then twisted to free the base.

A tightly wadded ball of brown bag paper serves equally well, and does not leave you with a ball full of glass fragments to hide from children.

LEAVING LOOSE WIRES

Sometimes an electrical repair will not go as quickly as expected, and it will be necessary to leave the wiring loose in a switch receptacle or a junction box.

If you have to walk away from a job at the halfway point, and cannot leave the circuit defused while you are away, follow these steps: (1) Tape all bared wire with plastic electrician's tape so that no short circuit can take place no matter how much pressure two wires may exert against each other. (2) Tape all the loose wires together in parallel to minimize the chances of one tip being forced through the insulation of another wire. (3) Cover the receptacle or junction box with a face plate so children will not be attracted to the wires, or pets will not chew them.

• Fixing Fluorescent Light Fixtures

Fluorescent light fixtures do not use house current directly, but set up a current within themselves to produce light. The means is a component called the "ballast," which frequently plays some part in a malfunction.

There are three types of fluorescent fixtures in which ballasts (as well as tubes) cannot be interchanged. Getting a wrong part into a fixture is easy to do, but almost always causes the fixture to work badly or not at all.

The three types of fluorescent fixtures are Pre-heat, Rapid Start, and Instant Start. Each has its own type of ballast, and the Pre-heat has a separate piece called the starter. (Its function is to heat the electrodes in the tube so they can begin to produce light. The other types of fixtures get heat directly from the ballast.)

The ballast is the key source of information about the fixture. Printed on it is the capacity of the individual fixture, its type, and other information needed to choose replacement parts.

The following troubleshooter's guide should allow you to isolate any trouble, although some of the cures are in the province of the professional electrician.

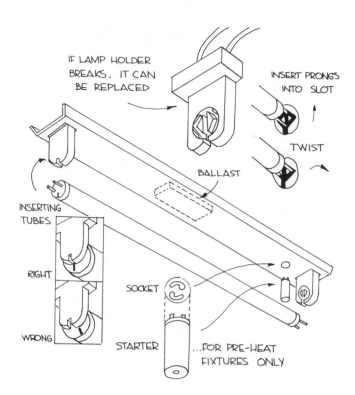

No start or slow start: Tube is damaged. Usually a broken electrode or a loss of vacuum in the tube. *Replace.* Broken lampholder breaks circuit. *Replace lampholder, usually a matter of loosening one screw and disconnecting two wires. Be sure current is shut off in circuit before beginning.* Use old holder guide for buying a replacement. Temperatures well below 65° around lamp may be causing the light to malfunction. (Light level diminishes 2% per degree below 65°.) *Warm room or enclose lamp.* Rapid-Start fixtures will not light if too much dirt accumulates on tube. *Wash tube in mild detergent solution, then rinse in clean water.* Dry thoroughly and replace in fixture. In a Pre-heat fixture, starter may be failing or may have failed. *Replace with one of identical ratings (see sketch for technique).*

If none of these succeeds, the ballast may be improperly installed, the fixture may have been repaired with the wrong ballast, or the circuit supplying the fixture may be operating at lower-than-normal voltage. Consult an electrician.

Lamp blinks on and off: This is one sign that a tube is about to burn out. If replacing the tube does not cure the blink, these are other possible causes. Lampholder (socket) is mis-adjusted so pins do not make firm contact. *Adjust holder so it fits against end of tube.* Low temperature (below 65°) around lamp. *Try first to warm room, then to enclose the lamp partially.* In a Pre-heat fixture, the wrong type or rating of starter may be in use. *Replace with the correct type (identified on ballast housing).*

If none of these succeeds, the ballast may be of an improper rating (not matched to wattage of tubes), the ballast may be improperly installed, or the circuit may be operating at lower-than-normal voltage.

Only tube ends light: In a Pre-heat fixture, the starter has failed. *Replace with one of identical ratings.*

Other causes are an improperly installed ballast, or failure to ground the fixture during installation.

Middle of the tube dim or dark: Low temperature below 65°. *Try first to warm room, then to enclose the fixture partially.* Direct current operating without reversing switches. *Swap tube end for end as temporary expedient.* Have switches installed.

Pronounced flicker or swirling effect: Sometimes new tubes flicker for a time after installation, but stop with seasoning. Also, any lamp may begin to flicker, but will stop if shut off for a few seconds then turned on again. In a Pre-heat fixture, the starter may be failing. *Replace.*

If these are not the causes, the fixture may have an improperly connected ballast; may have been repaired with the wrong type of ballast; or may be on a circuit operating at higher-than-normal voltage.

New lamps fail: Wrong tube type for fixture. *Replace (proper tube specified on ballast housing.)*

Other causes of repeated new lamp failure are improper type of ballast, improperly installed ballast, failed ballast, or a short in the fixture wiring. Consult an electrician.

Loud hum: Improper type of ballast, or improper installation. Consult an electrician.

Overheated ballast: Wrong type of tube. *Replace (proper tube specified on ballast housing).* High temperature in lamp housing. *Improve ventilation for ballast.*

Other causes are wrong type of ballast, a short in the ballast, improper connection of the ballast, a short in the circuit wiring, or higher-than-normal circuit voltage. Consult an electrician.

Radio interference: Aerial or radio too close to fixture. Keep both at least 10 feet from fixture. Aerial lead-in unshielded, not well grounded.

If the fixture and the radio are on the same branch circuit, interference can feed back through the circuit. A filter can be installed on the fixture to halt this.

• Some ABC's of Wiring

The National Electrical Code, supplemented by local codes, specifies that circuit wiring and protective fuses be matched in capacity.

The size of a wire determines how much electrical current can pass along it, just as the size of a pipe limits the flow of water through it. Wires are coded with numbers. As the numbers become larger, the size of the wire decreases. The commonest interior wiring sizes are No. 12 with 15-amp fuses, and No. 10 with 20-amp fuses. (An extension cord can be the equivalent of No. 14 or even No. 16 wire—not large enough to carry the heavy load of an appliance such as a heater.)

The greater the length of a circuit in feet, the less power it can carry. For this reason, some 15-amp circuits use No. 10 wire to compensate, and some 20-amp circuits use No. 8. Electricians have elaborate tables that tell them which wire to use in any circumstance; it is never a matter of guesswork.

In addition to the question of wire size, there are the requirements of insulation and installation.

No splice can be made outside of a junction box as a safe-guard in case of short circuiting or other failures.

A type of cable called BX can run exposed in walls or ceilings where conditions are dry according to some community codes. Many codes still require either lead sheath or thin-wall tubing. Where cable runs in damp conditions or through any kind of masonry, a lead sheath is required by all codes. Lead sheath can be either rigid or flexible.

Two wires carry alternating current in 110- or 115-volt circuits. The insulation of one is color-coded black to indicate that it is the "hot" wire. The other wire is either white or natural gray; it is the "neutral" or "grounding" wire. If there is a third wire colored green, it is the ground wire, and not to be confused with the grounding wire. The green wire carries no current under normal operating conditions. Its purpose is to divert current to a safe place in the event of a short circuit.

Circuits of 220- or 230-volts have three wires; two are hot, and the third is neutral. Black is the first hot wire, red the second, and white or grey the neutral wire. The hot wires must be attached to terminals in sequence, a task usually made simple by the color coding of the terminals themselves. If there is no color code on the terminals, get advice from a professional.

• Splicing Electrical Wire

There are several basic ways to splice electrical wire (or "cable" to call it by its proper name). Each method does a specific job.

Western Union splice: It is used to lengthen wire, and is the only appropriate splice when some pulling strain will be exerted on the wire in service. Offset the cuts as shown. Make each turn tight.

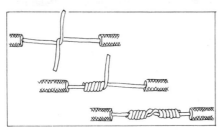

Solder the finished joints. Tape each wire separately, then cover the wire with a second layer.

Pigtail splice: It joins two wires in junction or outlet boxes where no pulling

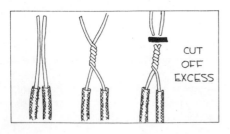

strain is to be exerted. Twist wires tightly together, starting at the point where the insulation is stripped away and work toward the tip. Four turns are enough. If the splice turns out longer, snip off the excess at the tip. Wrap the exposed wires with three layers of tape.

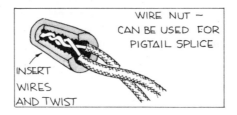

WIRE NUT — CAN BE USED FOR PIGTAIL SPLICE
INSERT WIRES AND TWIST

Tap splice: It allows a new line to branch away from an existing one at any point. Offset the cuts. Make each turn tight. (If the wire is stranded, start the splice in the middle of the wire bundle as shown.) Solder the finished splice.

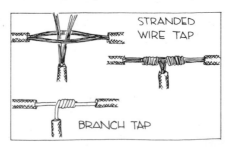

STRANDED WIRE TAP
BRANCH TAP

This is not a strong joint, and needs the extra support of the solder. Tape each

cut separately so that no wire is exposed.

With tap splices, you need to consider the potential burden on the parent circuit and also the size of the added wire.

All splices must follow the black-to-black and light-to-light coding of the insulation on the wires.

The wire that is used to form the splice should be scraped shiny bright before the joint is formed to assure good contact.

In scraping, avoid nicking the copper wire. This weakens it.

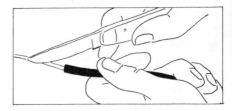

WIRE SOLDER
SOLDERING IRON

When you solder, heat the copper wire. You get a good joint only when the wire is hot enough to melt the solder on contact.

• Repairing or Replacing Electrical Cords

Because cords on appliances and lamps are subjected to regular pulling and twisting, the wires sometimes break, or the insulation breaks down.

When a wire breaks inside the insulating material, the lamp or appliance will not work.

When the insulation breaks down enough to allow bared wires to touch each other, the circuit shorts out, and may result in a fire. Persons touching the bared wire may suffer electrical shock.

Broken wires can be spliced if the break can be located. Failures in insulation can be repaired with electrician's tape. Or the whole cord can be replaced rather than repaired. The choice depends on the general condition of the cord. An old one, especially if its insulation is brittle, might as well be replaced.

HOW TO SPLICE A CORD

A spliced cord is never quite as good as a single length, but careful work will yield a perfectly serviceable and safe result. Whether you are lengthening a cord or repairing a broken one: (1) Stagger the cuts so that no part of the cut for one wire adjoins the cut for the other. (2) Form Western Union splices on each wire (a detailed drawing is on page 26). (3) Solder the splices as shown on page 26. (4) Using plastic electrician's tape, wrap each wire separately until tape is as thick as the insulation it replaces. Then wrap three layers of tape over the entire section. All turns should overlap by half the width of the tape.

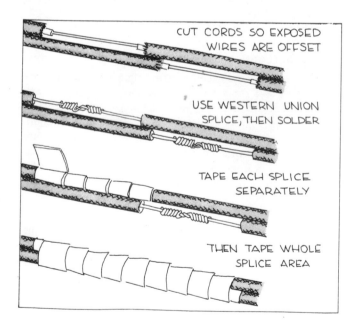

CUT CORDS SO EXPOSED WIRES ARE OFFSET

USE WESTERN UNION SPLICE, THEN SOLDER

TAPE EACH SPLICE SEPARATELY

THEN TAPE WHOLE SPLICE AREA

HOW TO REPLACE INSULATION

The key purpose of insulation is to keep the two wires in a cord from becoming wet or touching each other. Depending on use, types of insulation vary considerably.

The technique for replacing insulation is at right. For a heater cord, or one used in a dry place, the wrapping need cover only the exposed wire plus an inch in each direction to take care of the inevitable scuffing that comes with use. For a wire that must resist moisture, wrap the two wires carefully. Then wrap several inches on each side of the splice. Make each turn tight, overlapping the previous turn by half or more.

HOW TO REPLACE CORDS

In replacing an appliance or lamp cord, match the one that came with the appliance both for its capacity (amperage or wattage limits are marked on a tab) and its type of insulation.

Lamp cord, rubber insulation over stranded wire, is manufactured to carry 1500 watts or fewer. Heavy appliance cords have two or more layers of insulation, one of asbestos if it is a heater cord. These cords may have an outer layer of fabric for use in dry places; for use in damp places, the outer insulations are of rubber or plastic. Their wires are scaled to carry up to 2500 watts on 110-volt appliances, and more for three-wire cords that serve ranges or shop tools.

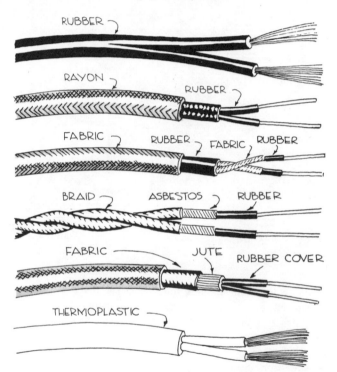

RUBBER

RAYON — RUBBER

FABRIC — RUBBER — FABRIC — RUBBER

BRAID — ASBESTOS — RUBBER

FABRIC — JUTE — RUBBER COVER

THERMOPLASTIC

Once you have the proper cord, replacement problems depend upon how easily you can reach the terminals of the appliance.

Some appliances carry their cords well inside the frame to a switch. Some have channels or clips to guide the cord or guard it against strain. For these, and for lamps with bulky or long bodies, attach a fishing line or string to the old cord as you withdraw it, then use the string to pull the new cord into place.

In light sockets, the terminals are not coded for hot or ground wires. It makes no difference which wire goes where. For appliances, wires will be coded white or gray for ground wire, black for hot wire. If the cord carries three wires to serve a 215-volt appliance, the third wire will be red. Terminals are colored correspondingly.

Loop wires so they fit clockwise around terminals.

• Repairing Doorbells

When a doorbell does not ring, there are four parts of the system to check: Push-button, chime or bell, transformer, and wiring. The transformer is there because doorbells operate on low voltage—12 to 24 volts—which makes them much easier and less hazardous to work with than regular 110-volt circuits. The voltage is probably 12 if there is but a single push-button at the front door. Separate buttons at front and back door usually are supplied with 16 or 24 volts. The latter, though not lethal, gives a painful enough shock to make it worth avoiding. It is just as well to de-fuse the circuit once you have diagnosed the trouble.

The sketches show how wiring runs in single-button and two-button systems in a stylized way. The inset panels show a more realistic view of the wiring you will encounter.

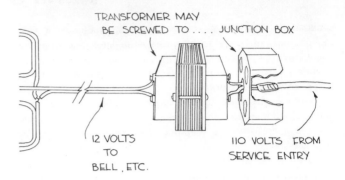

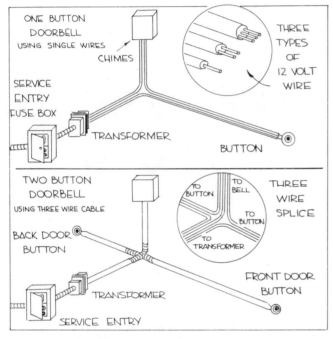

When a bell quits ringing, follow this sequence of steps to pinpoint the cause, then to repair the problem.

(1) Unscrew and remove the push-button face plate. The button is the commonest failure point because its exposed location allows contacts and wires to corrode. Disconnect the wires from the terminals, and touch the bare tips together. If the bell rings, the trouble is at the button. Scrape wires and contacts (or sandpaper the contacts lightly), and reconnect the wires. If the button still does not cause the bell to sound, it will have to be replaced. If the bell did not sound when the wires were crossed, the trouble is elsewhere.

(2) Check the bells. Make sure that each wire is securely attached to its terminal. Short the wires by laying a piece of scrap wire across two terminals. If there is power at the chimes, one of the moving parts is probably stuck by dirt or grease. If there is no power, move to the transformer.

(3) The transformer usually backs onto a junction box near the service entry or near the push-button. The sketch shows a typical arrangement in detail. Using a scrap of wire, short the terminals on the low-voltage side of the transformer. If there is power, a small spark will occur, and this will mean that the short is in the wiring between the transformer and the

bell. If there is no power, de-fuse the circuit and check the terminals on the 110-volt side of the transformer. To do this you will have to remove the cover-plate of the junction box. See page 21 for a method of de-fusing the circuit.

(4) If there is power at the transformer, but not at the bell, there is a break in a wire somewhere between. Trace as much of the wiring as is exposed, especially looking for tap splices or other potentially loose connections. Chances are very good that the break will be where the wire has been worked.

If you cannot find the break in an exposed spot, you will have to replace the entire length of wire. Check the exact voltage of the system (it will be stamped on the chime unit or the transformer), and be sure you have the right size wire.

Low-voltage wire comes in single insulated strands, or in the form of two-wire and three-wire cable. The latter is used in most contemporary installations.

To replace the bad wire, disconnect it at both the transformer and at the chime. Also, dismantle the splices that lead to the push-buttons at the doors. Then tie the new wire to the old, and use the old wire to pull the new into place.

WHEN A BELL RINGS STEADILY

If a doorbell rings constantly, or a chime unit buzzes constantly, there is a short in the push-button or its wires. Check to make sure the button has not gotten stuck with its contacts closed, then check the wiring to make sure there is no short. If the wiring has to be replaced, disconnect the splice where this wire joins the wires leading to the transformer, and disconnect the wire from the button terminals. Tie the new wire to the old, and use the old wire to pull the new into position.

OTHER LOW-VOLTAGE WIRING

Low-voltage wiring can crop up in other places in the home than the doorbell circuit. Contemporary garden lighting systems are frequently low-voltage, and many light fixture switches are low-voltage.

Wherever low-voltage circuitry crops up, it has two distinctive marks: The wiring is very thin—usually No. 16 or No. 18—and there is a transformer separating it from the regular household circuits of 110 volts.

Aside from this, however, circuits are wired identically with household circuits in terms of splices, insulation, and other techniques. If a circuit fails, use the earlier material in this chapter as a guide for troubleshooting and repair except in the matter of choosing materials. In choosing, the safest bet is always an identical replacement for the part that has failed.

Warm air heating

The two basic types of warm air furnaces are *gravity* and *forced air*. Gravity furnaces require basement installation so that the heated air will circulate upward through vents and the cool air will sink downward into the furnace to be reheated. Forced air furnaces, which use a blower to circulate the heated air, can be installed almost anywhere: basement, wall, closet, alcove, even in the attic. Both operate on either natural gas or liquid propane.

The great majority of minor malfunctions in either type of furnace are due to accumulated dirt, which ranges from a thin layer of dust in a thermostat to a deep mound of it in a blower chamber. Following the techniques outlined on pages 32-33, a homeowner can alleviate a great many seemingly serious malfunctions in a furnace.

Once you learn where to look for it, dirt is obvious. If a problem develops in a heating system that is not obvious and easy to correct, it is a good idea to call a furnace repairman (or a public utility service department if you live in an area where the utility company keeps men on call). The troubleshooting chart on page 30 should help you to identify the scope of your problem. Page 35 discusses dangerous problems in detail.

Aside from cleaning parts of the furnace, the homeowner's knowledge of his system should govern just how far he goes in attempting repairs. Thermostats and pilot lights are the only parts of the electrical and fuel system an amateur should tackle. Certain adjustments of fan belts are in reach of a non-professional.

BALANCING A HEATING SYSTEM

To get the most out of a heating system, it is important to control the cold at its source. Such things as adequate insulation, weather stripping, double windows, and storm doors can cut heating requirements—and fuel bills—dramatically. (Procedures for weather-stripping, installing doors and windows can be found in the chapters on those subjects.)

Dampers which are normally found on the ducts near the furnace (they are sometimes placed higher up, near the room registers), regulate the flow of warm air into various rooms and sections of the house, and they should be adjusted as required. A distant room may require a wide-open damper, a room near the furnace an almost-closed one. Some systems have no dampers and must be regulated at the warm air outlets in the rooms. The fireplace damper should also be closed when not in use. If open, it can leak 25% of the heat input.

Good air circulation is important. Some doors are so airtight that air flow is inhibited. Trimming a half-inch or so off the bottom will often resolve a cold room problem.

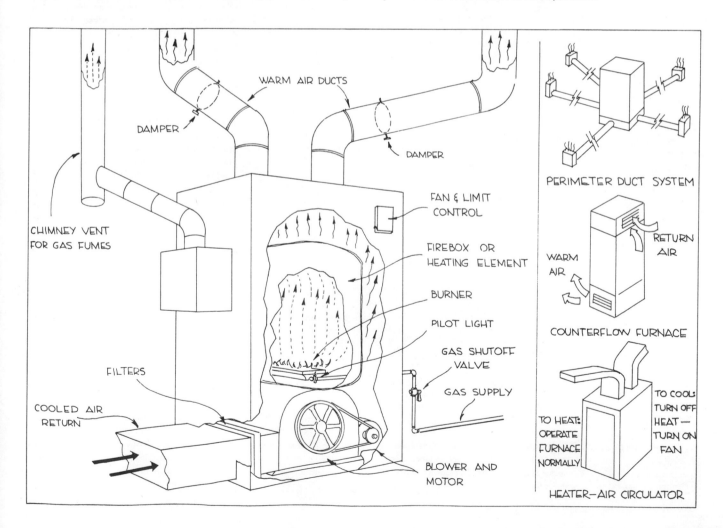

WARM AIR DUCTS

DAMPER

DAMPER

CHIMNEY VENT FOR GAS FUMES

FAN & LIMIT CONTROL

FIREBOX OR HEATING ELEMENT

BURNER

PILOT LIGHT

GAS SHUTOFF VALVE

GAS SUPPLY

FILTERS

COOLED AIR RETURN

BLOWER AND MOTOR

PERIMETER DUCT SYSTEM

WARM AIR

RETURN AIR

COUNTERFLOW FURNACE

TO HEAT: OPERATE FURNACE NORMALLY

TO COOL: TURN OFF HEAT—TURN ON FAN

HEATER-AIR CIRCULATOR

TROUBLESHOOTER'S CHART FOR WARM AIR HEATERS

Listed here are some of the problems or conditions that can be encountered in a warm air heating system—as well as possible causes.

Some of the corrective action is well within the capability of the home repairman and we list the most obvious and easily corrected causes first. Often, however, corrective action is difficult and complicated and should not be attempted by most home-owners. *A good rule of thumb:* If the problem cannot be easily detected and corrected (furnace switch off, clogged filter), it is best to call in an expert for corrective action. (Remember that public utility companies will normally respond to calls concerning problems in furnaces and other gas appliances.)

PROBLEM	POSSIBLE CAUSES
Pilot flame out	Pilot gas supply off; excessive draft (pilot unshielded), pilot burner orifice clogged. (If the above checks do not reveal cause, call a serviceman. Problem may be: thermocouple or thermopile bad; pilot flame improperly set; heat exchanger cracked or burned through.)
Pilot does not relight after several attempts	Not following relight instructions carefully (pilot gas supply not turned on, main control knob not set at pilot position, pilot reset not being held down). If pilot still does not relight, call a serviceman. Problem may be that the gas line is not purged of air; or any of the serious causes listed above.
Burner will not light	Main gas off; furnace switch off; power plug not connected to wall outlet; burned out fuse; defective thermostat. If the above checks do not reveal cause, call a serviceman. The problem could be a defective limit switch; poor electrical connections, a defective gas valve; or output too low on thermopile.
Delayed burner ignition	Burner ports near pilot may be clogged with dirt. Other causes requiring the services of an expert could be: pilot flame too small or improperly located; cracked heat exchanger.
Burner will not turn off. (This condition calls for immediate action — turn main furnace gas valve off.)	Thermostat defective, or poorly located. If this is not the cause, call an expert because the problem may be with a defective or maladjusted limit switch, a short circuit, or a defective or sticking automatic valve.
Rapid burner cycling	Clogged, dirty filters; poor thermostat location. More serious, and requiring the services of an expert, could be excessive anticipation, or limit setting too low.
Blower noisy	Fan blades loose; belt tension improper; pulleys out of alignment; bearings dry; defective or rubbing belt; or motor loose on its mounting.
Blower won't stop	Dirty, clogged filter; manual fan switch on. If these are not the cause, call a serviceman as the fan switch may be defective, or there may be a short circuit.

PROBLEM	POSSIBLE CAUSES
Blower won't run	Power off or disconnected; broken belt. If these checks do not reveal cause, call a serviceman as the problem may be caused by fan control adjustment set too high, loose wiring, defective motor overload protector, or a defective motor.
Rapid fan cycling	Call a serviceman for this condition. It may be caused by a fan switch differential that is too low, excessive blower speed, or a faulty limit switch.
Room temperature overshoots thermostat setting	Thermostat improperly located (cold wall, exposed to drafts, not exposed to circulating air), improperly installed (wiring hole not plugged, not mounted level); or incorrect for the furnace. If these checks do not reveal cause, call a serviceman. The problem may be that the thermostat is not properly calibrated); or that the heating plant is too large or its input excessive.
Room temperature doesn't reach thermostat setting	Thermostat improperly located (warm wall, exposed to sun or other heat source); not mounted level; dirty thermostat contacts; clogged filter. If above checks do not reveal cause, call a serviceman, as the problem could be that the blower is not set to deliver enough air (fan speed too low); limit control is set abnormally low; bad terminals, splicing, or soldering in the wiring; improper thermostat calibration; or a heating plant that is too small.
Gas smell Immediate action: turn off main gas valve, open windows for air, extinguish all flames, and call a serviceman.	A dangerous situation which may be caused by a gas leak, a loose connection, or a break in the gas line—call your public utility company or a serviceman immediately.
Combustion smell Immediate action: turn off furnace, open windows, and call a serviceman.	This serious condition may be caused by a cracked heating element, a cracked or leaking flue or vent, or an excessive amount of dirt and dust fouling the burner area. Call your public utility company or a serviceman.

• Checking Furnace Output and Efficiency

The rating plate which appears on the furnace indicates, among other things, the temperature rise the unit is approved for. The approved rise will vary according to the type and size of furnace. There is a simple home test you can perform to determine whether your heating system is operating efficiently. All you need is an accurate room thermometer.

A rating plate looks like this:

Approved for	70°F to 105°F	X
	50°F to 70°F	NO

Your furnace is approved for the rating followed by an "X," and is *not* approved for the rating followed by "No."

Assuming that your furnace is rated as the sample plate shows, it should add at least 70° and no more than 105° of heat to air that passes through it.

To test the furnace's performance, take the temperature of the air at the point where the return air vent enters the furnace—the filter slot is a good point. Let's assume it is 60°. Then take the temperature at the room outlet which is nearest the furnace. Assume this reading is 135°. Add 5° to compensate for heat loss in the duct and the difference in temperature between the incoming cool air and the outgoing heated air should ideally fall at the low end of the rise indicated. In our example it is 80° (135 + 5 − 60 = 80), acceptable for the sample furnace. If your furnace test results in a reading that is higher or lower than the approved rise, it is a good idea to consult with a heating expert. An experienced handyman can bring the rise within the limits by adjusting motor speed (see page 34). Higher blower speeds will lower the temperature rise.

• Dirt—the Number One Problem

Careless housekeeping which allows dirt, dust, and lint to build up and foul the working parts of the furnace causes most problems with heaters. Here are the periodic tasks the homeowner should perform:

Change filters. Replace filters (forced air only, gravity systems have no filters) as often as required. Some experts recommend a change at least three times a year. A good visual check is to hold the filter up to the light to see the accumulation of dirt and lint. Change it long before it is blocked completely. In extremely dusty or heavy industrial areas, you will have to change filters more often. The procedure is simple:

Remove filter. It may be in a slot where the cool air returns to the furnace or it may be inside the blower compartment. There may be more than one. Replacement size is marked on the edge.

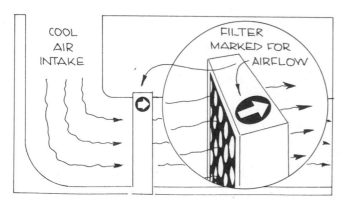

Place new filter in position. Be sure the arrows indicating airflow are pointed in the right direction (into the blower). If it is reversed, the filter will become clogged with dirt and be worthless in a very short time. An oversize filter can make an acceptable replacement—cut it down and bind the edges with masking tape. Be sure to close doors if you have opened any on the blower compartment.

Vacuum and dust. Keeping the filter and all other components of the heating system clean is the most important—and simplest—thing a homeowner can do to prevent problems. Pay particular attention to the areas below.

Blower and motor area. (Caution—turn down thermostat and turn off furnace switch before working around the fan and motor.) Filters do not stop all the dirt and lint from entering this section so it should be vacuumed and dusted periodically. Blower blades clogged with dirt move very little air. If excessively dirty, they can be washed with hot detergent and rinsed, being careful not to get the motor wet. (For a thorough job, have the motor and belt removed at each annual inspection before washing the blades. See page 35.)

Burner and pilot area. The combustion area must be kept clean for efficient operation. Proceed by first turning thermostat and manual control to off, burner and pilot control knob to off. Vacuum or brush away dirt around pilot and burner ports. Relight pilot according to the instructions posted near it.

Warm air outlets and cold air return. Keeping these areas clean should be part of normal housecleaning routine with vacuums and brushes.

Don't use furnace area as a closet. Most building codes call for a certain amount of space around and above a closet furnace (these space requirements are noted on the furnace rating plate), and this open area should not be used for storage. Besides creating a fire hazard, such storage also affects the operation of the furnace by inhibiting air circulation and reducing the volume of air the system requires. You should also keep all basement clutter a good distance away from a furnace there.

ABOUT FILTERS

Several different types of filters for forced air furnaces are on the market. Least expensive and most widely used are the disposable types which are thrown away when they become dirty. Slightly more expensive are the permanent filters which are designed to be cleaned and re-used. Both types perform well when clean and new, but their efficiency drops off rapidly as they become dirty.

More expensive—and much more efficient—are the electrically-charged filters which trap particles electronically, including the microscopic ones which pass through a mechanical filter. These filters must also be cleaned periodically.

• About Thermostats

Thermostats are simply switches that are activated by a temperature-sensing device, and in turn activate another switch at the furnace to turn it on.

The two most common household thermostats are the 24-volt thermostat which uses a transformer to operate off normal household current, and the millivolt thermostat, which is not dependent on household current, but is powered by the very low-voltage produced by a pilot generator in the furnace. (120-volt thermostats are used in some commercial and apartment type installations. Extreme caution should be exercised when working on appliances and fixtures using high voltage.)

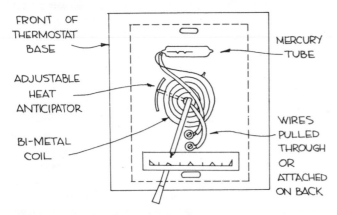

FRONT OF THERMOSTAT BASE

ADJUSTABLE HEAT ANTICIPATOR

BI-METAL COIL

MERCURY TUBE

WIRES PULLED THROUGH OR ATTACHED ON BACK

The three principal working parts of a thermostat are the heat anticipator, the heat sensor, and the switch. The anticipator heats the sensor faster and more accurately than the room temperature could. The sensor, usually a bi-metal coil, contracts as it cools, which in turn trips the switch to "on." The sensor expands as it warms, tripping the switch to "off."

Many heat anticipators are adjustable. Heat sensors, usually bi-metal coils, cannot be repaired or adjusted. Some magnetic switches can be cleaned; mercury switches can be leveled to give better performance. The specific techniques are given below.

Most adjustable heat anticipators have an ampere scale, and should be set during installation to match the ampere rating printed on the furnace primary control (which is located near the pilot light assembly). Some old-fashioned thermostats have a pointer and a plus-or-minus scale, usually mounted on the base plate. This scale should have been set by an expert at the time of installation, and should not be tampered with since it must be checked with special test equipment to determine the effect of any change.

Switches are either mercury bulb, open-contact magnetic, or glass-enclosed magnetic. Mercury bulbs function properly only if installed in perfect level. If a check reveals that your base plate is not level, adjust it using the instructions for installing a new unit (see at right). The points on a magnetic switch with open contacts can be cleaned this way: Turn thermostat control down to open contacts, place a business card between the points; turn the thermostat back up to close points, then rub the card back and forth several times with light gentle pressure.

Thermostats are precision instruments, and they should give years of trouble-free service. Oil should be kept away from them, and the only maintenance required is the occasional removal of accumulated dust and lint under the cover. This should be done by blowing (a small rubber ear syringe, available in drugstores, works well) or by careful, very light brushing. Do not use a vacuum cleaner.

Thermostats merely control room temperature—not the amount of gas supplied to the furnace. The latter supply is constant when the burner is on. Therefore, turning the thermostat way up to a higher-than-normal setting will not heat the house faster than turning it just to the temperature desired. To change the way the furnace operates requires professional adjustment of the primary air on the fan-limit switch, which is located on the furnace itself (see page 35).

REPLACING A FAULTY THERMOSTAT

It is not difficult to replace an existing thermostat. Detailed installation procedures should be included in the packaging of a new thermostat. These will vary with different manufacturers, but generally are as follows:

Remove old unit. The protective cover will snap off or come off with the removal of one or two screws. This will usually expose the two or three mounting screws. Some models have an additional cover over the scale, which will also have to be removed to expose the screws. Remove the mounting screws and pull base plate from wall. The wires leading to the furnace will be attached to the front or back of the base plate. Unscrew terminals to free the old thermostat (be careful not to let the unattached wires fall into the wall).

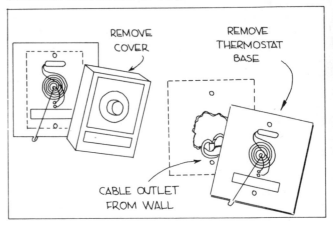

REMOVE COVER

REMOVE THERMOSTAT BASE

CABLE OUTLET FROM WALL

Connect wires to new unit. (Important: be sure the new thermostat operates on the correct voltage for the system.) Clip wire ends and strip ½ inch of insulation to expose fresh wire. Scrape and clean these ends thoroughly with a knife blade. A good check at this point is to touch the loose wires together to be sure the burner ignites. If it does not, there is a problem elsewhere. Connect the wires securely to the proper screw-type terminals on the thermostat. (Caution: Keep the two wires well-separated—if they touch continuously after installation the thermostat cannot shut off.) Push excess wire back into the wall, plugging any free space around the wire with a rag or paper to prevent drafts from affecting the thermostat.

Mount thermostat base. Take base plate of new unit and mount on wall with screws provided. If thermostat is the mercury bulb type, it is important, for proper calibration, to level the base carefully with a spirit level or plumb line. Then tighten one screw, correct level, and tighten all the screws. Replace thermostat cover.

Check operation. Move thermostat indicator above room temperature. Check to see that the main burner lights, then turn indicator back down below room temperature. The burner should shut off. (The fan may not shut off instantly.) Once the room temperature has stabilized, it should remain at the setting on the indicator lever. (Thermostat thermometers are calibrated at the factory and should not require further adjustment. Instructions for calibrating those that are adjustable will normally be provided in the package with the new thermostat.)

SPECIAL CARE WITH MILLIVOLT INSTALLATION

It is extremely important to scrape and clean the wire ends until they are shiny before attaching them to a millivolt thermostat. A pen knife works well. A small amount of dirt or even the dull oxidized coating on the wire can render a millivolt thermostat inoperative. Proper cleaning of wire ends is also important in the case of splices—the wires must make a clean contact.

• Floor Furnaces and Wall Heaters

These installations, because of certain inherent design characteristics, are particularly vulnerable to problems caused by neglect. These compact units are adaptable to many situations where a conventional furnace is not practical, and with periodic attention they function well.

Floor furnaces. Because they are situated beneath an open floor grill, floor furnaces are dirt collectors. (In extreme cases, a pileup of dirt and dust can choke off the air flow at the base and create a potential fire hazard.) Be careful not to put anything on the floor grill. The burner flame is covered, but anything lying on the grill could create a fire hazard by causing the

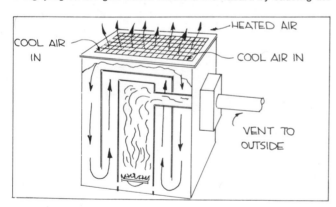

unit to overheat. (Check also to be sure the isinglass window covering the pilot flame is in place.) Beware of throw rugs in the area which can be skidded on top of the unit by running children and pets.

Installations in houses without a basement and only shallow crawl space beneath the floor may have their bases under ground level. Though the unit is enclosed, it is not necessarily waterproof, and you may have a messy situation in a heavy rainstorm. If there is flooding, shut off the unit and do not attempt to use it until it is clean and dry. You may have to call in a furnace repairman to clean it and put it in operation. As with other types of furnaces, make sure the outside vent is tight and is not leaking combustion gases up into the room.

Vented wall heaters. This type of furnace forms high BTU's between studs and therefore needs high air velocities to move the heat and prevent it from becoming a fire hazard. The heater thus acts as a vacuum cleaner and sucks dust and dirt into the blower. It is extremely important to clean this unit often. Otherwise, in a surprisingly short time, you'll get improper combustion and perhaps soot blockage. Continued neglect could cause the burner flame to back out the bottom and emit toxic combustion products. Be sure there is sufficient combustion air for wall heaters. It is a good idea to leave a window cracked about 1 inch in a room housing this unit.

Warning signals:

• Soot deposits at lower opening.
• Black soot at top of heater.
• Black soot on roof vent cap. If it is sooty—like the fireplace vent—there is a problem.
• Highly luminous yellow-tip flame reflecting under heater.

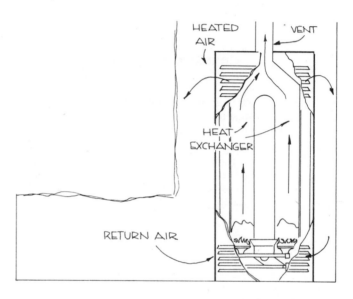

CLEANING WALL AND FLOOR FURNACES

Wall Heaters:
   1. Set manual control (or thermostat) to "off" position.
   2. Open panel at the base to get access to the burner area.
   3. Place burner and pilot control in the "off" position.
   4. Using attachment on vacuum (or a long-handled brush) clean all lint and dust from the burners, controls, and other accessible surfaces inside compartment.
   5. Carefully follow printed instructions to re-light pilot.
   6. Replace burner compartment panel.
   7. Turn manual control on and set thermostat as desired.

Floor Furnaces:
   1. Set manual control (or thermostat) to "off" position.
   2. Remove floor grill.
   3. Use long attachment on vacuum to remove lint and dust from bottom of furnace and from all exposed surfaces.
   4. Retrieve all foreign objects which may have fallen through the grill and into the heating unit.
   5. Replace floor grill and place manual control to "on" position.
   6. Set thermostat as desired.

• Re-lighting the Pilot

If the gas pilot goes out, proceed as follows:

1. Turn off gas to the main and pilot burners. (The knob on the pilot accomplishes this.) Allow at least five minutes for any accumulated gas to dissipate before attempting a re-light. If the system utilizes LPG fuel, use extreme caution since it does not vent upward naturally.

2. Turn room thermostat to a setting well below room temperature.

3. Open warm air registers; be sure that cold air return grills are unobstructed, and that the filter is in place.

4. After at least five minutes have elapsed since you turned off the gas supply, re-light the pilot by following the step-by-step instructions you'll find posted on the furnace.

These instructions will vary slightly, depending upon the type of furnace and pilot installation. If, after following instructions carefully, you are still unable to light the pilot, shut off the gas and call a furnace repairman or your public utility company.

• Checking the Flame

The pilot and burner flame is the heating system's "body temperature." A deviation in burning often provides the first clue to a problem in your furnace. A healthy flame should be blue with perhaps just a hint of yellow at the tips, and burning strongly, but not hard and sharp. If the flame has any of the following characteristics, it may be a simple and obvious problem—or it may be serious and even dangerous. Improper burning not caused by dirt should be regarded as hazardous and the problem referred to an expert.

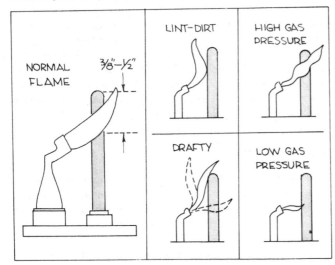

This type of flame:	May be caused by:
Lazy yellow flame	Too little primary air. Clogged ports. Dirt, soot, and dust on pilot and burner. Incorrect or blocked vent.
Noisy flame	Too much primary air. Dirt or burr in orifice. High gas pressure.
Lifting, blowing flame	High gas pressure. Blocked vent. Improperly set manifold pipe angle.
Waving, blue flame	Excessive draft. Re-circulation of combustion products. Cracked heat exchanger.
Small blue flame	Low gas pressure. Clogged orifice.

• Preventive Home Maintenance

A service call at least once a year (see checklist on the next page) is good insurance for a heating system. These annual "physicals" should be routine and inexpensive if the home-owner keeps his furnace clean and performs some basic preventive maintenance. Changing of filters, covered on page 31 is one of these jobs. Here are some others:

Blower and motor. *(Caution—turn thermostat down and turn furnace switch to "off" position before working in this area.)* A prime cause of motor problems is the failure to oil them regularly. Generally, motors with belts should be oiled; those with direct drive are normally oiled and sealed at the factory for the life of the motor. Instructions for oiling should be posted on the motor, but a quick examination will usually reveal the oil cups which need filling. Use SAE 20 or a similar good grade of automotive oil. Do not over-oil or spill oil on other parts. You should lubricate the motor at least once a year (preferably just before the peak operating season). If you use the blower motor year-around, you will have to oil it at least every six months.

Fan belt. The fan belt should be checked regularly for cracks and tears, and it should be replaced if worn. (Remember to turn the furnace switch off before working in this area.) The fan belt should also be kept in proper adjustment for efficient and quiet operation. Belt adjustment affects blower speeds—a loose belt gives slow speeds, a tight belt faster speeds, thereby moving more air. A belt that is too tight can overload the motor.

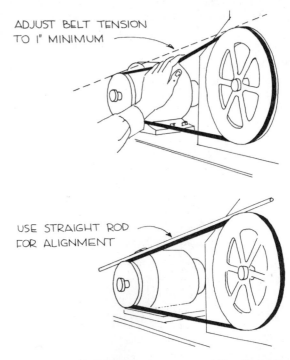

Adjustment of the belt requires some skill with tools and a knowledge of the installation. On some motors, the belt can be adjusted by loosening a set screw on the pulley and widening or narrowing the groove for proper adjustment (wide grooves give slower speeds). On other types, adjustment may be made by means of a cradle belt beneath the motor. To check adjustment, press down between the pulleys. Belt should deflect ¾ to one inch.

• Furnace Parts for Professional Care

Most of the control mechanisms on warm air furnaces should be adjusted or repaired only by professional servicemen. However, it is most useful to know how these work—and how they go wrong—so emergencies can be diagnosed correctly and dealt with.

FAN AND LIMIT CONTROL

One of the most important controls built into a forced air heating system is the fan and limit control. This is a temperature sensing device with two functions. Normally it is housed in one compact unit on the furnace but can be installed as two separate controls.

The fan control automatically turns the blower fan on and off. The limit control is set to shut off the gas supply should the furnace overheat or should the pilot light be extinguished.

The temperature settings of these controls are adjustable within a certain range. The settings are selected and made during installation. They should not require later adjustment unless there is a major change in the system.

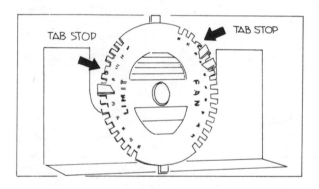

The fan control portion of the unit has two temperature settings. One starts the fan when heated air from the furnace reaches the selected temperature. The other setting shuts the fan off when the air temperature drops to a selected level. Thus the fan operates only when the air is properly warmed, and will not circulate cooled air.

On some installations, a manual switch on this control permits the fan to be turned on to circulate cool air during the summer.

The limit control has one temperature setting which is higher than the fan setting. When this temperature is exceeded, the limit shuts off the gas supply. If this happens, switch the manual furnace control to "Off" and call a repairman. Overheating can indicate a dangerous problem. The condition should be corrected before the furnace is used again.

A separate sensor attached to the pilot light assembly shuts off the gas supply if the pilot goes out.

PRIMARY AIR

To burn properly, a flame must have just the right mixture of

---

ANNUAL INSPECTION CHECKLIST

Annual tuneups have the same value for furnaces as they do for automobiles. They help prevent major breakdowns caused by needless wear. The following checklist contains 15 steps every competent repairman should include in his tuneup service.

1. Check for proper pressure on gas valve.
2. Check for proper millivolt output of thermocouple.
3. Tighten and clean thermocouple connections.
4. Check setting of pilot. Flame should be high enough to generate current through thermocouple.
5. Tighten all gas connections. Check for leaks.
6. Thoroughly check heat exchanger for cracks and holes caused by high temperatures.
7. Remove and clean burners, reset, and adjust air shutters for a proper flame.
8. Check burner and pilot alignment.
9. Clean blower blades for full capacity. An extremely dirty fan may have to be dismounted and its blades washed with detergent in hot water. If it is washed, the fan should be coated with light oil before being replaced.
10. Oil motor bearings.
11. Check fan belt tension and wear.
12. Check fan and limit switch operation and settings.
13. Check flue for leaks and proper connection to outside vents.
14. Check thermostat location, operation, anticipation setting.
15. Check thermostat wiring for tight, clean connections.

---

air and gas. The air control on furnaces is checked and set at the factory by the manufacturer and adjusted by the installer if necessary to accommodate local variations in gas supply. It should not require further adjustment. However, if your flame is burning improperly, this unit may be the problem. The air shutters should be checked for proper adjustment by a furnace repairman.

HEATING ELEMENT

A crack or break in the heating element (firebox) of a furnace is a serious and dangerous situation. Fortunately it is also a rare one. It is usually a result of metal fatigue resulting from many years of expansion and contraction in this part of the furnace.

When this failure occurs, fumes containing carbon monoxide and carbon dioxide spill out of the heating element and mix with the warm air stream that circulates throughout the house. The problem may be compounded because this can result in soot buildup and blockage, which in turn can cause the burner flame to lick out the front of the furnace. The flame then becomes a fire hazard.

If you have reason to believe you have a problem in this area, call in a repairman or a public utility serviceman at once. The first hint is an odor around the registers that is very much reminiscent of automobile exhaust. The professional test is to burn some sulphur in the heating element as a more specific test of odor.

Doors

In theory a door that is fitted carefully and hung with proper clearance should function indefinitely without binding or sticking. But houses settle, wood swells and shrinks, and doors are abused by people, causing door problems in most households.

The most common causes of door trouble are:

● Hinges that are loose or not set properly (mortises cut too deep or not deep enough).

● Improper fitting and hanging of the door at installation.

● Warping, swelling or shrinking of wood.

● Settling or shifting of the house that results in an opening that no longer accommodates the door.

Planing or sanding a sticking, binding door is an obvious solution to a familiar problem. But it may not be the best solution because most door problems in the first two categories can be corrected more effectively at the hinges by resetting them firmly, shimming them out, or cutting their mortises deeper.

Start any diagnosis of a balky door by taking a good look at how it sticks. Close the door if possible, and check the sides, top, and bottom by sliding a five cent coin or a thin (1/16-inch) strip of wood along between the door and jamb to see where it is loose and where it sticks.

Second, use a carpenter's square to check the shape of the door and the jamb.

If the jamb and door are both true and the sticking parts are small in area, chances are good that you will be able to correct the situation at the hinges.

If both are square but the door fits too tightly in general, you will have to sand or plane it down to fit.

If either the jamb or the door is out of square, you may be able to compensate at the hinges, but you will probably have to saw or plane the door down to fit (rather than attempting to work the jamb back into square—a demanding job even for a journeyman carpenter). A door jamb that is very far out of square may indicate serious settling in your house. You may be well advised to call in a carpenter for a check. There could be some way to stop the settling before it begins to cause all kinds of trouble in the frame, the foundation, and the plumbing.

If the door has shrunk until it fits too loosely in its frame, adjusting the hinges and latch strike plate can be of some help. In most cases weather stripping serves best to fill the cracks.

A warped door can be towed back into line in some cases, as described on page 40, but usually has to be replaced. Broken doors also are best replaced rather than repaired. The method for hanging a replacement door is described on pages 40-41.

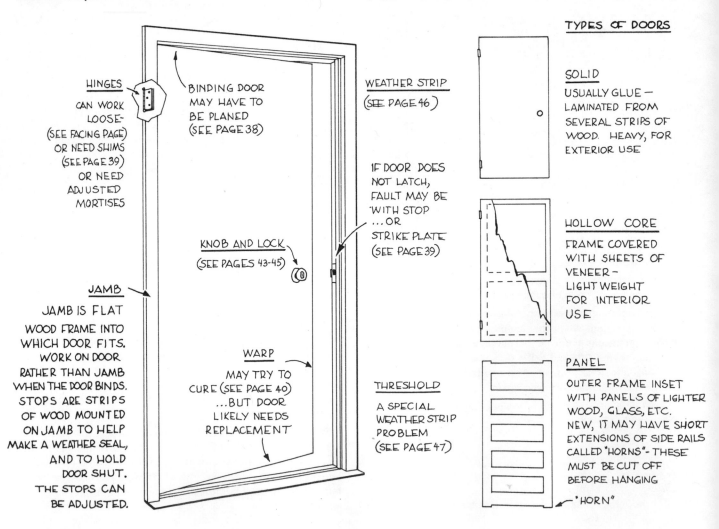

HINGES
CAN WORK LOOSE- (SEE FACING PAGE) OR NEED SHIMS (SEE PAGE 39) OR NEED ADJUSTED MORTISES

BINDING DOOR MAY HAVE TO BE PLANED (SEE PAGE 38)

KNOB AND LOCK (SEE PAGES 43-45)

JAMB
JAMB IS FLAT WOOD FRAME INTO WHICH DOOR FITS. WORK ON DOOR RATHER THAN JAMB WHEN THE DOOR BINDS. STOPS ARE STRIPS OF WOOD MOUNTED ON JAMB TO HELP MAKE A WEATHER SEAL, AND TO HOLD DOOR SHUT. THE STOPS CAN BE ADJUSTED.

WARP
MAY TRY TO CURE (SEE PAGE 40) ...BUT DOOR LIKELY NEEDS REPLACEMENT

WEATHER STRIP (SEE PAGE 46)

IF DOOR DOES NOT LATCH, FAULT MAY BE WITH STOP ...OR STRIKE PLATE (SEE PAGE 39)

THRESHOLD
A SPECIAL WEATHER STRIP PROBLEM (SEE PAGE 47)

TYPES OF DOORS

SOLID
USUALLY GLUE— LAMINATED FROM SEVERAL STRIPS OF WOOD. HEAVY, FOR EXTERIOR USE

HOLLOW CORE
FRAME COVERED WITH SHEETS OF VENEER— LIGHT WEIGHT FOR INTERIOR USE

PANEL
OUTER FRAME INSET WITH PANELS OF LIGHTER WOOD, GLASS, ETC. NEW, IT MAY HAVE SHORT EXTENSIONS OF SIDE RAILS CALLED "HORNS"- THESE MUST BE CUT OFF BEFORE HANGING

"HORN"

• How to Un-stick a Sticking Door

If a door is tilted in its frame, the points at which it binds will be easy to spot (using the coin or wood as a guide as explained on the opposite page).

The sketches show how to diagnose the problem and how to start remedying it.

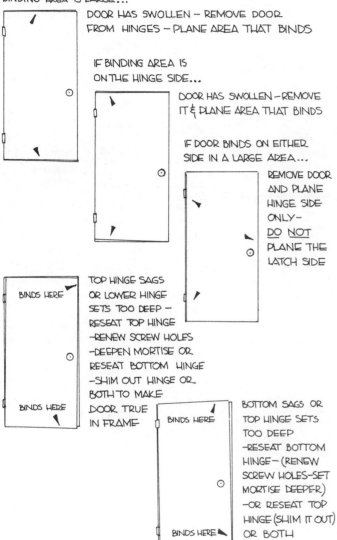

WHEN TOP OR BOTTOM
BINDING AREA IS LARGE...

DOOR HAS SWOLLEN — REMOVE DOOR
FROM HINGES — PLANE AREA THAT BINDS

IF BINDING AREA IS
ON THE HINGE SIDE...

DOOR HAS SWOLLEN — REMOVE
IT & PLANE AREA THAT BINDS

IF DOOR BINDS ON EITHER
SIDE IN A LARGE AREA...

REMOVE DOOR
AND PLANE
HINGE SIDE
ONLY —
DO NOT
PLANE THE
LATCH SIDE

BINDS HERE

TOP HINGE SAGS
OR LOWER HINGE
SETS TOO DEEP —
RESEAT TOP HINGE
—RENEW SCREW HOLES
—DEEPEN MORTISE OR
RESEAT BOTTOM HINGE
—SHIM OUT HINGE OR
BOTH TO MAKE
DOOR TRUE
IN FRAME

BINDS HERE

BINDS HERE

BOTTOM SAGS OR
TOP HINGE SETS
TOO DEEP
—RESEAT BOTTOM
HINGE— (RENEW
SCREW HOLES–SET
MORTISE DEEPER)
—OR RESEAT TOP
HINGE (SHIM IT OUT)
OR BOTH

BINDS HERE

Some general hints:

In working with the hinges, attempt to get the hinge side of the door perfectly aligned with its side of the jamb. The rest will follow automatically if the door and jamb are square.

If you plane, concentrate first on the hinge side. Avoid planing the latch side if possible since it is bevelled to allow tight fit. If the hinge side cannot be planed to un-stick the door, proceed next to the top or bottom.

Do not be too hasty to plane. Coarse sandpaper followed by finer sandpaper is easier to control. A belt sander is best. Otherwise wrap the paper around a block to keep the sanding as even as possible.

The techniques for each operation are described below.

REMOVING A DOOR

Regardless of the problem, you likely will have to remove the door from its hinges to make repairs.

Open the door to an angle that gives easy access to the loose pins that hold each set of hinge leaves together. Remove the pin from the bottom hinge with a hammer and a nail set (or screwdriver, or even a sturdy stick). The pin should not be loose enough to be pulled out by hand but should come out easily with several solid upward blows. Next, remove the top pin the same way. Then lift the door out of its jamb.

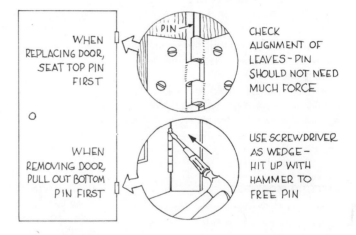

WHEN
REPLACING DOOR,
SEAT TOP PIN
FIRST

WHEN
REMOVING DOOR,
PULL OUT BOTTOM
PIN FIRST

PIN

CHECK
ALIGNMENT OF
LEAVES – PIN
SHOULD NOT NEED
MUCH FORCE

USE SCREWDRIVER
AS WEDGE–
HIT UP WITH
HAMMER TO
FREE PIN

When you replace the door, start the top pin first, then the bottom one. Drive the pins home only after both hinges are correctly aligned.

If you are going to plane the hinge side of the door, unscrew and remove the hinge leaves before you begin. Remember that you may have to deepen the mortises after planing.

REPAIRING WORN SCREW HOLES

The screws holding hinge plates to the door and jamb carry the full weight of the door, so are prone to wear. Once the screws work loose, the door will sag against its jamb.

A simple, fast way to repair a worn-out, oversize screw hole is to drive wooden matchsticks or bits of wood into the hole. The screw bites into and expands this

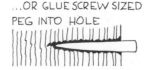

PACK MATCH STICKS
INTO HOLE...

packing for a tight fit. If you use this method, it is a good idea to use slightly longer screws than the originals. The method works best with lightweight doors.

...OR GLUE SCREW SIZED
PEG INTO HOLE

...TRIM PEG FLUSH WITH
CHISEL

The strongest, most durable repair is to trim a wooden peg to size, dip it in woodworking glue, and drive it into the hole. After the glue dries, trim the top of the peg flush, then replace the hinge.

PLANING DOOR EDGES

Planing the side of a door is simpler than planing a top or bottom, because on the side you go with the grain rather than across it.

The following are general rules for planing:

● Use the plane with the longest sole if you have a choice. In any case, use one with a blade wider than the edge of the door in order to keep the cuts level.

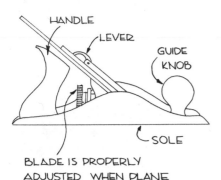

JACK OR BENCH PLANE

HANDLE
LEVER
GUIDE KNOB
SOLE

BLADE IS PROPERLY ADJUSTED WHEN PLANE CUTS A LONG PAPER THIN CURL

● Keep your weight on the handle at the rear of the plane, not on the guide knob at the front.

● Make your strokes parallel with the edge you are planing, and keep the plane at the same angle as the direction of the stroke, as shown in the sketch.

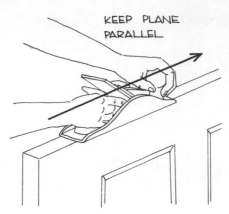

KEEP PLANE PARALLEL

● If you are planing across the grain (that is, across the ends of the side rails), work from the edges toward the center and do not go all the way across the edge. An end will often split under outward pressure from the plane.

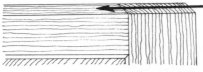

ACROSS SIDE RAIL – PLANE TOWARD CENTER - NOT OVER THE END

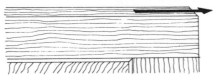

ALONG SIDE RAIL - PLANE OVER END

If you do not have a bench vise, this simple device can be assembled to hold a door steady:

Nail two scraps of 2 x 4 to a strip of ¼-inch-thick hardboard or plywood, just far enough apart to accommodate the door easily. Then nail two more scraps to the opposite face of the hardboard,

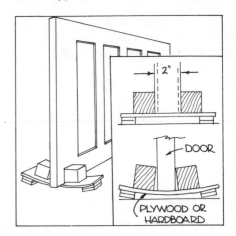

2"
DOOR
PLYWOOD OR HARDBOARD

preferably farther apart than the top two.

Make two of these, one for each end of the door.

When the door is set edgewise into the device, its weight will bend the hardboard and thus press the top blocks together as a vise does.

An extra advantage is that the device keeps the door edge off the ground, so it is not marred, or does not pick up dirt that will dull your plane.

CUTTING MORTISES

A mortise is the chiselled recess into which a hinge leaf is fitted. Frequently a mortise has to be made deeper to reset a door truer in its frame, or a full mortise has to be cut in a replacement door.

The full process: (1) Use the hinge leaf as a template, and score guide lines with a knife blade. Also use the hinge leaf to mark the depth of the cut. (2) Make

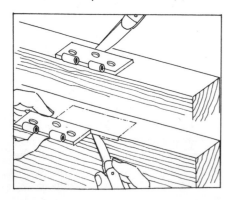

a parallel series of shallow cuts to the desired depth, hammering on the chisel almost vertically, with the bevelled face away from you. (3) Decrease the angle to about 30° and carefully chip out wood to

HAMMER CHISEL IN THIS STEP ONLY

the desired depth. (4) Make the final smoothing cuts with the chisel almost flat, working from the side. This would be the first step in deepening an existing mortise. (5) Place the hinge leaf in

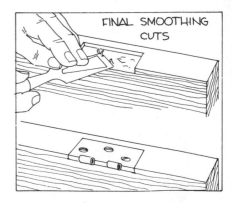

FINAL SMOOTHING CUTS

the cut and check it. It should be uniformly flush with the edge of the door or jamb. If the cut is not deep enough, continue working from the side, paying special attention to the corners. If you have cut too deeply, shim with a thin sheet of brass or a hard-finished cardboard (such as is used for file folders).

See page 41 for details on how to locate a hinge leaf.

SHIMMING HINGES

Hinges can be built up from their original depth with any of several materials in order to reset a door so it will not bind.

The most durable material is sheet brass, sold in small squares in many hardware stores. The metal comes in varying thicknesses for fine work, as in cabinets.

Shims also can be cut from any non-compressible cardboard, particle board, or similar material.

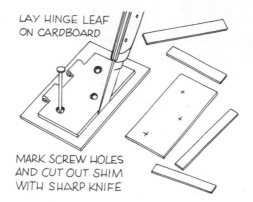

LAY HINGE LEAF ON CARDBOARD

MARK SCREW HOLES AND CUT OUT SHIM WITH SHARP KNIFE

Use the hinge leaf as a template. Cut the shim so it is minutely smaller in each dimension, using tin snips, old scissors, or a sharp knife and a straight-edge. Use a drill or a nail to start screw holes in the shim. Take care to center them in the holes drilled in the hinge leaf.

In general it is not advisable to glue the shims in place since you may need to replace them in time, or may wish to replace the entire door at some later date.

• Doors That Will Not Latch Properly

Doors that will not latch properly are sprung or warped slightly, or are in frames that have settled. A sprung door pushes up against its stop before the latch can seat in the strike plate out of alignment.

Dealing with a warp: There are two possibilities—partial shimming of the hinges, or resetting the stop.

If you shim the hinges, the point is to change their angle slightly by shimming one or both leaves only on the side nearest the hinge pins. This turns the door slightly inward, perhaps enough to allow it to latch. The method works best if the warp is at top or bottom of the door.

Resetting the stop serves best if the warp is near the latch, and if the warp is too much for shimming to correct. If the door will latch when you slam it hard, but not otherwise, this technique should work. (1) Score the paint between the stop and the door frame to minimize its chipping. (2) Starting at the bottom, use a wide chisel to pry the stop away from the frame. (3) Once it is free and the old nails are driven out, close the door and prop the stop lightly against the door. (4) Insert a thin cardboard shim between stop and door. (5) Pressing the stop against the shim, nail it into place using 6d finishing nails. (6) Repaint to seal the stop against weather.

If this resetting of the stop moves it much more than 1/16-inch, you also may need to shim the hinges at an angle as described above in order to avoid forcing them, since you will have changed the angle at which the door closes.

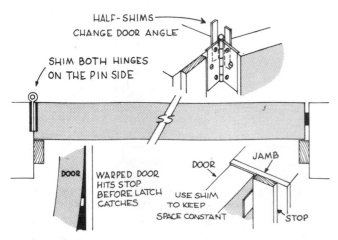

HALF-SHIMS CHANGE DOOR ANGLE

SHIM BOTH HINGES ON THE PIN SIDE

WARPED DOOR HITS STOP BEFORE LATCH CATCHES

DOOR

JAMB

USE SHIM TO KEEP SPACE CONSTANT

STOP

Dealing with a latch plate: Close the door carefully to see how the latch meets the strike plate. Depending on how the frame has settled, the latch will strike either too high or too low to fit the hole in the strike plate. (Often scars in paint on the strike plate will give a precise clue.) Once you have discovered the degree of mis-alignment, file the hole in the strike plate so the latch can seat, or remove the strike plate and cut the mortise higher or lower to accommodate the changed position. Fill the

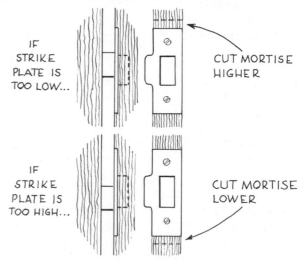

IF STRIKE PLATE IS TOO LOW...

CUT MORTISE HIGHER

IF STRIKE PLATE IS TOO HIGH...

CUT MORTISE LOWER

vacated part of the original mortise with wood putty, or a slurry of sawdust and woodworking glue, and paint over the area once the glue has dried.

For more detailed notes on cutting a mortise, see the section titled "Cutting Mortises" on the facing page.

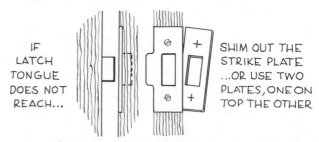

IF LATCH TONGUE DOES NOT REACH...

SHIM OUT THE STRIKE PLATE ...OR USE TWO PLATES, ONE ON TOP THE OTHER

Occasionally a latch will fail to reach a strike plate because the door has shrunk. To make the latch reach, shim the strike plate out with any suitable material (see above). If the gap still exists, shim the hinges of the door as well.

• Straightening Warped Doors

Occasionally a homeowner will find reason to try to straighten a severely warped door. There is no guaranteed success, but there are three separate methods to try.

One is to dampen a door and put it out to dry in the sun on levelled sawhorses with weights piled on the warp. The door should be left to dry for at least two days. The weight should be enough to flatten the warp while the door dries.

For a door that has bowed anywhere but at a corner, the solution is the same as that used for curing a sagging gate—a wire and turnbuckle. Locate the extreme point in the outward bulge of the warp. Plot a diagonal from that point to the nearest jamb-side corner. Extend the diagonal in the other direction to the hinge side. Attach screw eyes to the door at the two indicated points. Attach the wires and a turnbuckle loosely. Then place a 2x4 on edge at the extreme point of the warp, and cinch the turnbuckle tight. As the door begins to straighten, take additional turns to maintain pressure.

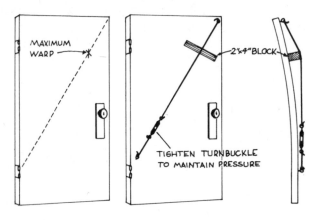

If the warp is toward the top or bottom of the door, try this adaptation of the way boat builders bend oak boat ribs. Soak oak strip—a 1 x 1 or 1 x 2 as long as the warp—in boiling water. Clamp it down over a block that will produce a bend about four times greater than the bend of the warp. Then pour boiling water over it again. When dry, this rib will have a pronounced bend. When screwed into place, it will tend to pull the door into a straight line.

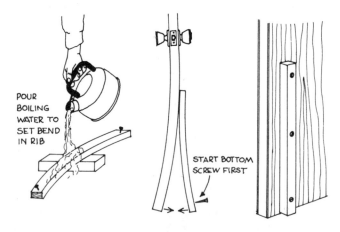

If the door fits close against closet shelves, you may have to notch some shelves to give clearance to the rib.

• Replacing a Door

Replacement doors, readily available in building supplies stores, should require only slight adjustments to fit into standard doorways.

Although no individual step is complicated in itself, hanging a replacement door requires patience. The secret of success is taking the steps in logical order, and using a few small tricks to make the work go faster. The steps can be divided into five major jobs: the preliminaries; trimming the new door; locating and installing the hinges; hanging the door and making final adjustments; and installing the latch and lock hardware. The following section follows that organization.

The preliminaries: Remove the old door, leave the jamb-side hinges in place if you are salvaging the hardware. Measure the opening from top to bottom on both hinge side and latch side. Also measure it across at two or more points. Knowing the exact shape of the opening will help you choose the best-suited replacement, and will also tell you if you will have to make substantial trims.

With the replacement door purchased, make any rough trim. (Some doors come with "horns" at top and bottom—untrimmed extra lengths of the side rails. Non-standard openings also require cutting for rough fit. The latter can be a crucial point with hollow-cane doors, which have only a ½-inch trim margin.)

Trimming to fit: (1) Hold the door in the opening. With the sides in approximate alignment, the top of the door should fit squarely against the top of the jamb. If it does not, align the latch side. Measure the gaps, transcribe the measurements to the door, then sand or plane until the top does fit squarely. Remember to plane in from the edges toward the middle to avoid splintering the side rails. (2) Measure the exact distance from the top jamb to the door sill at both the hinge and latch side. Subtract ⅝ inch from these measurements, more if the rug is deeper than the sill on an inward-opening door. (3) Transcribe these measurements onto the door. Trim the excess off. (Rule of thumb: Plane or sand any excess up to ¼ inch; saw any excess more than that.)

The above approach requires precise measurement and sawing. A more cautious method: Place the door in the opening with shims at the top to give a clearance of 1/16 inch. Prop the door up on shims at the bottom if necessary for the top clearance to be correct. With a straight-edge, mark the bottom of the door to establish desired clearance, then trim the excess. (4) Prop the door into place so it is snug against the latch side, using shims on the hinge side to force it into place, and at the top to keep a 1/16-inch clearance there. Use a scribe or ordinary pencil compass to mark a trim line on the hinge side that allows a total of ⅛-inch clearance along the side. Trim if necessary. (5) Plane the latch side to a slight bevel toward the inside. About ⅛ inch is enough on a 1⅜ door. This is to allow easy opening without sacrificing a tight fit. (6) Prop the door into position, using shims on all four sides, and check all clearances. The top clearance should be ⅛ inch. Each side should be 1/16 inch. The bottom should be ½ inch or enough to clear the rug. A few spots may need light sanding at this point.

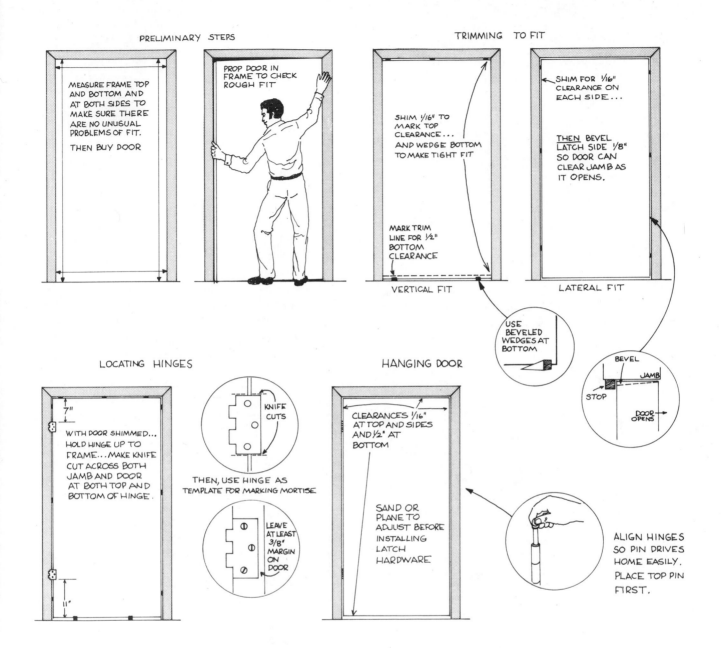

PRELIMINARY STEPS

MEASURE FRAME TOP AND BOTTOM AND AT BOTH SIDES TO MAKE SURE THERE ARE NO UNUSUAL PROBLEMS OF FIT.

THEN BUY DOOR

PROP DOOR IN FRAME TO CHECK ROUGH FIT

TRIMMING TO FIT

SHIM 1/16" TO MARK TOP CLEARANCE... AND WEDGE BOTTOM TO MAKE TIGHT FIT

MARK TRIM LINE FOR 1/2" BOTTOM CLEARANCE

VERTICAL FIT

SHIM FOR 1/16" CLEARANCE ON EACH SIDE...

THEN BEVEL LATCH SIDE 1/8" SO DOOR CAN CLEAR JAMB AS IT OPENS.

LATERAL FIT

USE BEVELED WEDGES AT BOTTOM

BEVEL

JAMB

STOP

DOOR OPENS

LOCATING HINGES

7"

WITH DOOR SHIMMED... HOLD HINGE UP TO FRAME... MAKE KNIFE CUT ACROSS BOTH JAMB AND DOOR AT BOTH TOP AND BOTTOM OF HINGE.

11"

KNIFE CUTS

THEN, USE HINGE AS TEMPLATE FOR MARKING MORTISE

LEAVE AT LEAST 3/8" MARGIN ON DOOR

HANGING DOOR

CLEARANCES 1/16" AT TOP AND SIDES AND 1/2" AT BOTTOM

SAND OR PLANE TO ADJUST BEFORE INSTALLING LATCH HARDWARE

ALIGN HINGES SO PIN DRIVES HOME EASILY. PLACE TOP PIN FIRST.

Locating and installing hinges: With door propped in position as described in Step 6, remove the hinge-side shims and push door tight against hinge side jamb. (2) Using old jamb-side hinges as a guide, mark hinge position on door. If no hinges are in place, make knife cuts on both jamb and door to locate the hinges. It is standard practice for the top of the upper hinge to be 7 inches from the top of the door, and the bottom of the lower hinge to be 11 inches above the bottom of the door. (3) Using a hinge leaf as a guide, use a knife to cut an outline for each mortise. (4) Fashion the mortises as described on page 38. (5) Install hinge leaves securely.

Hanging the door: A helper is welcome at this point, but an adept foot at the bottom of the door can replace extra hands. (1) Ease the door into position so hinges begin to align. (2) When the hinge butts are together, start the top pin through its guides. Do not force it. (3) Once the top pin passes through two or more loops of the hinge butts, start the bottom pin. (4) Jostle the door until both pins slip into place.

At this point the best of professional door hangers usually needs a bit of judicious sanding to free a tight spot or two. The rest of us frequently have to take the door back down for some vigorous sanding or light planing to compensate for slight mis-measurements along the way.

Installing latch hardware: The position of the existing strike plate on the jamb usually determines the location of the door-knob and lock. See page 45 for details.

Before painting or finishing the door, take it down and seal the top and bottom edges with a sealer (or prime coat if you are going to paint). This will prevent moisture from seeping into the door and causing swelling or warping later.

• Sliding Doors

Though all sliding doors operate basically the same way, regardless of their purpose, the variety of their hardware is almost unlimited. All of these doors, whether they lead onto patios or into closets, are supported by top and bottom tracks. Nearly all of them roll on wheels. The major difference in installation is that some are hung from the top rail, while others rest their weight on the bottom rail. Lightweight closet doors and extremely heavy garage doors tend to be top-hung. Most other moderately heavy doors (patio doors, etc.) rest on their bottom rails.

If doors jump off their rails, the source of difficulty may be an obstruction in the track or may be a missing guide. Doors that bind may be running in dirty or bent tracks or may be pressed too tightly by a guide. Doors that drag heavily or sit crookedly in their frames usually have one wheel or more out of adjustment.

Maintenance: All tracks, especially those which support the wheels, must be kept free of foreign objects and dirt. This is most important with bottom-supported doors where dirt from foot traffic can easily clog the tracks, causing the door to bind. Inspect all hardware periodically and tighten any loosened screws in the frame or track. Because most of the wheels used on sliding doors are self-lubricating nylon, they should not be oiled.

Removing doors: Removing sliding doors for maintenance or repair is simple, although there are several variations in design that affect the process. Some bottom-supported doors can be removed by lifting them straight up (far enough to clear the bottom tracks), then angling the lower part of the door outward. (Patio doors especially are heavy; lifting them takes a stout pair of arms.) Some top-hung doors can also be lifted straight up and off the tracks, but most require additional positioning or angling because the top wheels are usually locked into their

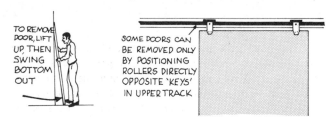

TO REMOVE DOOR, LIFT UP, THEN SWING BOTTOM OUT

SOME DOORS CAN BE REMOVED ONLY BY POSITIONING ROLLERS DIRECTLY OPPOSITE 'KEYS' IN UPPER TRACK

tracks to prevent them from jumping off the rails every time they are jarred. Some doors employ a spring-loaded cover mechanism for this purpose. Others have key openings, so it is possible to lift the door up and out only at one point along the track. These openings are usually located so the door is about halfway open and thus easy to grab at each side.

Doors that jump off tracks: All sliding doors have some sort of guide that keeps them vertical and aligned with their tracks, rather than free to sway off line. In bottom-supported designs, the frame usually overlaps the sash enough to keep the sash firmly in place. Top-hung doors, however, frequently have only one or two guides to keep the bottoms aligned as the door slides. The principal guide is at the center of the opening. The secondary one, if any, adjoins the jamb where the door closes.

When these break or are too small to perform their job, they should be replaced, or the door will jump off its track frequenty. The sketch shows some typical guides.

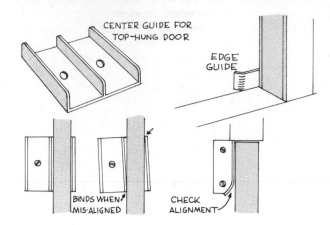

CENTER GUIDE FOR TOP-HUNG DOOR

EDGE GUIDE

BINDS WHEN MIS-ALIGNED

CHECK ALIGNMENT

If these guides appear to be properly positioned, check the wheel track of a top-hung door. A piece may be missing from the assembly that helps keep the wheels locked in place.

Dragging or tilted doors: All sliding doors of substantial manufacture roll on adjustable wheels. The range of adjustment allows compensation for slight changes in the shape of the frame due to settling of the house, or swelling or warping of the wood frame. The illustration shows three typical wheel assemblies and the method for adjusting each.

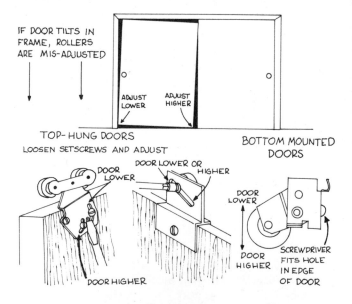

IF DOOR TILTS IN FRAME, ROLLERS ARE MIS-ADJUSTED

ADJUST LOWER

ADJUST HIGHER

TOP-HUNG DOORS
LOOSEN SETSCREWS AND ADJUST

BOTTOM MOUNTED DOORS

DOOR LOWER

DOOR LOWER OR HIGHER

DOOR LOWER

DOOR HIGHER

DOOR HIGHER

SCREWDRIVER FITS HOLE IN EDGE OF DOOR

The best basic approach is to adjust all wheels to their fully retracted position, then to proceed to align the door and set the clearances by measurement.

Replacement for worn out wheels can be a problem because many small manufacturers producing them have gone out of business over the years. Take the broken part and as much information about the door as you can to a dealer. Get his advice on the best way to proceed.

If the door is too far out of adjustment for the wheels to compensate, it is necessary to reposition the runners or modify the basic frame. Both jobs take professional skill.

• Adjusting or Replacing Locks

Lock problems are apt to cause a great deal of inconvenience. They usually require immediate attention.

Although failures seem sudden, lock problems tend to develop gradually. Many of them can be corrected before they become serious with some preventive maintenance at the first sign of trouble. Over a long period of time, locks will age and wear out. When this happens, and the lock mechanism fails or malfunctions, it is often simpler and less costly to replace a lock than to attempt repairs.

Replacing a lock is not difficult. Lock replacement kits are available through locksmiths, building suppliers, and hardware stores. These come with all the parts and complete installation instructions. The task has been greatly simplified with printed templates which are included and drilling rigs (which can be rented or borrowed from dealers) which assure correct positioning and size of drilled holes.

Almost all residential exterior door locks fall into two categories—they are either mortised or bored into the door. Chances are that if a house was built in the past 20 years, its locks are the bored-in variety. Locks of this type are easier to

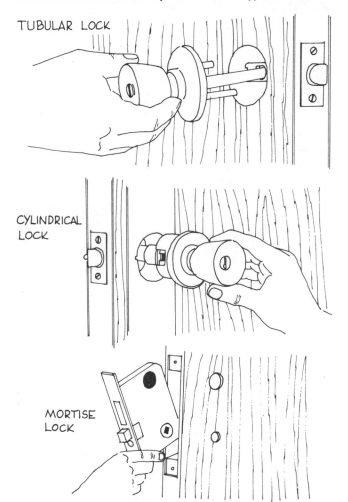

TUBULAR LOCK

CYLINDRICAL LOCK

MORTISE LOCK

install and require relatively small drilled holes rather than the big hollowed-out space in the door required by mortise locks. Locks can also be surface mounted, but these are usually auxiliary locks such as night latches, sliding bolts, and chains.

Replacement mortise locks are still available, but most homeowners prefer to convert their doors to a bored-in tubular or cylindrical lock assembly. This conversion is relatively easy and a typical installation is described and illustrated on page 45.

Tubular and cylindrical locks are similar in construction and in installation. The major difference is that the tubular kind is simpler and usually less rugged in construction and has a smaller locking mechanism than a cylindrical lock.

The three basic parts of bored-in locks are the strike, the latchbolt, and the lock mechanism. The simplest lock problems, and the easiest ones to correct, occur in the area of the strike (or striker) plate. Sagging, warped or shrunken doors, or settling of the house can result in the latch and strike being out of alignment. Curing the door problem (see page 37) will normally put two parts back into alignment. If a door has shrunken excessively, it may be necessary to shim out the strike to narrow the gap. (You can also shim out the door hinges or even use two strike plates, one on top of the other.)

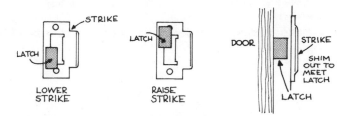

LATCH / STRIKE — LATCH / LOWER STRIKE — LATCH / RAISE STRIKE — DOOR / STRIKE / LATCH / SHIM OUT TO MEET LATCH

An improperly functioning latchbolt can often be traced to some of the strike problems above. Mis-alignment will prevent it from latching or sliding properly into position in the strike. It may also be sticking, a condition which can often be cured by cleaning or lubrication.

If a lock problem occurs in the lock's tumbler mechanism, it is usually beyond the repair capability of the home handyman and will call for a locksmith or replacement of the lock. Removing the lock and taking it to a locksmith is far less expensive than having the locksmith come to you.

CLEANING A LOCK

Locks are lubricated during assembly and may not require additional lubrication. However, the original grease in the interior can become gummed up by dirt and dust, resulting in slow response or improper operation of the lock (especially true in extremely dusty areas). When this happens, it is a simple matter to correct.

Remove the lock from the door. Thoroughly wash the lock chassis in a petroleum solvent and then apply a small amount of cup grease or a penetrating oil to the various moving parts (the retractor, the outside spindle, the button unit, bearings—if any—and the latch unit). Do not over-lubricate because this will trap dust and gum in the lock again in a short period of time.

Never use oil or grease in the keyway. The tumblers must exert a certain degree of friction to work the latchbolt. Only graphite should be used—you can often apply enough to do the job by scraping ordinary pencil lead onto the key. Be careful of using too much graphite if you live in a moist climate, as it may also become sticky.

In extremely dusty areas, it is a good idea to attach a keyway shutter to prevent dust and dirt from entering.

HOW TO REMOVE A DOOR LOCK

The typical modern lock is easy to remove. Illustrated is the step-by-step procedure for removing a typical cylindrical door lock. Some other cylindrical locks are removed the same way except that they have a tiny hole in the knob's shank instead of a button or catch. You push a nail into that hole to release the knob.

TROUBLESHOOTING BALKY LOCKS

The list of probable causes of lock troubles can be divided about equally between poor fit between the lock and its strike plate, and malfunctions of some part of the lock mechanism. In fact, adjustment of the fit is a more frequent solution to trouble.

PROBLEM	PROBABLE CAUSES AND SOLUTIONS
Lock sticks or is slow in responding	Original grease in lock interior is dirty and gummy. *Remove lock from door and clean as described below.*
Key does not insert smoothly	Keyway and tumbler area dirty. *Blow a pinch of graphite into the keyway, or scrape an ordinary pencil lead onto the key's teeth. Do not oil.* Foreign object in keyway. *Attempt to dislodge it with a key extractor or hatpin.*
Lock is frozen	Extremely cold weather has caused accumulated moisture to freeze solid. *Hold match to key until it is hot to touch, then insert key in lock and work it gently until the ice melts. Spraying windshield defroster into keyway will prevent re-occurrence.*
Key is broken in lock	Key inserted improperly or not pushed all the way in before turning, or attempting to force an ill-fitting replacement key. *Attempt first to remove broken part of key with a key extractor or hatpin. If this does not work, remove lock cylinder and push key fragment out from the reverse side with a hatpin.* (If the key went all the way in before breaking and you are locked out, it is sometimes possible to unlock the door by turning lock with pliers or a screwdriver.)
Latch bolt will not engage or disengage without jiggling door	Door loose on hinges or otherwise misaligned because of warping, shrinking, or setting. *Correct basic door problem, then make any adjustments required to realign latchbolt and strike plate.*
Latchbolt engagement in strike is too shallow	Door has probably shrunk, widening gap between door and jamb. *Shim out door or strike plate, or both. Or place second strike plate on top of original.*
Key turns freely but does not operate locking mechanism	Tail piece of cam (which connects cylinder to locking mechanism) is loose or broken. *Normally requires services of a locksmith.*

If your lock has exposed screw heads on the inside rosette, simply remove these screws and both knobs will come off. The remainder of the mechanism will slip out from the edge of the door with the latch.

Removing a mortise lock. The simple type used on interior doors is removed in a manner similar to removing a cylindrical lock. You remove one knob by loosening the set screw on its shank. Pull the square spindle and second knob out from the other side of the door. Then you can unscrew and slip the latch and lock mechanism out from the edge of the door.

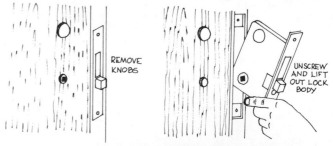

The type of mortise lock for an exterior door which has a thumb latch for an exterior handle is more complicated. (1) First you remove the interior knob, the turn knob for the deadbolt, if any, and the exterior handle. (2) Look closely at the interior knob's square spindle. It is a two-piece hook spindle. One half, when wiggled around, will unhook itself from the other half, then can be removed. The outer half, which has a hooked end, will then come out freely. (3) Remove the exposed screws, if any, on the cylinder lock on the outside of the door. (4) Look closely on the latch face of the lock (on the edge of the door) for a long set screw that is in line with the cylinder lock. After loosening this, you can unscrew the cylinder from the lock body. (5) Finally, remove the screws of the lock body from the edge of the door and slip out the body with the latch.

REPLACING A LOCK

Before you purchase a new unit, jot down a few notes about your existing lock installation. This will help the dealer in advising you in your selection of a replacement. This information should include:

- Type of lock—mortised or bored-in.
- Diameter of lock mechanism hole.
- The distance of the backset—this is the distance from the edge of the door to the center of the doorknob and is normally 2¾ inches, but can vary.
- Type of latch front—the shape and dimensions of the part of the latchbolt which shows in the edge of the door.
- Thickness of door—most locks are designed to accommodate standard doors (1⅜ and 1¾ inches thick). Thinner or thicker doors will require one of the locks which are capable of adapting to them.

This installation procedure will vary, depending upon the replacement, and step-by-step procedures will be provided with the kit you purchase.

Described below is the procedure for replacing an old mortised lock with a new cylindrical unit. Other installations will be similar.

(1) Remove interior and exterior knobs and hardware from old lock. A screwdriver—and perhaps a pair of pliers—should do the job. (2) Remove screws from latch face on door edge and slide out old mortise lock mechanism. (3) Using template supplied with new lock, mark off size and location of new hole for cylindrical lock. (4) Drill new hole. Avoid splitting by completing drilling from the other side when point of drill breaks through. (5) Extend old mortise on door edge as necessary to accommodate new latch face plate. (6) Install and screw in place the new reinforcing unit inside the old mortised area. (7) Remove old strike plate from door jamb. (8) Mortise as required to accommodate new strike plate and new latchbolt. (9) Attach new strike plate in its proper position on jamb. (10) Cover old lock holes with larger escutcheons provided with new lock. (11) Slide cylinder into place from the outside with the keyhole properly positioned (serrated edge of key should be up for insertion). Be sure that the lock housing engages correctly. (12) Attach inside escutcheon and hardware. (The inside knob and rose will snap into place on the end of the cylinder.)

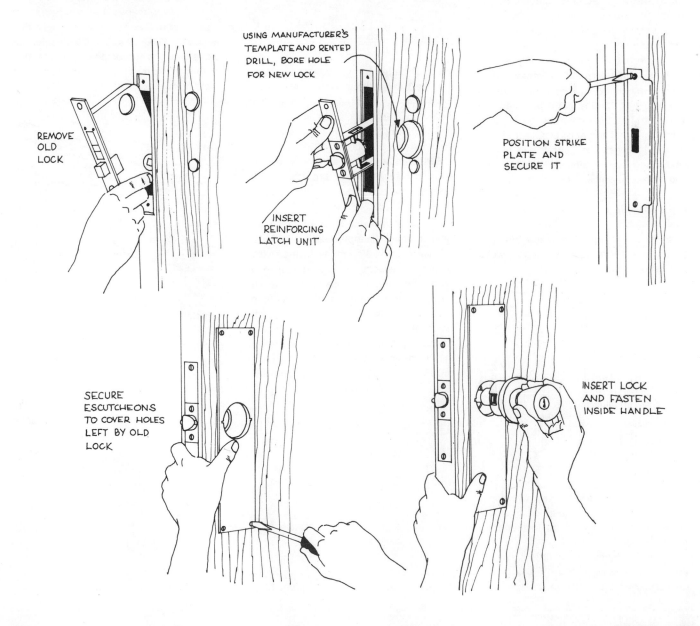

REMOVE OLD LOCK

USING MANUFACTURER'S TEMPLATE AND RENTED DRILL, BORE HOLE FOR NEW LOCK

INSERT REINFORCING LATCH UNIT

POSITION STRIKE PLATE AND SECURE IT

SECURE ESCUTCHEONS TO COVER HOLES LEFT BY OLD LOCK

INSERT LOCK AND FASTEN INSIDE HANDLE

• How to Use Weatherstrip

Exterior doors and windows require more and more weatherstripping to block out moisture and drafts as a house settles and shifts with age. The more weatherstrip a house has, the more it needs replacement owing to wear or damage.

Weatherstrip materials specifically designed for home installation are readily available at hardware and building supply stores. They can be grouped into three broad categories: interlock, pliable gasket, and gasket clinched in a rigid strip. There are other specialty types that require professional installation; they are not described here because they must be fitted with special tools and techniques.

Because different materials and procedures are used to weatherstrip the top and sides of a door than for the threshold, the two are described separately.

JAMB WEATHERSTRIP

The two crucial points to watch are how the door presses against the strips as it moves toward or past them, and how the strips abut each other at the corners.

Interlock: It is generally considered to be the most effective type—while it is in good condition. The interlocking strips are set into the door and the jamb. Original installation requires special equipment and precise fitting, but repair or replacement is possible for a home handyman.

Anyone who has interlock will probably either have to repair it or replace it at some time since the type is prone to damage with rough usage or when the alignment of a door changes in its frame.

First correct the door problem, if any. At a point when the door is already off its hinges, force damaged strips back into rough alignment using pliers, or a block and hammer to work the kinks out. If the strip is damaged beyond repair, yank it out. You need pliers and brute force to free it, but a delicate touch to avoid splitting the narrow edge of wood that adjoins the mortise.

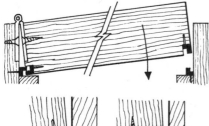

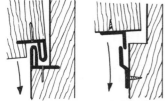

Replace the destroyed strip with identical material. You will need a small nail set to drive the nails home in their narrow channel.

Once the replacement strip is nailed and the salvageable strip roughly reconditioned, re-hang the door. It will take several trial-and-error fine adjustments to get rid of all the spots that rub.

Pliable gasket: Nearly always bought in rolls, most of this weatherstrip is made of felt; some is of vinyl. The two are installed differently.

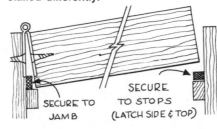

SECURE TO JAMB SECURE TO STOPS (LATCH SIDE & TOP)

Felt is nailed to the edge of the stops that meet the window sash on all but the hinge side of a casement window. It is nailed to the frame next to the stop there. (Some felt is self-adhesive and does not need nails.)

Felt with serrated aluminum nailing edge and tubular vinyl are attached in the same positions as the rigid gaskets described below.

Rigid strip gaskets: Most of these are tubular vinyl or neoprene clinched in an aluminum strip. Variations include vinyl or non-absorbent sponge glued to a wood strip. All are screwed or nailed to the stop, then painted to match the stop.

The metal type is cut to length with tin snips or a hacksaw. The technique for mounting metal or wood is as follows: (1) Cut the top piece so it is flush against the side stops. (2) Cut the side strips so

SECURE TO FACE OF STOP

they butt against the top strip. (3) Close the door, place the top piece in position, and nail or screw it into place. (4) Attach the side strips in the same manner. The seal should be a light one if the strip is to have long life. Some models have elongated screw holes that permit adjustment of the pressure.

Springy metal strips: Shaped to form a cushion either by a V-fold or a simple crimp, these strips are made of bronze, aluminum, or stainless steel.

Both the V-shaped and crimped strips provide good control of drafts. They can, however, make doors hard to open or close and are subject to being deformed or torn by hard use. Also, wind can make them hum.

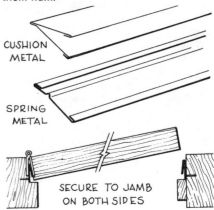

CUSHION METAL

SPRING METAL

SECURE TO JAMB ON BOTH SIDES

Installation is not difficult. The main thing is not to kink them. The procedures: (1) Beginning with the hinge side, nail strip on jamb. With the V-shaped type, the long leg should be nailed to the frame so that it butts against the stop. The crimped type should be positioned so that it can lie flat against the frame without quite brushing the stop. Tack

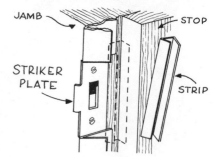

JAMB STOP STRIKER PLATE STRIP

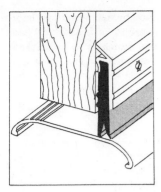
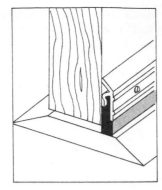

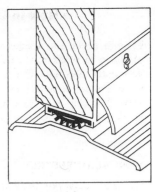

SWEEP THRESHOLD STRIPS

GASKET THRESHOLD STRIPS

either at both top and bottom to hold the strip in place for accurate nailing. (2) On the latch side, attach the piece that adjoins the strike plate, then attach the pieces above and below it. The side pieces should reach to the top of the frame. (3) Attach the top piece in the same way after mitering the corners about ⅛ inch to allow clearance for the side pieces. (Failure to do this will compress the side pieces, breaking the weather seal.)

THRESHOLD WEATHERSTRIP

Of the many threshold weatherstrips on the market, most are packaged in easy-to-install kits. The types range from simple vinyl gaskets to retractable models which raise to clear the rug when the door opens, then lower to seal the door against the threshold when the door closes.

The home handyman trying to seal off an air leak or replace a worn unit, is going to have easier success with one of the gasket types.

One gasket combines the threshold and weatherstrip in one piece. A vinyl hump or bubble runs the width of the threshold so that it compresses when the door closes. A two-part threshold attaches the vinyl bubble (called a "boot" or "shoe") to the bottom of the door. The matching threshold is of sturdy metal, but most of these gaskets will operate with an existing threshold. The advantage of this type is that it protects the vinyl from the wear and tear of foot traffic.

Installing any of the metal thresholds is relatively easy. The following instructions will work in general for the two-piece type: (1) If a wood threshold is worn, drive the nails through it using a nail set and lift the old piece out. (2) Trim the ends of the new threshold to fit with a

AFTER TRIMMING THRESHOLD TO FIT AROUND DOOR JAMBS AND STOP, CAULK BOTH ENDS

hacksaw. The highest point of the threshold should rest directly below the closed door. (3) Screw the threshold into place and caulk the ends as a protection against moisture. (4) Mark the door to allow required clearance (usually ½ inch)

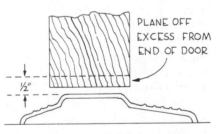

PLANE OFF EXCESS FROM END OF DOOR

½"

between door and threshold so boot can fit into the space. (5) Remove door from hinges and cut or plane excess from bottom. Remember to plane from the latch and hinge sides toward the center to avoid split edges. (6) Hold the shoe in place against the bottom of the dismounted door and mark shoe for width.

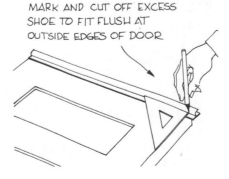

MARK AND CUT OFF EXCESS SHOE TO FIT FLUSH AT OUTSIDE EDGES OF DOOR

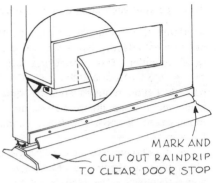

MARK AND CUT OUT RAINDRIP TO CLEAR DOOR STOP

(7) With a hacksaw trim the shoe to fit flush against each outside edge of the door. Then, if there is a raindrip, trim it at both ends to clear the door stops as shown in the sketch. (8) Replace door

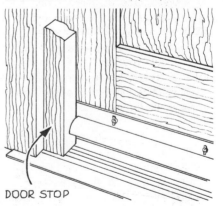

DOOR STOP

on hinges *without* attaching the shoe. (9) Close door and fit shoe in place. (10) Attach the shoe so it brushes lightly against the threshold. The crucial point is for the gasket to form a seal with the threshold and *not* for the metal carrier to fit flush against the door bottom.

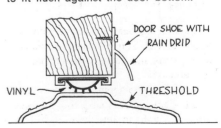

DOOR SHOE WITH RAIN DRIP

VINYL

THRESHOLD

• Overhead Garage Doors

Most garage doors of post-war vintage slide on overhead tracks. There are two types: sectional and one-piece. Both get their lifting power from coiled metal springs, requiring only minimal human or motorized effort to operate them.

Their problems stem mainly from their great weight being unsupported in the middle when they are in the raised position.

Keeping all the moving parts properly lubricated is the best insurance against overhead door problems since this minimizes undue strains caused by forcing the doors past balky spots. On sectional doors, pay particular attention to all the many hinges, all the roller wheels, and the bearing plates which hold up the spring shaft and drum assembly. (Sectional doors roll up on curved tracks whereas one-piece doors swing out and up on straight tracks. The latter require fewer and less complex moving parts.)

If the moving parts are kept in good condition, the two principal possibilities of failure are tracks that have worked loose or otherwise gone out of alignment, or structural failure of the door itself.

The tracks: If the door does not move smoothly, check all the lag screws that hold the door hardware to the wood, and the track supports to the ceiling joists. These heavy screws are loosened by the drying of new wood and simply through use. Tighten any loose screws with a wrench. If a hole has worn until the screw no longer grips firmly, remove the screw and insert a glued peg as described on page 37. Do not remove more than one screw at a time in this circumstance.

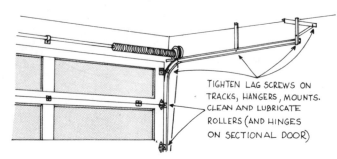

TIGHTEN LAG SCREWS ON TRACKS, HANGERS, MOUNTS. CLEAN AND LUBRICATE ROLLERS (AND HINGES ON SECTIONAL DOOR)

Also, inspect the big coil springs from time to time. If the coils become unevenly spaced or develop bulges it is a sign of impending failure. Replacing them is not a home repair job. Call a professional. These springs are loaded under lethal pressures with special equipment.

If these two elements are in proper condition, the door should operate well. It would be rare for properly installed tracks to go out of alignment for any other cause except extreme settling in the house. Warp in the door is a more likely cause of binding.

Latches: The locking latches on most overhead doors are spring-loaded ears that catch on metal plates set into the side

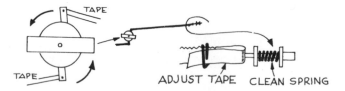

TAPE
TAPE
ADJUST TAPE   CLEAN SPRING

jambs. Steel tapes connect them to the handle at the center of the door. If a door fails to latch, either the latch assembly has become clogged with dirty grease or the steel tape has broken or slipped out of adjustment. In the case of tape failure, a proper adjustment retracts the ear just enough to clear the stop when the handle is turned as far as it will go.

The door: One piece doors are susceptible to warp, especially if they are made of dimensioned lumber to match siding.

Sometimes the solution is to trim the door to fit the opening. A portable disc sander will trim an edge or bottom of a wood door efficiently. On a fiberglass or metal door, the job is likely to require more tools and experience than an average handyman can bring to bear.

One-piece doors that are frequently left in the "up" position tend to sag in the middle. To correct this condition, attach a metal reinforcing rod or strap across the top and bottom as shown in the sketch. Most of them are designed to attach to

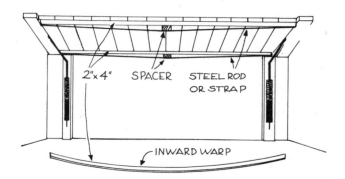

2"x 4"   SPACER   STEEL ROD OR STRAP
INWARD WARP

eye bolts at each side; a turnbuckle permits adjustment. (Set the door with a ½-inch outward warp.) The rods are available in varying sizes at hardware and building supply stores.

Warped or split individual boards, or decomposing plywood can hinder the operation of overhead doors. Any split wood should be glued with woodworking glue and re-nailed. The

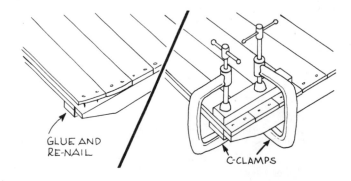

GLUE AND RE-NAIL
C-CLAMPS

patch should be put under pressure with a C-clamp while it dries to assure a firm bond.

Weatherstrip: The most familiar weatherstrip for overhead doors is a black rubber raindrip type that is nailed to the outside of the door on both sides and along the bottom—and to the face of the overhead jamb at the top of the door. An alternative method for the bottom is a tube nailed to the bottom of the door. Discarded lengths of garden hose can substitute for commercial weatherstrip.

• Repairing Torn Screening

Door and window screens split or are torn from their frames by over-active use.

It is possible to patch a screen for the sake of utility, as described below, but there is no such thing as invisible mending of this product. If a damaged screen must be made as good as new, the screening must be new.

PATCHING SCREENING

There are two ways to patch screening: By shellacking a piece of mosquito netting into place over the hole, or by "sewing" a patch into place with lengths of wire identical or similar to that in the screen. Neither patch is permanent, but both are adequate temporary solutions, especially in screens not prominently in view.

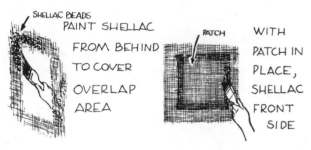

SHELLAC BEADS

PAINT SHELLAC FROM BEHIND TO COVER OVERLAP AREA

PATCH

WITH PATCH IN PLACE, SHELLAC FRONT SIDE

If the tear is a small one, the shellacking method is effective. Cut the hole square. Cut a piece of mosquito netting so it overlaps the hole by one to two inches on all sides. Coat the overlap with shellac working from each side of the screen, back side first. Apply two extra coats to the front side after allowing drying time. (Coat the mosquito netting with one coat if you wish to make it stiff.)

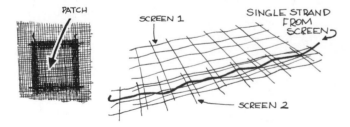

PATCH

SCREEN 1

SINGLE STRAND FROM SCREEN

SCREEN 2

For a larger hole, buy a piece of screening of the same type as the torn piece. Trimmed, the patch should be two inches larger in each dimension than the hole after the hole has been trimmed to a neat rectangle. Thread single strands of wire along each side to tie the patch to the main piece of screening as the sketch shows. This job will be easier if you work on the screen while it lies flat.

The closer the stitch, the sturdier the patch will be. Also, close stitches afford more protection against insects creeping through a gap.

For any patch to be tidy, its mesh should align with that of the main screen.

REPLACING SCREENING

Three materials are in general use for screening: aluminum, brass, and nylon. All three are serviceable, but most people choose the replacement that matches other screens around the house.

Before going to buy, measure the dimensions of your screen to include the channels in a metal frame, or the outside edge of the molding in a wood one. To these figures, add at least an inch—preferably more—to each dimension. This minimum will provide a working margin.

The key to replacing screening in a frame is in the original alignment. If your first side is secured crookedly, you will not be able to correct the situation except by starting all over. Lay the frame on a floor or level patch of lawn, then lay the screening over it. If you are confident of your eye, you can work without marking. But it is easier to keep a straight line by making a chalk mark the length of your first side where the screening will fit into its channel.

Work down one long side of the frame first, then go down the other side. Secure the ends last. Working on a long side first is the surest way to keep a straight line. Taking the opposite side next minimizes sag.

Metal frames almost universally use a strip of neoprene that locks into a metal channel to secure the screening in place.

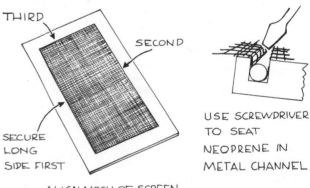

THIRD

SECOND

SECURE LONG SIDE FIRST

ALIGN MESH OF SCREEN

USE SCREWDRIVER TO SEAT NEOPRENE IN METAL CHANNEL

The sketch shows how this works. A screwdriver serves to push the neoprene into place. The first inch serves as an anchor so you can keep the screen stretched taut as you work.

Wood frames use quarter-round or similar molding to secure the screen. With these, it is useful to lightly tack the top of the

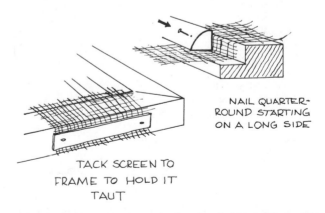

NAIL QUARTER-ROUND STARTING ON A LONG SIDE

TACK SCREEN TO FRAME TO HOLD IT TAUT

screen to the frame as shown in the sketch to provide tension as you work along the first side.

Once you have finished securing all sides, there will be a narrow strip of excess along two or more edges. An old knife can be used to trim these.

Windows

There are three principal types of window frames, and two main materials used to make them. The three types (shown in the sketches below) are double-hung sash, casement, and sliding windows. They are either made of wood or metal (steel or aluminum).

The troubles that usually beset windows are broken glass, broken locks, and improper fit of sash in frame. Except in the cases of molded metal frames—especially in sliding windows —most failures can be repaired, or at least improved to the point where they no longer are a nuisance.

This section discusses methods of replacing broken glass and locks, and fixing windows so they fit and move properly— along with information on a fourth type of frame, the jalousie, and some cures for failures of the hardware connected with shades, screens, and other window coverings. Skylights are covered in the section on roofs (see page 83).

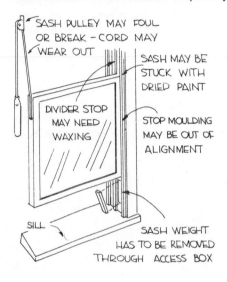

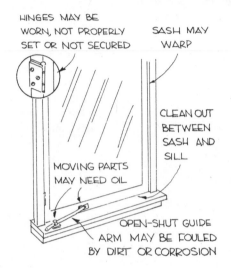

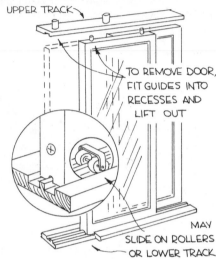

WHEN YOU BUY GLASS

When you buy replacement glass for one of your average-sized windows, it is almost certain to be a type called "sheet glass" or "window glass."

It comes in several thicknesses and quality grades. In addition, you may run into any of several other types of glass.

Sheet glass. Formed when molten glass is drawn vertically. The faster the speed, the thinner the glass. Finished product has some wave or distortion. Sheet glass from about 3/32 inch to 1/8 inch thick is used to glaze most residential windows and doors. The term *single strength* refers to glass 3/32 inch thick, weighing about 19 ounces per square foot; *double strength* glass is 1/8 inch thick, weighs 26 ounces. Quality grades are AA (special order), A (superior), B (standard), and greenhouse.

Thicker sheet glass (3/16, 7/32, and 1/4 inch thick) is called *heavy sheet* or *crystal sheet* and is used in large windows.

Float glass. A relatively recent method of manufacture, float glass is formed on molten tin, then cooled and conveyed through an annealing oven. It is exceptionally flat and free of distortion. Available in ¼-inch thickness.

Plate glass. Molten glass is rolled into large, continuous flat sheets, then ground and polished on both sides to a uniform thickness. There is little wave or distortion. *Regular polished plate* usually refers to clear ¼-inch plate, widely used in building construction. *Heavy polished plate* is ⅜ inch, ½ inch, and thicker. It is used for large uninterrupted window areas. *Rough plate* has not been ground and polished on both surfaces, so it is not clear. It is available regular or tempered, tinted or not, with both sides rough or one side polished.

In addition, there are several specialty glasses manufactured from the basic types.

Heat-strengthened glass. Partly tempered to increase its strength, which is about double that of the glass from which it is made. It is not a safety glass.

Insulating glass. Two pieces of glass with a dry air space between and all edges sealed.

Laminated glass. Two pieces of clear or patterned glass with a clear or tinted plastic between, sealed together into a single unit. If broken, glass fragments are held together by the plastic interlayer.

Light-diffusing glass. Patterned, normally in a prism-like design, or coated so light rays passing through are diffused.

Patterned glass. Made like regular plate, except passed through patterned rollers. Designs range from finely pebbled to deeply fluted.

Reflective glass. A transparent metallic oxide is fired to the surface of a ¼-inch plate glass, providing a light and heat-reflecting mirror-like coating.

Tempered glass. Controlled heating and cooling produces a compression layer on the glass surfaces, and a tension layer inside. This glass is as many as five times stronger and more impact-resistant than unprocessed glass of the same type.

Tinted glass. Formed by the introduction of coloring agents into molten glass. Transmission of visible light is lowered. Various shades of green, gray, bronze are available.

Wired glass. Glass with wire mesh incorporated within the body of the glass during manufacture. When glass breaks, the wire holds it together.

• Re-glazing Puttied Windows

The difficulty in replacing broken glass in wood-sash windows grows in direct proportion to the size of the pane.

Small windows can be glazed with their sashes in place. For larger ones, it is often necessary to remove the sash from the window frame so it can be placed flat while the work goes along. (See pages 52-53 for ways to dismount sashes.) Some panes are just too big to handle without professional glazier's equipment.

Tools and equipment you need: Hammer, glazier's points, linseed oil (or wood sealer), chisel, putty knife, putty, paint brush (½-inch trim brush), and paint to match the existing trim. If you do not buy glass cut to size, you will also need a glass-cutting tool. You may need a propane torch or similar heat source to soften old putty that held the broken glass.

Buying new glass: Most common window sizes can be fitted with pre-cut glass now, saving the trouble of special order or of cutting your own.

When you go to buy it, know which type of glass you want (see facing page), and know the exact dimension of the window. Glass is sold so that irregularities run in the horizontal direction (your gaze sweeps from side to side more than it runs up and down).

The pane will be cut ⅛ inch smaller than the opening so that it can fit easily even if the wood has irregular bumps (see sketch #3).

If you buy putty when you buy glass, you can buy the real thing—which comes dry and has to be mixed with linseed oil — or you can get a synthetic, which comes ready for use and stays pliable longer.

To remove shards: Work from the top of the frame so that no shards are left to fall onto your hands as you work along the bottom. Wiggle shards back and forth the same way you wiggle a child's loose tooth to free glass from putty. Since putty is on the outside, work from the outside if possible. If you cannot, push the shards outward.

Subsequent steps are shown in the sketches below.

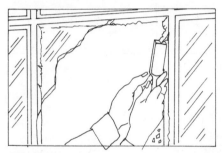

Chisel bits of glass and old putty out of frame. Propane torch will soften hard putty. Then, coat wood with linseed oil so putty oils are not drawn out causing putty to become brittle.

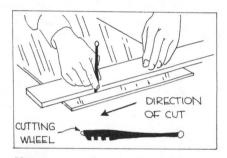

Measure opening, and cut glass ⅛ inch smaller in each dimension, if you must cut glass to fit. Score deeply with glass-cutting tool. Then snap edge by gripping it with pliers.

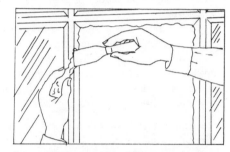

Lay a bead of putty around the frame so it fills the groove in which glass rests. This cushions the pane and corrects irregularities in the frame. Make the bead ⅛ inch thick.

Glazier's points (or spring clips in a metal sash) secure pane in place. Tap points into place with hammer and setting tool, two to a side in small panes, one each six inches in big sashes.

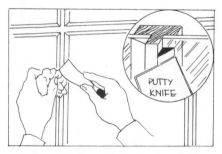

Apply sealing bead of putty. Bead should be flush with outer edge of molding and should come as high as inner edge (inside of glass). Press firmly for good seal; trim excess as you work.

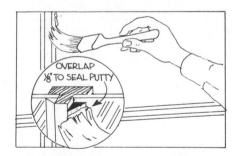

Paint putty color of window trim after it has dried 7 to 10 days. Paint should reach 1/16 inch up glass to assure a weather seal. After paint dries, clean paint, putty smudges with thinner.

• Re-glazing Metal Sashes

Most metal windows sandwich the glass between the halves of their sashes. In these cases there is no putty, but rather some form of a rubber seal.

The simplest of these sashes are two nearly flat pieces of metal screwed or riveted together. If screws hold the pieces together, re-glazing is simple. The pane is cut with the standard ⅛-inch allowance and laid in the dismounted sash (see page 54). The rubber seals are usually attached to the sash already. The two halves of the sash are then screwed together, and the sash re-mounted in its frame. Many casement windows are of this type.

Sliding windows are usually of molded parts (to form the track). Glass is held in place by a neoprene rubber gasket. These nearly always have to be re-glazed by professionals because of the complex interlocking of parts around the glass and its seal.

• Double-hung Sashes

Double-hung sashes frequently become troublesome with age on two principal counts: They begin to misfit their frames too snugly or loosely, or the weights that hold them open become fouled by failed pulleys or broken cords.

Because these windows are limited in size by their design and because their mechanical parts are simple, fixing any of their failures requires few tools. A chisel or similar prying device, a hammer, a screwdriver, and a few finishing nails will serve in most instances. A sharp, short-bladed knife is handy.

PAINT-STUCK SASHES

Because window frames are so thoroughly exposed to weather, they get frequent painting. One inevitable result is that sashes occasionally become frozen in place by dried paint.

If a sash becomes paint-stuck, recondition as much of its track as you can before freeing the sash. It will be easier to move in the first place and will not stick in a new position once freed.

To condition the track: (1) Wrap medium-coarse sandpaper (2/0) around a small wood block and sand the stop molding, separator molding, and frame. If there are large globs of paint in the track, use a chisel to trim them down. (2) Coat all three surfaces of the track with paraffin—the most durable and cleanest lubricant for this purpose.

To free a sash: (1) Run a sharp, short-bladed knife between the sash and the stop molding to cut the paint that bonds the two units together. (The fresher the paint, the less it will chip.) (2) If the window is closed, use a lever between the sill and the sash to pry the sash into motion. Work from the outside. Use the widest prying device you can find to minimize damage to

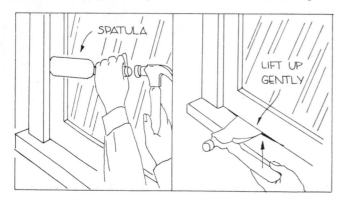

the wood. A hatchet is ideal. If the sash is canted in its frame, start on the side that sags lowest. Always work back and forth along the sill, trying to keep the sash as true as possible in the frame. OR: If the window is open too wide to be pried, place a block of wood on the top of the sash at one side, and hammer down on it. Alternate sides until the sash begins to move.

If the sash will not come free, remove the stop molding as outlined for jammed sashes.

FREEING JAMMED SASHES

Sometimes sashes or stop molding will swell until the sash binds against the track. Rarely the sash will swell until it binds against the frame.

To adjust stop moldings: (1) With a wide-bladed chisel, begin at the bottom or top to pry the stop molding away from the window frame. Score the paint first where the molding joins the frame to minimize chipping. Unless the wood has become brittle with age, it should come away undamaged. (2) Once stop molding is off, chisel paint flat if any has ridged up, or else the molding will not fit in its new position. (3) Reseat the stop molding to give the sash increased clearance. A sheet of cardboard from the back of a tablet can be used as a guide by inserting it between the stop and the sash as you nail the stop in place. Use 6d finishing nails. (4) If necessary, repaint the stop molding to cover the crack between it and the window frame.

If the old stop molding breaks during removal, you should be able to replace it identically from lumber yard stocks. Take a piece along to match.

If paint has gummed the edge of the stop that faces the sash, clean it, then paraffin the edge before nailing the stop back in place.

To sand a sash: Occasionally a sash will swell tight against the sides of the frame rather than the stops. When this happens, dismount the sash by removing a stop and lightly plane sand each side. Continually retest the fit as you go; if you take off too much, the sash will leak air. As little as 1/16 inch may do the trick.

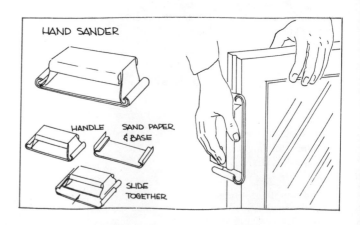

SASH TOO LOOSE IN TRACK

A sash-hung window too loosely fitted in its track allows cold air and wind-blown rain inside, and rattles, too.

If the gap is not too wide, cure as follows:

You will need a block of wood as a hammering surface, a hammer, and a can of touch-up paint. You may need some 6d finishing nails. It is very useful to have a shim. A length of cardboard from an old writing tablet serves well. Then: (1) Place shim between stop molding and sash. (2) Place block of wood against outer surface of stop molding, and hammer until the paint breaks between stop and frame, and the stop rests snugly against your shim. Go from top to bottom of frame in this way. (3) If the stop shows a tendency to spring back toward its original position, secure it in the desired position with three or four finishing nails. (4) Touch up paint wherever necessary. Countersink and putty new nails before painting.

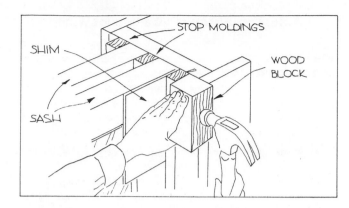

When the gap is too wide to be overcome by this method, pry the stop off the window frame and reseat it using the sequence of steps outlined in the section on jammed sashes.

FOULED SASH WEIGHTS

Sash weights foul either because the pulley at the top of the window frame has broken, or because the cord suspending the weight has stretched or parted.

If the pulley has failed, it can often be replaced without removing the sash from the frame, but a parted cord requires removing the sash.

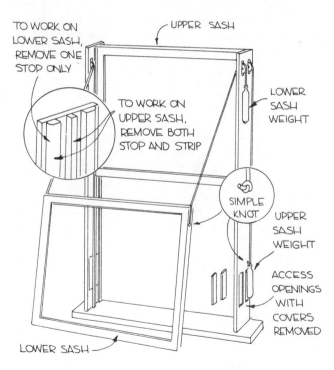

To replace a sash cord: (1) Pry stop molding off same side of window as broken cord. Method is described in section on jammed sashes. (2) Ease sash out of frame, exposing knot pocket on sash. (3) Remove broken rope. At same time, free the opposite cord so you can put the sash out of the way of your work. You may want to replace both cords at once in any case so this job comes up as infrequently as possible. If it is the upper sash, use pliers to pull the separator stop out, working from bottom to top, then remove the upper sash as described above. (4) Unscrew and remove the cover that gives access

to the weights. If paint covers the track, tap with a hammer until cracks reveal the outline. You may need to finish sawing out the cover if it has never been removed before. Use a keyhole saw. (5) Untie cord from weight. (6) Use old cord to measure length for new one. The new cord can be about three inches shorter than the old one to compensate for the stretching that comes with age. If you want long wear, replace the cords with sash chain. Available at many hardware outlets, the chain has snap links to secure it to weights and knot pockets. (7) Loop new cord over pulley and guide it down the channel to the weight. (8) Tie the weight on. (9) Rest sash on window sill, and secure other end of cord in knot pocket. (10) Raise the sash to the top of the frame, and check to see that weight hangs at least three inches above sill. If not, adjust length of cord. (11) When weight is properly adjusted, nail stop molding back in place. Use a piece of cardboard as a shim. (12) Screw access covers back in place.

To replace a pulley: (1) Raise the window so access cover to weight is exposed. (2) Remove cover and untie weight from cord so pulley is free of weight. (3) Pull cord out of pulley. (4) Unscrew pulley face plate and pull or pry unit out of frame. The axle may be frozen by rust, or broken. If it is rusted, oil and work it until the pulley turns freely. If the axle is broken, purchase and install a new unit. (5) Put the pulley unit in rough position, but do not screw it in place until the cord is in proper position. This way you can tie a washer or other weight to a balky cord to help guide it down its channel. (6) When cord is in position, secure pulley unit in window frame. (7) Tie weight to cord. (8) Screw access cover in place.

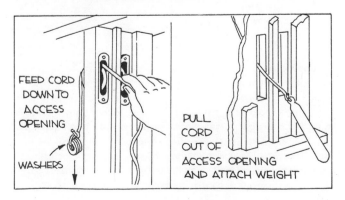

• Adjusting Sashes In Casement Windows

When casement windows do not fit properly, the probable causes are: Sash has warped, hinges have sagged, wooden frame or sash has shrunk or swollen (or been deformed by too much paint), or the house has settled so the window frame is out of square. All but the last can be cured with simple techniques and tools.

Warped sash: If the sash is wood and the warp severe, the only genuine cure is a new sash. Once wood has set, it will not re-shape itself without unreasonable effort. Mild warp can be compensated by adjusting the stop molding, using the method outlined on page 52 in the section called "Freeing Jammed Sashes." Flat metal sashes—as opposed to molded ones—are prone to warp but can be cured by counter-warping. To do

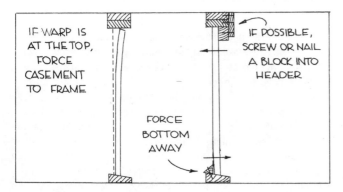

IF WARP IS AT THE TOP, FORCE CASEMENT TO FRAME

IF POSSIBLE, SCREW OR NAIL A BLOCK INTO HEADER

FORCE BOTTOM AWAY

this, close the sash until some part of it meets the frame. Set a small wood block, ⅜ inch thick, at this point to force it outward. At the same time, wedge the lagging corner of the window tightly closed. Leave the sash under this stress for as long as possible—up to a week. This over-compensation for the warp should leave the sash approximately true.

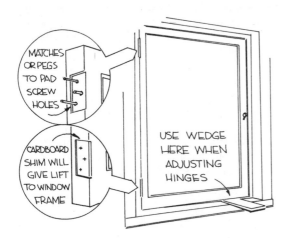

MATCHES OR PEGS TO PAD SCREW HOLES

CARDBOARD SHIM WILL GIVE LIFT TO WINDOW FRAME

USE WEDGE HERE WHEN ADJUSTING HINGES

Sagged hinges: If a window rides unevenly on its hinges, or rests askew, the hinges need adjustment or replacement. If a hinge pin is loose in its guides, replace the entire hinge with an identical model. If a hinge has screws loose, tighten them. If they will not tighten, renovate the holes with glued pegs (see page 37 for detailed steps), then re-mount the hinge. If the sash sits askew in the frame in spite of properly tightened hinges, one of the hinges will need to be shimmed. See page 37 in the section on doors for symptoms and cures.

Shrunken sash: Occasionally a sash becomes so loose fitting in its casement that cold air passes easily through the cracks. The usual cure is springy metal weatherstripping. See the boxed material for types of weatherstrip and ways to employ them.

Swollen sash: When a sash binds before it comes flush against its stops, either some wood member has swollen or paint has thickened extremely. Check all the way around, starting with the hinged side, to find where the rub is located. Chisel away any large globs of paint. Sand a wood sash as a first resort, using a very coarse grade of sandpaper (No. 50). Plane lightly as a second attempt if the first does not work. If you expose bare wood, coat it with wood sealer to prevent new swelling, then repaint.

• Fixing Levers In Casement Windows

Wood casement windows usually have some type of sliding rod to control their opening and closing. Most metal casement windows use a crank and worm gear system for the purpose. Either of these can be repaired or replaced without much fuss.

Fixing a sliding rod: There are two variations. In one, the rod slides through a fixed mount (see sketch). If the rod does not slide freely, lubricate it lightly with paraffin. Also, check to see that the mount is lubricated where it pivots, and that its base is securely attached to the sill. Finally, check the screws that secure the pivot at the other end of the rod to the window sash.

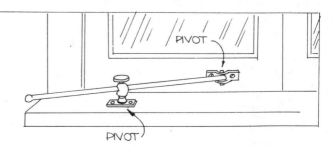

PIVOT

PIVOT

The variation rod assembly uses a shoe that slides along within a channel. These channels become dirt-clogged, or paint seeps into the channel. Balky action can usually be cured by unscrewing the channel from the sill, and cleaning both channel and sill so that shoe has no bumps in its way. Lubricate the sill with paraffin before replacing the channel. Also, check the pivot plate screwed to the sash to be sure it is not loose.

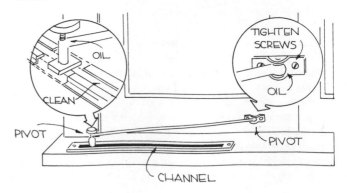

TIGHTEN SCREWS

OIL

OIL

CLEAN

PIVOT

PIVOT

CHANNEL

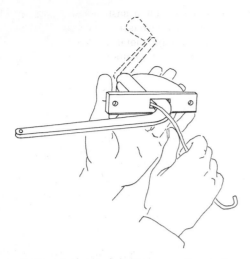

gear is dirt-clogged; or the gear is worn out. If a window is balky, open it as wide as possible and check the track in the bottom of the sill. With a wire brush, clean out any foreign matter and lubricate lightly with paraffin. If this does not do the job, you will need to dismount the gear assembly as follows: (1) Unscrew the setscrew that holds the handle in place and remove the handle. (2) Unscrew the two screws that hold the gear housing against the window frame. (3) Slide the lever arm along until it comes free from the sash. In most designs there is an enlarged hole at one end of the track that lets the arm pop free. (4) Once the unit is free of the window, check inside it to see whether the gear is dirt-clogged or damaged. If it is dirt-clogged, use a piece of stiff coat-hanger wire with its tip bent (see sketch) to dislodge dirt in the gear grooves, or the teeth on the lever arm. Lubricate the gear. Using the handle, work the gear to see if it turns smoothly. If it does, replace the unit by reversing the above steps.

If inspection shows the gear to be damaged, the only recourse is to purchase and install a new unit. Compare the old gear with the new one to be sure critical dimensions (lever arm length, distance between screw holes) are identical.

Fixing a crank and worm gear: There are three primary causes of a breakdown in one of these. Either the channel in the bottom of the sash, where a shoe slides, has gotten clogged; the old lubricant in the gear assembly has become rigid, or the

WEATHERSTRIPPING WINDOWS

No type of weatherstripping is permanent, but it is still the best material for closing the air leaks around window sashes, and well worth the trouble of installation and periodic replacement.

There are three basic types: Springy metal; compressible felt or rubber, and pliable gaskets, mostly of vinyl. Some come in rolls; some come both in rolls and strips. Choosing between the types depends mainly on the type of window, how air leaks through it, and how important appearance of the window frame is to you. Price and durability may be other considerations.

Below are descriptions and installation techniques for the major types.

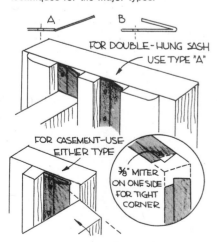

Spring metal: Usually copper, it comes either V-shaped or bent at a slight angle.

It is secured to the window frame with brads (except one length is sometimes secured to the bottom of a window sash rather than the sill).

The positioning is shown in the sketch for both double-hung sash and casement windows.

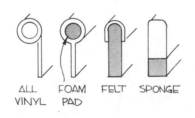

ALL VINYL   FOAM PAD   FELT   SPONGE

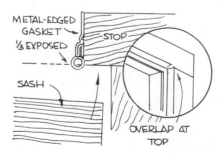

Pliable gaskets: Most of these are of vinyl. Some are metal-edged felt. Gasket types are attached with brads to the window stops so the sash presses lightly against them. As a result they are highly visible. Painting them to match the frame is a partial camouflage, but the gasket surface can-

not be painted or it becomes too rigid to do its job. The type works best on casement windows.

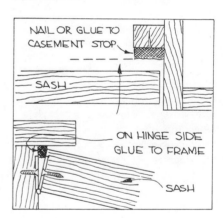

Compressible felt: Weatherstrip of this type adheres to the faces of the window stops where they meet the sashes, as shown in the sketch. Some types are tacked in place; some have adhesive backing. The material becomes permanently compressed after a time. It is the best choice in a warped casement window that cannot meet its stops tightly.

There are no weatherstrips made specifically for home installation in sliding metal windows. The manufacturer's weatherstrip is usually a bead of felt or neoprene gripped in a molded channel. It can be replaced only with identical material, and in most cases only by a professional glazier.

• Fixing Windows That Will Not Slide

When a sliding window ceases to slide freely, the probable causes are: the sash is stuck by dried paint; it has a dirty or bent track; or the rollers are broken or otherwise fouled. On occasion a sash will warp or bind, or a frame will be bent so that it binds.

Freeing sash stuck by paint: With a short-bladed, sharp knife, cut the paint by forcing the tip of the blade between sash and frame all around. Cutting the paint will minimize chipping. Then, grab hold of one side of the sash and push upward so

PUTTY KNIFE WILL SCORE DRIED PAINT AT SASH AND FRAME

ROCK SASH VERTICALLY TO LOOSEN

sash rocks into clearance built into top of frame. Repeat with the other side. In most sliding windows it is inadvisable to use a screwdriver or other pry except as a last resort since you risk bending the frame, thus losing some weatherseal and perhaps causing a new bind.

Track troubles: The sash will have to be removed from the frame to get at the track for cleaning or repairs. In many de-

signs, the sash will lift high enough to clear the bottom of the frame at any point. In some cases, however, the top rollers have to be aligned with key notches as shown in the sketch.

Once the sash is out of the frame, inspect the rail, the edges of the frame, and the bottom of the sash for dirt or deformities. Clean out any dirt with a wire brush. Dislodge stubborn particles with a screwdriver blade. Lubricate the track with paraffin.

If there are broken rollers, chances are you will have to take the sash to a glazier to have them replaced. Most designs recess the rollers inside a molded metal frame that is best disassembled and reassembled by a professional. If rollers are simply sticky on their axles, lubricate lightly with powdered graphite and work them until they turn free. (Many rollers are plastic and do not respond to oil as a lubricant.)

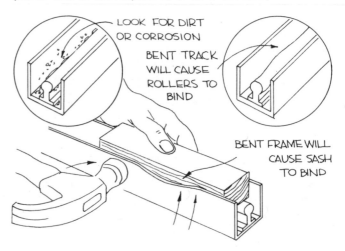

LOOK FOR DIRT OR CORROSION

BENT TRACK WILL CAUSE ROLLERS TO BIND

BENT FRAME WILL CAUSE SASH TO BIND

If the track or frame has been bent, you can try to hammer it back into shape. Hammer against a block as shown in the sketch, so as to guard against further bending of the metal, and also to give a true line for the place that is being bent back into shape. Tap as gently as possible, working from the sides of the bent spot toward its middle. You are not likely to get perfect cosmetic results, but you should be able to get the window moving adequately.

• Jalousie Windows

The glass in jalousie windows is easy to replace, but the direct-action lever systems common to most designs are more troublesome to fix.

To re-glaze, measure the broken piece, buy a replacement cut to size, and slide it into place. It is held by simple spring clips.

Lubrication can cure balkiness in a lever assembly, but worn or broken parts require replacement of the whole unit. The active side of the system has one fixed vertical piece and one movable one. The fixed piece anchors the control lever and also carries the pivots on which the glass carriers turn. The movable piece attaches to an off-center point on each carrier, and the lever drives it. The working parts can be hidden in a channel or left exposed. To replace a unit, dis-

mount all of the glass panes, then pry it away from the window frame. To install a new one, use a level to assure that the carriers are properly aligned.

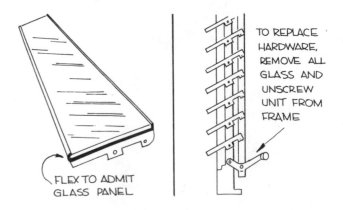

FLEX TO ADMIT GLASS PANEL

TO REPLACE HARDWARE, REMOVE ALL GLASS AND UNSCREW UNIT FROM FRAME

FIXING CATCHES ON SLIDING WINDOWS

Most catches on sliding windows are some variation on the old-fashioned hook-and-eye that used to fasten screen doors.

A few are more complicated devices that use a catch-plate and a spring-loaded "dog." Most of these are found on heavy, molded frame windows.

The hook-and-eye variations are simple. A lever pivots on a point so that its hook can fasten onto some part of the window frame. If the lever fails, it has to be re-shaped to get a hook back in functioning condition, has to be replaced, or has to be resecured to its pivot point. Since most simply screw into place, replacement is often the most satisfactory approach.

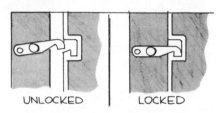

UNLOCKED | LOCKED

The catch-plate and dog assembly usually fails because use has bent the catch-plate under the rail until the dog cannot strike it squarely, or because the dog has gotten loose from its position in the bottom of the sash.

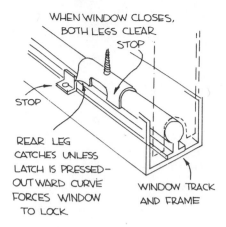

WHEN WINDOW CLOSES, BOTH LEGS CLEAR STOP

STOP

REAR LEG CATCHES UNLESS LATCH IS PRESSED—OUTWARD CURVE FORCES WINDOW TO LOCK

WINDOW TRACK AND FRAME

If the catch-plate has bent: (1) Unscrew it from its position alongside the rail after noting how far it will have to be bent to bring it flush with the widest diameter of the rail. (2) Clamp it in a vise and use pliers or a hammer to bend it to the needed angle. (3) Replace. If it is properly adjusted, the latch will click as the window closes, then will have to be depressed fully for the window to open again.

Trying to bend the catch-plate in place risks bending the rail.

If the catch-plate is properly in place, the trouble is with the dog. To get at it, you have to remove the sash from the frame. With the sash out, check to see if the dog has gotten loose, or if it is in place but worn or broken.

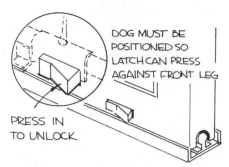

DOG MUST BE POSITIONED SO LATCH CAN PRESS AGAINST FRONT LEG

PRESS IN TO UNLOCK

If it is loose: (1) Retrieve the dog and the screw that holds it in place. (2) With the sash flat on a stable work surface, place the dog in position and secure it. The dog rides at an angle to the rail, its front leg away from the rail on the side where the catch-plate is, and its hind leg tight against that side of the rail. The hind leg is shaped to slide past the catch as the window is closing, but to hook on it as the window opens. Depressing the latch turns the dog parallel to the rail so both legs pass freely.

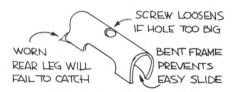

SCREW LOOSENS IF HOLE TOO BIG

WORN REAR LEG WILL FAIL TO CATCH

BENT FRAME PREVENTS EASY SLIDE

If the dog's hind leg is broken or worn, unscrew the dog from the sash and take it to a glazier's as a model when you buy a replacement.

• Fixing Window Shade Mechanisms

Window shade rollers, venetian blinds and the valance, rods for drapes all get balky at one time or another. Most of the problems that beset these devices are within the realm of home repair. Most repairs, in fact, do not even require tools.

ROLLER SHADES

The usual failures of roller shade mechanisms are: bent or loose brackets that bind the roller, too much or too little spring tension in the roller, or a dirt-clogged part in the spring-and-lock assembly.

Bad brackets: Check these first if a shade does not turn freely. If nails or screws have worked loose so that the bracket is not held tightly against the window frame, tighten them. If a bracket is bent so that it does not stick out at right angles to the window frame, straighten it so there is a uniform clearance about 1/16 to 1/8 inch) between bracket and roller tip. Bare fingers can bend most brackets, but a pair of pliers makes the job easier. If the clearances are too great or too little when the brackets are straightened, dismount one bracket and resecure it to give proper clearance.

Wrong spring tension: If the tension is too great, roll the shade to the top, take the roller out of the brackets and *unroll* six to eight inches of shade. Put the roller back in the brackets. Work the shade up and down several times to establish the

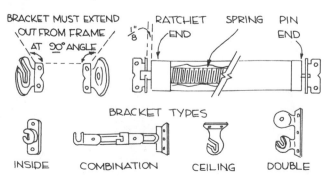

BRACKET MUST EXTEND OUT FROM FRAME AT 90° ANGLE

RATCHET END   SPRING   PIN END

1/8"

BRACKET TYPES

INSIDE   COMBINATION   CEILING   DOUBLE

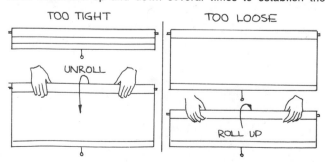

TOO TIGHT | TOO LOOSE

UNROLL

ROLL UP

tension. If shade still winds up too fast, repeat the maneuver.

If the tension is too weak, pull the shade about half way down and let the ratchet catch. Remove the roller from the brackets and roll about six to eight inches of shade *onto* the roller. Replace the roller in its brackets. Work the shade up and down several times. If it remains sluggish, repeat the process.

Shades that will not catch: The ratchet that locks a shade in position is housed inside a metal cap at the end of the roller with the flat blade (not the round pin). In most cases, dirt has jammed one or more of the little "dogs" that catch in the ratchet teeth. Without attempting to remove the protective metal cap, brush out any foreign particles and lubricate the moving parts with a very light oil. If this fails, remove the cap and try a more thorough cleaning job. Try not to let the spring release.

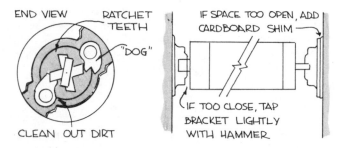

If the ratchet teeth are worn, or the spring has broken, you will have to buy a new roller. The shade attaches to the roller easily with a series of staples or brads, so the old one can be salvaged for re-use. The shade must be stapled evenly, or it will wind off center.

VENETIAN BLINDS

Because venetian blinds have so many moving parts and so much flexible material, they tend to be the most troublesome of all window covering devices. The ladder tapes that hold single slats in place grow fragile with age and break, causing slats to fall out of position. The two cord systems that tilt the blinds and raise or lower them grow frayed or break after protracted use. And the tilting gear itself can be clogged by dirt. Replacing the tapes or cords is tedious but not complicated. Cleaning the gear is simple.

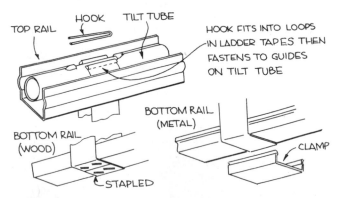

Ladder tapes: To remove the old ones, undo the clasps on a metal bottom rail or the staples on a wood rail. This will give access to knots that anchor the cords that raise or lower the blinds. Untie the knots and pull the cords out of the slots through the blinds all the way to the top. Remove all slats. At the top, unhook the tapes from the tilt tube.

To install the new tapes, attach them to the tilt tube just as the old ones were. Place the slats in rough position. Thread the cords down through them taking care that the cords alternate on each side of the tapes that hold the individual slats (this minimizes sideways sliding by the slats). Tie knots in the cords so they are taut when the blind is lowered as far as it will go, then close the metal clasp or re-staple the tapes to a wood rail.

Replacing raise-or-lower cords: If a blind does not raise and lower smoothly, check for a broken or fouled pulley, then for a worn cord. Any worn spot on a cord is likely to be near a pulley or the sharp-toothed locking device. Lubricate the pulleys if you suspect they are contributing to the wear, then replace a worn cord.

To replace it, unclasp the ladder tapes from the bottom rail and untie the knots that anchor the cord. Withdraw it by pulling on the loop as if you were going to raise the blind.

To install a new cord, begin at the bottom rail at the far end from the locking device. Thread the cord up through the slats (passing on alternate sides of the ladder tapes), over the pulley and across the top, down through the locking device, back up over the second pulley, then down through the slats. The sketch shows the course the cord should take.

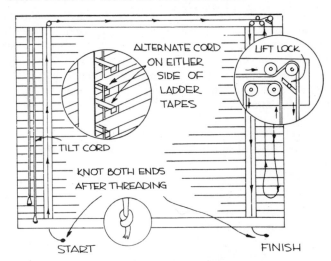

Balky tilt mechanism: The tilt cord simply loops over a pulley. The pulley drives a worm gear directly. The gear turns a tube. The ladder tapes are attached to the tube and tilt with it.

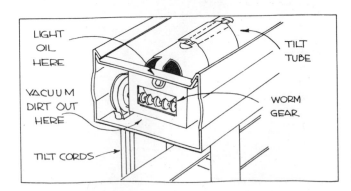

When something goes wrong, it is usually in the gear. Brush out any foreign particles. Lubricate lightly. Check to make sure the gear surfaces mesh properly. If they do not, you will have to replace the blind.

VALANCE RODS

When valance rods bind so that drapes do not draw easily, the probable sources of difficulty are: bracket loosely fixed on wall, brackets unevenly adjusted so that one end of rod is farther away from wall than the other, cord is frayed and fouling pulley, or there is a broken glide or other obstruction in the track.

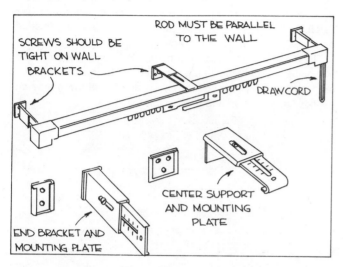

SCREWS SHOULD BE TIGHT ON WALL BRACKETS

ROD MUST BE PARALLEL TO THE WALL

DRAWCORD

CENTER SUPPORT AND MOUNTING PLATE

END BRACKET AND MOUNTING PLATE

Brackets: Check first to see if one or more of the brackets holding the rod is coming loose from the mounting surface. If nails are working loose, replace them with screws. If screws are working loose, turn them tighter. If the screw holes have become over-large, pack them with wooden match sticks, then re-drive the screws.

If the brackets are firmly mounted and the rod still seems to bend or twist, measure each of the brackets to see how far it is set from the wall. All brackets are adjustable with set-screws, which sometimes work loose. If you get varying measurements, adjust the brackets all to the same measurement.

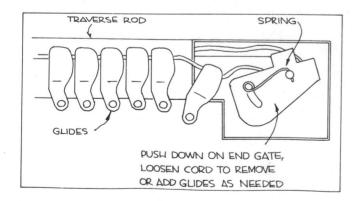

TRAVERSE ROD

SPRING

GLIDES

PUSH DOWN ON END GATE, LOOSEN CORD TO REMOVE OR ADD GLIDES AS NEEDED

Cord and track: If all of the brackets are in good condition, make a running check of the track for obstructions such as broken glides, frayed strands from the cord, and the like. Using a wire hook, try to fish any foreign matter out. This

requires patience since the rod is formed with only a small opening on the side facing the wall. You may have to open the gate through which glides are put into the track, and move everything to the end to get rid of the block.

On occasion the draw cord will go out of adjustment, or one slide will not work. If a slide does not draw, it is because the cord has become detached from it. If the drapes do not open evenly, it is because the cord has slipped, then caught again on the master slide.

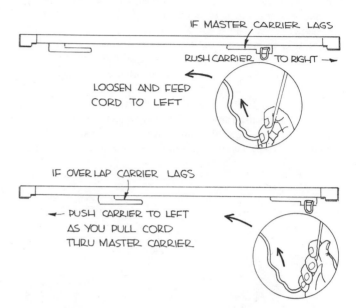

IF MASTER CARRIER LAGS

RUSH CARRIER TO RIGHT →

LOOSEN AND FEED CORD TO LEFT

IF OVERLAP CARRIER LAGS

← PUSH CARRIER TO LEFT AS YOU PULL CORD THRU MASTER CARRIER

To get the cord and slides in proper adjustment, move both slides as far to the outer ends of the rod as the glides will allow. Unhook the master slide in order to let the lagging slide get to the end of the track, then hook it again.

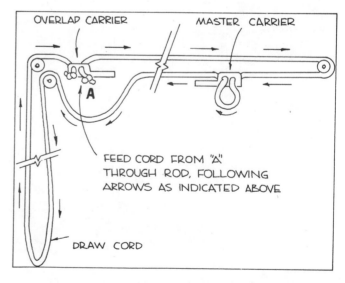

OVERLAP CARRIER

MASTER CARRIER

A

FEED CORD FROM "A" THROUGH ROD, FOLLOWING ARROWS AS INDICATED ABOVE

DRAW CORD

If you must replace a worn cord, the sketch shows how it should be fed through the rod. Tie a simple half-hitch around a knitting needle or long nail to tow the cord along the rod from one side to the other.

In this and all other work on a traverse rod, progress will be much faster and easier if you remove the drapes before you begin.

Walls and ceilings

Walls and ceilings develop a surprising number of cracks and holes, even when the walls are made of concrete. Most cracks come from settling in the house foundations or frame. A few holes are accidental. Most are made on purpose during the hanging of pictures and the installation of light fixtures, becoming troublesome when the decorations are changed.

Gypsumboard and plaster continue to be the two commonest wall surfaces. The materials and methods used for patching are easy to manage, but the work goes slowly and perfection is hard to achieve. (Pages 61-63 cover the essentials. The complications added by wallpaper are noted on page 64.)

Assorted wood, particleboard, vinyl, and other decorator panels that go on walls or ceilings can be far more problematical when repairs are required. They may be applied over other, earlier wall coverings, and may have patent locking systems that are extremely mysterious when you cannot see which one

you are dealing with. Page 64 explains how to make simple in-place repairs of cracks. Larger troubles almost always require the assistance of a professional carpenter.

The ways to repair ceramic tile walls and masonry walls are identical to the methods used with these materials on floors, so are covered in the chapter on floors (see pages 73-75).

One of the most persistent irritations of an average household may be the wall fastener device that is supposed to bear great weight but is torn from the wall by the weight of a simple calendar. There is no complete cure; some helpful information on choosing and using the devices is on page 65.

The many possible patching materials to use in all of these situations are outlined below and on the facing page. If you are faced with a patching job, one or another of these may be best-suited to the job and to your approach.

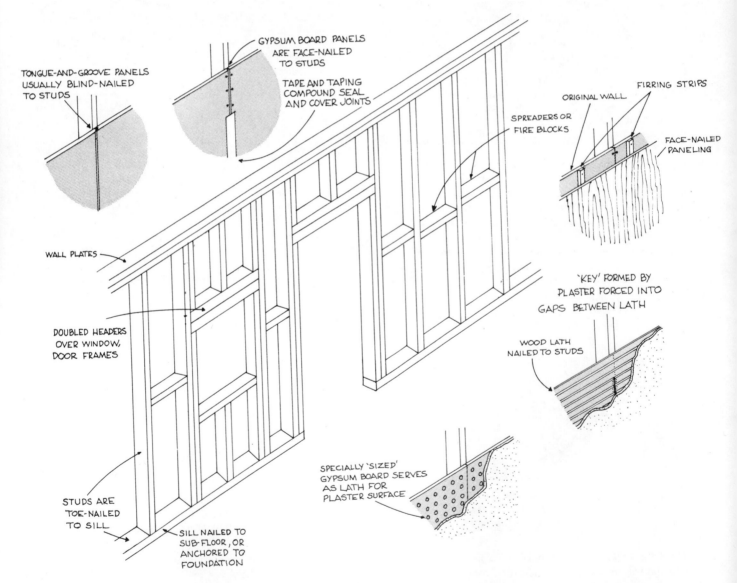

TONGUE-AND-GROOVE PANELS USUALLY BLIND-NAILED TO STUDS

GYPSUM BOARD PANELS ARE FACE-NAILED TO STUDS

TAPE AND TAPING COMPOUND SEAL AND COVER JOINTS

ORIGINAL WALL

FIRRING STRIPS

FACE-NAILED PANELING

SPREADERS OR FIRE BLOCKS

WALL PLATES

DOUBLED HEADERS OVER WINDOW, DOOR FRAMES

STUDS ARE TOE-NAILED TO SILL

SILL NAILED TO SUB-FLOOR, OR ANCHORED TO FOUNDATION

SPECIALLY 'SIZED' GYPSUM BOARD SERVES AS LATH FOR PLASTER SURFACE

WOOD LATH NAILED TO STUDS

'KEY' FORMED BY PLASTER FORCED INTO GAPS BETWEEN LATH

• Which Patch to Use

In recent years there has been a wide variety of wall patching materials that may be helpful but bewildering to the inexperienced.

This brief catalog sorts out some of the materials now on the market and gives recommended uses.

Spackle: Still a standby for patching cracks in gypsumboard and plaster, spackle is a mixture of chalk and plaster. It comes as a ready-mixed paste. This is the way to buy it for patching jobs. It also comes as a powder, but in this form is practical only for major construction work.

Small amounts of sand can be added to either type to match the texture of sand-finish plaster walls.

On occasion, especially when repairing holes in gypsumboard, spackle serves as a finish coat over patching plaster.

Spackle is spread onto a wall with a three-inch or wider putty knife. The exact technique depends on the type of repair, as described on the following pages.

Patching plaster: For any good-sized holes in either a gypsumboard or plaster wall, this is a useful material. It can also be used to cover minor cracks as an alternative to spackle.

Patching plaster comes as a powder and is mixed with water to form a paste-like texture. It can be colored to match a plaster wall by the addition of poster paint to the paste. (You add the powdered paint to the wet plaster and mix until you get an even tone just one shade darker than the wall. Smooth a thin layer onto a small part of the crack and let it dry for a few minutes, then adjust the color intensity upward or downward if necessary to match the wall. Do not anticipate precoloring a large patch this way; painting to match is the only solution once the area gets much larger than a few inches square.)

The plaster is mixed in a pan with a spoon or ladle, usually one pound of powder to ¾ cup of water. The plaster will set up within three hours and cannot be reworked thereafter, so batches are kept small.

Like spackle, patching plaster can be sharpened with sand to match a sand-finish plaster wall.

The paste is applied with either a broad putty knife or a plasterer's trowel. Excess and stains should be wiped off as the work progresses. A wet sponge is effective. Specific techniques are outlined on the following two pages.

White lead putty: In spite of the name, white lead putty comes in many wood colors. Its principal use is in filling nail holes, chips, or nicks in wood. Because of its small-scale application, it is sold in very small cans.

The putty can be painted over after it has dried if this is more effective than trying to match a natural wood finish or if the wood is painted. White lead putty cannot be used as a patch on plaster or gypsumboard. The oil in it leaches out and stains the plaster.

To apply a putty patch, the user just presses the material into the hole with one finger or a putty knife. It is sanded smooth after drying.

Lacquer-based wood filler: This material, also called wood dough, is used primarily for filling holes in wood but can be pressed into service to patch porcelain, cement, and tile. It is made either of wood or cellulose fibers.

You can buy this filler in cans, either left its natural color or stained to match any of several wood tones. No prime is needed before patching, but the hole into which it will go must be clean and slightly roughened.

Like putty, it can be pressed into a small cavity with no more than finger pressure. For larger holes a putty knife is in order. In the repair of deep holes, it is usually applied in layers. The finish coat is sanded to match the texture of the surrounding surface.

Because the lacquer base evaporates quickly in contact with air, it is important to keep the lid firmly in place on the can between jobs. Otherwise, the dough dries out and becomes unusable.

Latex caulk: Tubes or guns full of this material are widely used in interior finishing work and by painters. It can be used on almost any wall surface from metal to plaster and can be painted over after it dries. Because of its versatility, caulk is especially

valuable in dealing with a crack where gypsumboard has separated from a wood or metal window frame, or some similar situation.

The caulk is applied to a crack with the gun, then smoothed with finger pressure. Light sanding will give it some texture if it dries too smooth to match a coarse surface such as plaster.

Sink and tub caulk: This material is formulated somewhat similarly to the latex caulk described above but stays more flexible and has better resistance to water. Thus it is used principally to seal joints between tubs, sinks or shower pans and adjacent walls of whatever material.

It comes in tubes that can be squeezed with finger pressure or mounted in guns. The material is made white but can be painted over.

Although the texture is a little too smooth for many plaster walls, the material will bond properly to any commonly used wall covering.

Patented crack patchers: Several firms have launched patented crack patchers that use a material somewhat like latex caulk in combination with microscopically fine screening. The idea is that the screening bridges the crack with a flexible material that allows the crack to move beneath the patch without disturbing it. The adhesive keeps the screening in place at the same time that it hides the patch. The screening can be used on any surface, although there are differing adhesives for indoor and outdoor use. Paint covers the patch.

• Patching Gypsumboard or Plaster

Gypsumboard and plaster are made out of the same material at base, so the materials and techniques of patching are similar. Differences arise mainly in patching jobs that require attention to the underlayer, if any.

Gypsumboard is simply nailed to studs. Plaster is bound to a wall in several ways. In older buildings, wooden or metal laths have been nailed to the studs, and the first layer of plaster forced between and around them to form the bond. Gypsumboard drilled with holes and nailed to the studs is used in a similar manner. Plaster in newer buildings is usually applied to smooth wallboard panels which have been treated with an adhesive. A variation is porous wallboard that absorbs plaster into its fibers to form the bond.

REPAIRING GYPSUMBOARD

Cracks in gypsumboard can be patched with spackle, a patented crack patcher, or a caulk. Narrow cracks should be wire-brushed smooth. Wider, deeper cracks should have all loose material pried out with a can opener or screwdriver. A firmer bond results if the edges are undercut. The edges of the crack should be dampened so moisture is not drawn out of the patch (except in the cases of certain caulks with instructions that specify dry application).

PRY OUT ALL LOOSE MATERIAL, THEN FILL CRACK

FEATHER EDGES OF SURFACE

COAT WITH "V" STROKES

Fill a deep crack with a layer that comes almost to the surface, then follow with a thin finish coat that feathers out an inch or two on either side of the crack. The sketch shows how to feather edges with a putty knife.

Holes in gypsumboard are usually without backing. The facing page shows techniques for patching these. If a hole is very large, it likely will meet a stud. In this case, cut a piece of gypsumboard to fit the trimmed up hole, nail it to the stud, then tape and spackle the seams as if you were installing a wall from scratch.

SPACKLING WITH TAPE . . .

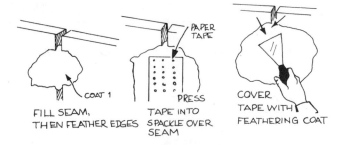

FILL SEAM, THEN FEATHER EDGES

COAT 1

PAPER TAPE

PRESS TAPE INTO SPACKLE OVER SEAM

COVER TAPE WITH FEATHERING COAT

REPAIRING PLASTER

Cracks in plaster are treated exactly as are those in gypsumboard, except that extra steps may be required to match surface textures.

Holes or wide cracks that go all the way to the lath or wallboard require more extensive treatment. (1) Knock out all loose, cracked plaster with hammer and chisel. Take care not to cause further cracking. Undercut the edges to strengthen the eventual bond. (2) Check the lath for damage or excessive moisture that could be decomposing the plaster. If you encounter signs of substantial damage at this point, it may well be advisable to call in a professional. (3) Having assured yourself of the good condition of the backing material, prepare a batch of patching plaster following the package instructions. (4) Using a sponge, dampen the area surrounding the patch. Dry plaster will absorb water from the patching material, weakening and shrinking it. (5) If the patch is smaller than four inches square, fill and surface it with one application of the

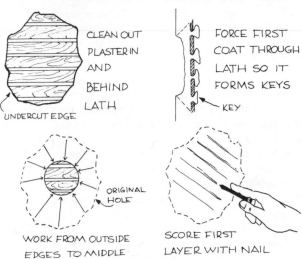

CLEAN OUT PLASTER IN AND BEHIND LATH

UNDERCUT EDGE

FORCE FIRST COAT THROUGH LATH SO IT FORMS KEYS

KEY

WORK FROM OUTSIDE EDGES TO MIDDLE

ORIGINAL HOLE

SCORE FIRST LAYER WITH NAIL

patching plaster. If the hole is larger than that, plan to fill it with three layers. The first one should fill a little more than half the depth, and should bond to the backing. Before it dries, it should be scored with a nail to provide "tooth" for the succeeding layer. The second layer, applied after the first has dried (about four hours), requires a re-wetting of the patch area. This coat should come within a half to quarter inch of the surface. The third coat is applied as soon as the second has dried, and the patch area moistened again. This coat has to be textured to match the rest of the wall. (6) For a smooth coat, pull a wide putty knife or a concrete float across the patch as flatly as possible. To achieve almost a glossy smoothness,

TO MATCH EXISTING WALL . . .

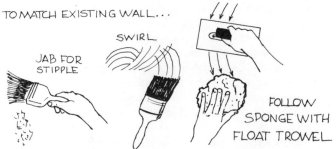

JAB FOR STIPPLE

SWIRL

FOLLOW SPONGE WITH FLOAT TROWEL

wipe a wet sponge across the patch with one hand just ahead of the float held in the other hand. For a rough surface, scour lightly with a paint brush—either in swirling strokes or jabbed straight at the wall—depending on the texture you are matching. (7) Seal the patch with shellac or another sealer before painting.

PATCHING DEEP HOLES

The method of patching shown in the adjoining photos will work with either plaster walls or gypsum wallboard, and is most useful for holes where there is no backing.

These holes usually follow the removal of an electrical fixture.

The maximum area this patch should be expected to cover is about four inches square.

You will need patching plaster, a piece of rust-resistant screen slightly larger than the hole, a length of wire, a stick, a pair of pliers, and a putty knife.

To prepare the hole, remove any cracked material. Dust as thoroughly as you can. Before beginning to apply the patching plaster, wet down the wall adjacent to the hole, or you risk shrinkage in your patching material.

After the patch has been finished according to the instructions with the photos, allow it to dry thoroughly. Then sand smooth with fine sandpaper. Brush patch with sealer before painting.

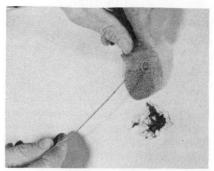
Loop wire through screen at the center, then fasten it with two twists.

Push screen through hole, then draw it up tightly. Fasten with wood stick.

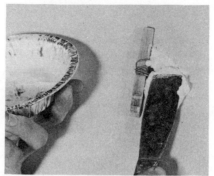
Fill hole to half thickness of wall with patching plaster.

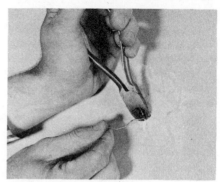
Cut wire off after patch dries. Fill hole flush with second layer.

FOR GYPSUMBOARD ONLY

The method of patching outlined in the sketches is much simpler than the one above but works only with gypsumboard.

It makes use of an extra margin of paper surface on gypsumboard as a sort of sealable flap.

Cut the patch to its gross size from a scrap piece of gypsumboard. Then, working from the back, cut a smaller plug without scoring the paper on the "good" side. A sharp knife used carefully will do the job.

To cut away the hole in the wall, a sharp knife or a hacksaw blade will serve.

When you apply spackle around the opening, cover the edges of the hole as well to give the plug extra purchase.

Once the patch is in place, press the excess spackle out from behind the flap, then paint a light coat of spackle across the entire surface, but taking special care to hide the seams.

After the spackle has dried, you will need to go over the patch with fine sandpaper for a final smoothing.

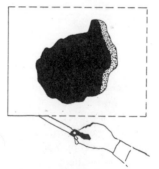
Mark wall and cut hole to neat rectangle same size at patch "plug."

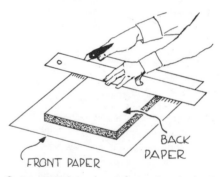
Cut gypsumboard patch to size desired, leaving extra margin of surface paper.

Spread a cement — spackle will do — around the hole in the wall.

Place the patch in position, then paint over the entire surface with spackle.

• Gluing Down Loose Wallpaper

Loose edges, blisters, and bubbles in wallpaper can be repaired with library paste, flour-and-water paste, or white glue. If it is vinyl wallpaper, only white glue should be used.

Tears in wallpaper can be patched with a matching piece, using one of the adhesives noted above.

To repair loose edges, simply apply glue to the underside of the paper and press it back into place. Do not use so much glue that it soaks through the paper and leaves a stain. A thin, even layer about as thick as a piece of notebook paper is about right. Sponge off any excess glue with water, taking care not to soak the paper so much that glue loosens behind the wet spot.

Simple tears can be repaired in a similar manner. If it is the peeling sort of tear that gets larger and larger, peel it up and apply glue to the underside, then press the paper back into place so the edges of the tear match as closely as possible.

If some paper is torn completely away, you will need a matching piece to replace the missing part. It will be almost impossible to get an exact tone match unless you bought some spare footage with the original purchase, but the following technique at least will allow you to match any pattern precisely. Cut a patch somewhat larger than the torn area making sure that the patch contains all of the pattern area you will need to replace. With masking tape, tack the patch directly over the hole. Align the patch so that it exactly matches the pattern beneath. Using a sharp knife, cut through both the patch and the paper on the wall in a neat rectangle. Remove the patch, and peel away the paper inside your knife cut. The patch will fit the hole exactly. Paste it in place following the instruction above for pasting down loose edges.

If wallpaper develops blisters or bubbles, the cure is to slit the paper and force glue through the slit, then press the paper

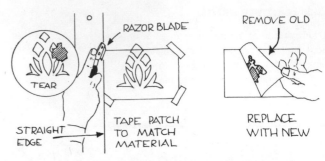

STRAIGHT EDGE — RAZOR BLADE — TEAR

TAPE PATCH TO MATCH MATERIAL

REMOVE OLD — REPLACE WITH NEW

tight again. A sharp razor blade produces the neatest cut. A single, straight cut will do for a small blister. Cut a V or L for a larger bubble so you will not risk tearing the paper when you force the glue into the bubbled area. To hide the cut as

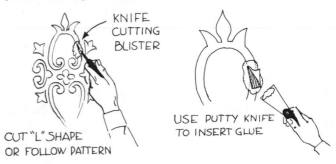

KNIFE CUTTING BLISTER

CUT "L" SHAPE OR FOLLOW PATTERN

USE PUTTY KNIFE TO INSERT GLUE

best you can, follow along a line in the pattern. Use white glue for vinyl wallpaper; for regular paper use white glue or library paste. Use a kitchen knife to spread the adhesive under the paper.

For any repair, a smoothing brush and seam roller are helpful in pressing the paper smoothly to the wall. These can be rented from many tool rental outfits. A sponge or straight-edge and a rolling pin can substitute.

• Paneling

Paneling is an easy-to-install interior wall material with great diversity of texture and design. It is, however, a material that is very difficult to repair.

This product is a manufactured "sheet" where, under strong pressure and glues, a veneer is laminated to a base material. Typically, the base material is some sort of pressed wood. The surfaces range from wood veneers to burlap to glossy vinyl. Because these surfaces are laminated to the base materials at the manufacturing plant, patching or other repair is difficult or impossible.

Wood veneers can be patched with caulking compound or with a putty if the crack is relatively straight and narrow. Many of the other materials—particularly fabrics—cannot be patched. The panels must either be replaced or the mar hidden by placement of furniture or decorations.

Patching cracks. Tub caulk is the best-suited of the several caulks for repairing cracks in wood-veneer paneling and vinyl-surfaced panels. It dries to a smooth finish and will accept wood stains or paint readily. In addition, it retains some flexibility—an advantage in cases where framing might shift, causing a more rigid putty to break loose.

A putty pencil colored to match the wood paneling is also a good repair item. The pencils, available in most building supply stores, look something like the big crayons primary school children use. The technique is similar, too: You just bear down hard and follow the line. A crack that crosses grain lines of widely differing colors may require two of the pencils for a careful blending job.

Replacing panels. Normally, this is a job for a professional or at least a seasoned amateur. The problem is that the panels may be attached in any of several different ways. In most cases, it takes very careful work to avoid damage to panels adjacent to the one being removed.

You can do some investigation to see what the probabilities of replacing panels yourself are. Start by taking the cover plates off wall switches, convenience outlets, or any fixture that will allow you to see how the wall is put together.

Plywood paneling may be nailed directly to the studs, may be nailed to firring strips that are in turn nailed to the old finish wall, or may be glued to either an old finish wall or a clean gypsumboard wall. The edges may be tongue-and-groove but are likely to be square-edged.

Composite paneling may be secured to a wall in any of the above ways. In addition, it may be secured with any of many patented interlocks that augment the tongue-and-groove.

• Fastening Devices For Walls

Wood, being resilient, clinches tightly around a nail or screw driven into it. Plaster, concrete, and other non-organic materials lack resiliency, making it difficult to attach shelf brackets, picture hangers, or anything else that must suspend weight.

There are two separate series of devices designed to compensate for the natural deficiences of inelastic wall materials. Hangers for gypsum or plaster wall depend upon a spreading frame that distributes weight over a larger surface than a nail or screw can provide. Hangers for masonry walls use a resilient sleeve that fits into a hole drilled to hold both sleeve and screw.

Once a hanger fails, abandon it. Move to an unbroken patch of wall and install the new hanger as carefully as possible. The less the wall is disturbed, the better the installation. Choices of hangers are described below.

GYPSUM, PLASTER WALLS

The choices among fasteners depend primarily upon the weight of the object to be hung.

For lightweight pictures—two pounds or less—a straight pin driven downward into the wall at a 45° angle is reliable and durable because it disturbs plaster the least.

The conventional picture hook, a nail seated in a metal hook, should hold frames up to 20 pounds. To minimize the breaking of the plaster or gypsum, drill a guide hole for the nail. Use the finest bit you have and drill using the hook as a guide (to assure getting the correct angle).

Shelf brackets and other weighty objects should be secured with wood screws driven into the studs. If a stud cannot be used, the next best choices are screws with expansion anchors or split-wing toggle bolts. In both cases, you drill a hole, insert the screw (or bolt), then tighten it to spread the anchor (or wings). The most frequent mistake in installation is turning

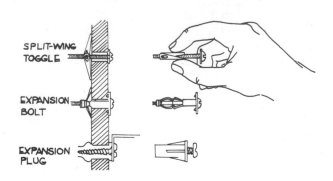

SPLIT-WING TOGGLE

EXPANSION BOLT

EXPANSION PLUG

the screw too far; this pulls the anchor into the wall material. And the deeper the cut, the weaker the device's grip.

If design permits, use two or three of the anchoring devices to secure a strip of wood to the wall, then fasten the shelf brackets or whatever to the strip of wood.

In purchasing these anchors, be sure to get the proper size. Expansion anchors, for example, have a solid shank designed to equal the thickness of the wall.

The design limit for a single anchor is 100 pounds of dead weight. Anchors are not intended to secure shower grab bars or anything meant to take sudden pulls.

If one of the devices is abandoned, remove the screw if possible, and sink the anchor shield into the wall deep enough for it to be covered with a caulk or spackle patch.

MASONRY WALLS

A wide assortment of expansion shields are available to secure screws in masonry. Length and diameter govern the carrying weight of these fasteners.

Expansion shields, like fasteners used in gypsum or plaster, can work loose in time. Like their counterparts, they should be abandoned and a new device inserted in sound wall near the original.

The key to a good installation is in the hole drilled to receive them. There are three tools: Star drills for small, accurate holes, electric drills for faster work, and electric hammers for big fasteners.

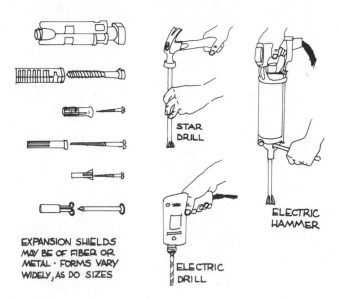

STAR DRILL

ELECTRIC HAMMER

ELECTRIC DRILL

EXPANSION SHIELDS MAY BE OF FIBER OR METAL · FORMS VARY WIDELY, AS DO SIZES

A star drill takes patience but is easy to use. You mark the exact point of the hole and hold the drill firmly while you make the first five or six hammer taps. Once the hole begins to form, you loosen your grip and let the drill tip dance a bit inside as you strike it. Diameters run from 3/16 inch to two inches. (For a hole larger than ¾ inch, first you drill a pilot hole, then the larger one.) In all cases, hundreds of light hammer taps rather than dozens of crushing blows result in a truer hole and fewer cracks.

Electric hand drills with carbide tips are faster than star drills, but they are limited in size. The drills can be rented, and the carbide tips bought.

For a ¾-inch hole or bigger, the electric hammer is the required power tool. These, too, can be rented.

Once the hole is drilled, you push the shield into it, and then insert the screw through the bracket (or whatever you are fastening).

Floors

There are two general types of flooring, "slab" and "suspended." Slab is concrete laid in direct contact with the ground at or below grade level. Suspended is a finish floor laid over wood sub-flooring and a system of joists, as illustrated below.

Slab floor repairs are relatively simple. If the concrete cracks, it is patched. The complication—beyond amateur skills—is in checking the cause of the cracks if they are persistent. The cures for simple cracks in concrete and for relaying loosened brick are described on page 73.

Repairs of suspended flooring are far more complicated. Most of the problems that matter show up in the surface of the finish floor. These include loosened or cracked linoleum or resilient tile (see pages 68-69), loosened or broken ceramic tile (see pages 74-75), hardwood floor that is somehow defective (see pages 70-72), and squeaking floors.

In any of these cases, the trouble may be rooted in either the joists or the sub-flooring. It is, therefore, useful to have a detailed understanding of the ways in which the elements of flooring go together. Even though some of the major repairs are in the realm of the professional, knowing the possibilities allows the home repairman to go ahead with confidence and to avoid endlessly repeated superficial cures for failures that are located in the frame of the house rather than the finished floor.

The basic construction of an interior floor is as follows: The finish floor is laid on sub-floor, which is in turn supported by joists.

Joists are 2x6 or larger in dimension, edge-laid with centers 12, 16 (most common), 20 or 24 inches apart. The sub-floor (also called rough floor) is either 1x6 or wider lumber, or heavy plywood of "2.4.1" designation. In older homes, the 1x6 sub-floor is usually laid at right angles to the joists. In later buildings, the 1x6's are laid at an angle of 45° to the joists. Recent buildings tend to have the plywood sheets laid in checkerboard pattern over the joists. Plywood does the best job of eliminating sub-floor squeaking. It also eliminates the need for underlayment between the sub-floor and certain finished floors—especially linoleum, cork, and asphalt tile—because it serves adequately as a moisture barrier where 1x6's do not.

Finished floors may be secured to sub-floors in any of several ways. Most hardwood floors are nailed or screwed to the sub-floor. Resilient floors (linoleum, vinyl tile, etc.) are secured to the sub-floor or to an underlayment with any of several paste adhesives. Ceramic tiles are set in a cement-like base.

Most home repairs concentrate on the successful removal of damaged finish flooring and replacement of that section with identical new material. The following pages deal with the techniques for doing these tasks.

Except for bracing an obviously weak joist against its neighbors, other floor repairs quickly go beyond "basic."

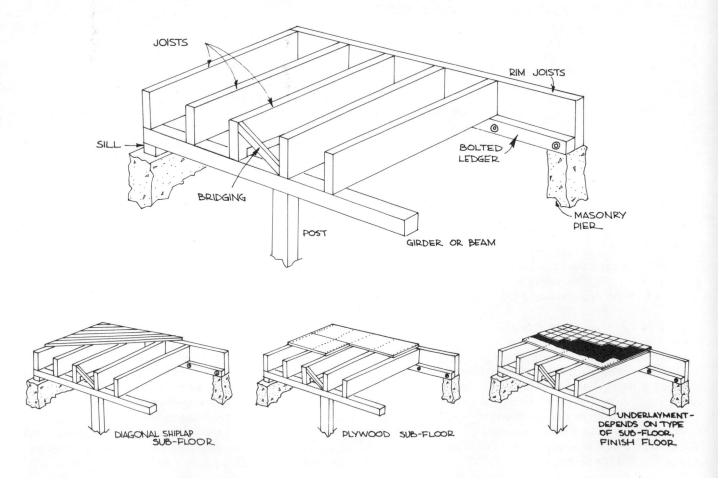

JOISTS

RIM JOISTS

SILL

BOLTED LEDGER

BRIDGING

POST

GIRDER OR BEAM

MASONRY PIER

DIAGONAL SHIPLAP SUB-FLOOR

PLYWOOD SUB-FLOOR

UNDERLAYMENT—DEPENDS ON TYPE OF SUB-FLOOR, FINISH FLOOR

• Squeaky Floor Repair

A loose sub-floor is the main cause of squeaks underfoot, but hardwood finish floors may also be sources of irritating noise.

SUB-FLOOR SQUEAKS

The nails in sub-floor sheeting loosen at the joists because of wood shrinkage or house settling. Play between the joists and sub-floor causes the annoying noise.

Repair is relatively simple if the joist area is exposed to view and is accessible. Locate the loose sheeting by having someone walk on the floor while you watch for sub-floor movement from below.

If only one board is loose, wedge a shingle between it and the joist to stop the play, as shown in the sketch.

SHINGLE WEDGE
JOIST

If several boards are loose, stop play by butting a 1x4 against the loose boards. Maintain upward pressure with the cleat against the sub-floor as you nail the cleat to the joist with two or more 6d common nails. Be sure that your helper is not still standing on the area above and forcing the sub-floor

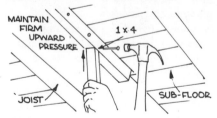

MAINTAIN FIRM UPWARD PRESSURE
1 x 4
JOIST
SUB-FLOOR

flush against the top of the joist. To be effective, the cleat must force the sub-floor upward against the heads of the old nails holding the sheeting to the joist.

If the nailing area is not accessible because it is covered from below by a ceiling, or because the crawl space under the house is too shallow, the job must be done through the finish floor surface.

The joist must first be located. This is difficult. The finish floor offers no clues because of the intervening sub-floor. Generally, joists run parallel to the short

axis of the house, but not always. This is particularly true of older homes with additions and of modern houses with complex room arrangements and split levels. However, with a sensitive ear you may be able to locate the joist by tapping the floor (or the ceiling below) with the handle-end of a wooden hammer. When you tap an area supported or backed by a joist, it returns a "solid" sound. If you locate the joist from the ceiling side, use a measuring tape and any walls extending through the floor above as reference points for finding the joist again from the other side.

With the joist in the squeaking area located, the next step will depend on the type of finish floor.

On a wood surface (strip, plank, block, or parquet), drive 10d finishing nails slightly toed-in through the finish floor into the joist. Use a nailset on the nailheads near the surface to avoid marring the finish floor. Countersink the heads and fill the holes with plastic wood. Sand lightly when dry.

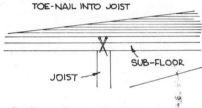

TOE-NAIL INTO JOIST
JOIST
SUB-FLOOR

Resilient floors (linoleum, cork, asphalt tile, etc.) require removal of the surface material over the joist area before toe-nailing the sub-floor as above. Removing, replacing, and/or patching such floors is described on pages 68-69.

FINISH FLOOR SQUEAKS

An obvious but infrequent source of squeaking floors is loose strips or planks in "hardwood" floors. The strip or plank fastenings loosen from the sub-floor because of warping, shrinkage, or house settling. One or more of the finish floor boards may be involved. The trouble spot is easily located by walking over it and noting the squeaks and "give."

The first remedy to try: Place a one or two-foot length of 2x4 on several thicknesses of newspaper (to avoid marring the finish floor). Place this over the area at right angles to the lay of the floor strips or planks. Rap the 2x4 sharply with a hammer while moving the block over the loose area in a steady rectangular pattern as indicated in the

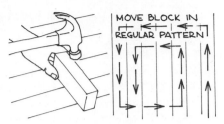

MOVE BLOCK IN REGULAR PATTERN

sketch. Caution: Avoid hammering the block on the same spot with repeated hard blows. The tongue-and-groove of the flooring directly beneath the hammer may split.

This treatment may cure the squeaking. However, if it fails, renailing the finish floor to the sub-floor may be necessary. To do this, locate the approximate center of the squeaking area. Nail in the lengthwise cracks running through the center of the area. Start by driving two 6d finishing nails into one of the cracks. They should be several inches apart and slightly angled in opposite directions (see the sketch). Use a nailset on the nailheads near the surface. Countersink the heads, then fill the hole with plastic wood. Sand the filler when it is dry.

6d FINISHING NAILS AS WEDGES
6"

If the first pair of nails fail to stop the squeaking, repeat the procedure, nailing in parallel crack to the left and right of the original pair until all of the loose finish floor boards are securely nailed to the sub-floor.

If cracks between boards in the finish floor are wide enough to admit a putty knife blade, gluing (alone or in a combination with nails as described above) may stop squeaking.

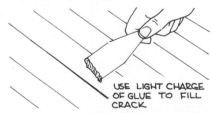

USE LIGHT CHARGE OF GLUE TO FILL CRACK

When one crack is filled, wipe excess glue off the floor surface with a clean rag. When the whole job is completed, place appropriate weight (bricks, heavy books) on the freshly glued cracks overnight, or until the glue has dried according to manufacturer's instructions.

• Resilient Floors

Resilient floors are the types of floors that are relatively pliable compared to wood. They include tile or sheet materials such as vinyl, asphalt, linoleum, rubber, cork, and various special compositions.

On a raised floor supported by joists, the resilient material may be directly on the sub-floor, on "felt" (building paper), on plywood or particleboard underlayment, or on a combination of these materials.

In basements or slab-floor homes, resilient floors are often laid on the concrete slab with an intervening polyethylene vapor barrier. In older homes, resilient finish floors may be found to lie atop earlier finish floors.

Resilient tile or sheet is held in place by emulsion, paste, cement, epoxy, or other adhesive specified by the manufacturer for the particular kind of surface and underlayment materials involved.

Repairs to resilient floors should be made with either the same materials and adhesives used in the original floor or with recommended substitutes. To get the correct material and adhesive for replacement, take a sample of the original tile or sheet to your hardware store or floor specialty shop. Also be prepared to advise the retailer on the type of existing sub-floor the finish material is to be laid on—that is, felt, vapor barrier, plywood, old wood, or whatever.

In addition to supplying you with the right materials, the retailer probably can tell you how best to loosen the particular adhesive under the existing material. The usual choices are water, heat, solvent, or a scraper. The methods to be used depend on the chemistry of the particular adhesive.

Floor type	Method of cutting
Asphalt tile	(1) Heat back of tile with blowtorch, then cut with tile cutter or tin snips. (2) Score unheated tile heavily on its front side with a linoleum knife guided by a metal straightedge. Snap the halves apart by bending toward the back of the tile.
Vinyl, vinyl-asbestos, rubber, cork	(1) Thin, lightweight tiles are cut with a sharp, short-bladed knife or sturdy kitchen scissors (*not* the type with serrated cutting edges). (2) Thick, heavyweight tiles are cut with a linoleum knife, tile cutter, or metal shears.
Linoleum, vinyl sheet	Linoleum knife guided by metal straightedge.

Note: When using a linoleum knife or other type of knife blade, cut the tile or sheet on an old board or other expendable surface that may be marred as each cut is completed.

REMOVING RESILIENT TILE

To remove one or several damaged resilient tiles, you will need a stiff wide-blade putty knife and a linoleum knife. In addition, it makes the job easier if you also have adhesive solvent recommended by your materials supplier, or for asphalt tile, a blowtorch. Proceed as follows:

(1) Using linoleum knife, cut completely through damaged tile to underlayment; make cut near tile edge and wide enough to insert putty knife as illustrated.

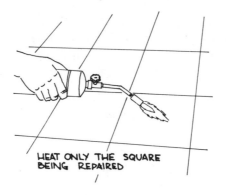

HEAT ONLY THE SQUARE BEING REPAIRED

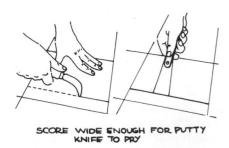

SCORE WIDE ENOUGH FOR PUTTY KNIFE TO PRY

On asphalt tile ONLY, first heat the face of the tile to be removed with blowtorch, taking special care not to scorch adjacent tiles that will remain in place.

(2) Using putty knife, remove strip of tile nearest edge; then reverse work direction and remove remainder of tile with help of solvent. For asphalt tile ONLY, keep tile face heated with blowtorch as you work.

(3) While the adhesive loosened by solvent is still semi-liquid, wipe off excess with rag; take special care not to let smudges of adhesive dry on adjacent, in-place tile faces.

REPLACING WHOLE TILES

To replace a whole tile or tiles that you have removed, you will need a serrated blade to spread the adhesive. If the tile is rubber, linoleum, or cork, you will also need an ordinary kitchen rolling pin. Asphalt and vinyl-asbestos tiles do *not* have to be rolled after laying.

You will also need tile and adhesive identical to the kinds removed. Proceed as follows:

(1) Using serrated spreader and following adhesive manufacturer's recommendations, spread adhesive on exposed work area; wipe off with a damp rag *im-

SERRATED SPREADER

mediately any accidental adhesive smudges on adjacent in-place tile faces.

(2) _SET,_ do not _slide_ tiles in place. Press new tile in place firmly with your

SET TILES...
DO NOT SLIDE

hands, especially at edges. With damp rag, immediately remove any excess adhesive forced out where in-place tiles butt against the replacements.

(3) Using rolling pin when all new tile is in place, firmly roll surfaces if tile is

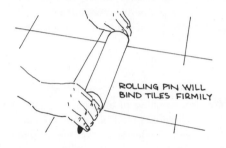

ROLLING PIN WILL
BIND TILES FIRMLY

rubber, linoleum, or cork. _Do not_ roll asphalt or vinyl-asbestos tile. Edges of asphalt tile may be slow to set properly, but don't worry: room warmth and foot traffic will flatten them in a few days.

Let newly placed area dry at least overnight before waxing or polishing surface and replacing furniture. Do not mop for at least one week.

PART TILES AND CUTOUTS

To cut resilient tile to fit, use tools as shown for the various materials. The following are some suggestions on easy ways to get proper fits.

Cutting partial tiles: To cut a partial tile for an edge row, use a full tile (Tile B) as a measuring tile in addition to the full one (Tile A) you are going to cut. Then:

(1) Lay Tile A in position on top of an in-place tile adjacent to the narrow edge strip.

(2) Position measuring Tile B over Tile A, then slide it so it covers the narrow strip, butting against the wall.

(3) Using Tile B as a straightedge, score Tile A with a linoleum knife.

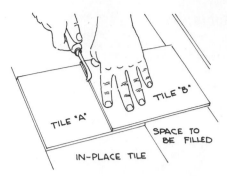

TILE "A"   TILE "B"

SPACE TO
BE FILLED

IN-PLACE TILE

(4) Remove Tile A and complete cut on scoring made by linoleum knife. One of the two should be an exact fit for the narrow edge strip.

Cutouts in tile: To make a neat job around obstructions, first experiment with scissors and light cardboard (shirt cardboard from a laundry is excellent) in tile dimensions. It may take several tries before you get a good pattern, which you then transfer to the tile.

Generally, the smaller the diameter of the curve to be cut, the more difficult it is to do neatly. To make the job easier on heavyweight tile, use a food can of appropriate diameter as a guide edge

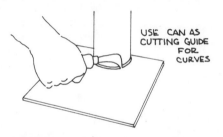

USE CAN AS
CUTTING GUIDE
FOR
CURVES

for the linoleum knife. Completely cut through the tile as you work continuously around the can. Make the circular cutout before straight cuts that may lead into the hole to fit around obstruction.

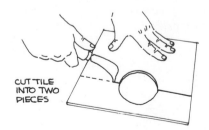

CUT TILE
INTO TWO
PIECES

Cut heavy tile in two pieces with a straight cut through center of hole to make fit around obstruction. Partially cutting tile on one side of hole and attempting to bend material in place often results in splitting or breaking it.

PATCHING LINOLEUM OR VINYL SHEET

It is relatively easy to put an inconspicuous patch in a badly damaged area of linoleum or vinyl sheet flooring. You will need:

- Flooring material of the same kind, thickness, and pattern from the same manufacturer as the original flooring.
- Adhesive recommended by the sheet manufacturer for the particular flooring.
- A sharp linoleum knife, metal straightedge for straight cuts, and/or food cans of appropriate diameter as guides for cutting curves in heavily patterned flooring.
- A hammer and handful of one-inch wire brads.

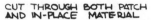

CUT THROUGH BOTH PATCH
AND IN-PLACE MATERIAL

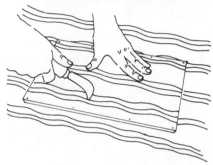

- A stiff putty knife and a serrated blade for spreading the adhesive (if work area is too small to accommodate standard serrated spreader, improvise with a piece of stiff sheet metal and use tin snips to make serrations as illustrated). Proceed as follows:

(1) Without removing the damaged area, lay a piece of the replacement sheet over the area to be repaired.

(2) Position replacement sheet to match any pattern in original floor and nail in place with the brads as illustrated.

(3) Using linoleum knife with straightedge or cans as guides, cut completely through the replacement sheet _and_ the in-place original sheet.

If flooring is plain or has a regular pattern, cut rectangular patch; if elaborately or boldly patterned, cut patch with irregular edges following pattern curves or angles to make repair inconspicuous.

(4) Pull out brads and put excess replacement sheet and new patch aside.

(5) Remove damaged area and replace with new patch.

• Understanding Wood Floors

To successfully repair a wood floor, it is necessary to know what kind of wood is involved, how it has been milled, and how it is secured to the sub-floor. The following primer will enable an accurate assessment of any typical floor.

STRIP FLOORING

Strip flooring is the wood surfacing commonly termed hardwood floor. Replacing sections of strip floor requires exact matching of the old and new strip by dimension and by kind and grade of wood.

Your flooring may be white or red oak, maple, beech, birch, or one of the less expensive softwoods such as hemlock, larch, or elm. Various systems are used to grade these according to quality. For example, oak comes in #2 Common, #1 Common, Select, and Clear. The latter is the highest quality.

Strip dimensions also vary greatly. Tongue-and-groove strip widths are given in the width of the face, not including the protruding tongue. Typical widths are 1½ inch, 2 inch, 2¼ inch, and 3¼ inch. Some floors are patterned by alternating strips of differing widths.

Strip flooring also comes in different thicknesses. The most common in oak is $\frac{25}{32}$ inch, but ⅜ inch, ½ inch, and ⅝ inch are among other standard thicknesses used.

Usually, strip is tongue-and-groove on the sides and ends. However—especially in an older house—you may find the less common square-edge type that is butted together without tongue or groove.

There is only one safe and easy way to get an exact match in replacement strip out of these many possible combinations: Take a sample of the original strip removed from the floor to the lumberyard when you order the new materials.

Methods of nailing: Before starting to repair a wood-finish floor, examine the surface closely for evidence of the method of nailing. There are several methods, each involving special considerations in removing and replacing sections of flooring.

If no evidence of nailing is found on the surface, the finish floor is probably "blind-nailed." This technique applies only to wood flooring milled with tongue-and-groove. In addition to being the commonest technique with strip flooring, it is also sometimes used with plank flooring and with block.

In blind nailing, the nails holding the finish floor to the sub-floor are driven at an angle through the tongue of each board. The overlapping groove of the adjoining board then hides the nail head from the finished surface.

The alternative to blind nailing is to nail straight through the exposed face of the flooring, countersinking the nail heads and filling the hole with plastic wood. This leaves visible but not conspicuous rows of nail marks on the finished surface.

Seldom are both blind and face nailing to be found in the same floor. Face nailing is most generally used with square-edge strips but sometimes is found in tongue-and-groove flooring.

The slim possibility exists that a floor is not nailed at all, but rather set in mastic or another adhesive.

PLANK FLOORING

Plank flooring is essentially strip flooring in wider board widths. It frequently has more complicated fastening methods to cope with in making repairs. In some floors, replacement is further complicated by the use of two or more widths randomly laid.

Plank flooring comes in about the same varieties and grades of wood as strip flooring. However, available widths are not as highly standardized as for strip and may range from 3 inches up to 9 inches. A few planks may be even wider. Thicknesses, however, vary less than with strip. The two commonest dimensions are $\frac{25}{32}$ inch and $\frac{13}{16}$ inch. Some veneered planks are ⅞ inch thick.

Plank flooring may be either tongue-and-groove or square-edge.

As with strip flooring, replacement of sections within an existing floor requires exact matching of old and new planks by dimension and by kind and grade of wood. With plank flooring, take samples of all widths removed from the original floor to your lumberyard. In addition, if the original lay of plank involves two or more different widths in patterned or random floor design, make a reference drawing of the replacement area showing sequences, widths, lengths, and numbers of new planks required.

Methods of securing: Planks may be fastened by blind or face nailing as described in the section above on strip flooring. They may also be secured by screws hidden beneath wood plugs. Most of these floors are secured by nails and two screws at each end of each board.

A few floors may be secured exclusively with screws at about 30-inch intervals.

To remove these, the plug must first be drilled out, then the screw head cleaned so it can be removed. The detailed instruction is shown on the facing page.

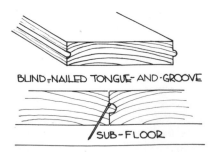

BLIND-NAILED TONGUE-AND-GROOVE
/SUB-FLOOR

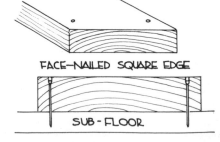

FACE-NAILED SQUARE EDGE
SUB-FLOOR

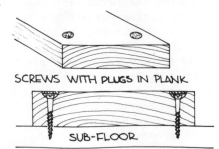

SCREWS WITH PLUGS IN PLANK
SUB-FLOOR

REMOVING TONGUE-AND-GROOVE FLOORING

You will need the following tools:
- Carpenter's square and pencil.
- Portable power cut-off saw with a hinged shoe for regulating depth of cut (or a curved floorboard saw if you wish to rent one). Do not figure to do the work with a handsaw.
- Hammer and sturdy wood chisel with at least a two-inch blade.
- A heavy pry bar with curved end.
- Pliers or wirecutters.
- Nailset or punch.

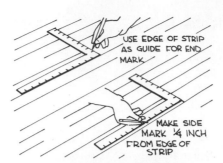

Mark out work area with square and pencil. Use a lengthwise crack to align square for end mark. Then use end mark to align side marks ½ to ¼ inch away from cracks (so saw will not hit nails).

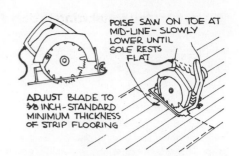

Make end cuts first. Put toe of shoe at mid-point of end cut, then slowly lower blade until shoe rests flat on floor before moving ahead. Work from center out to each edge, avoiding over-cut.

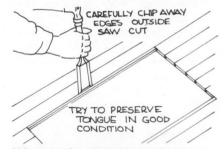

Next, make side cuts. To guide these, tack a strip of wood next to the pencil line toward the center of the area to be removed. Work from center toward ends. Adjust saw blade if shoe rides on strip.

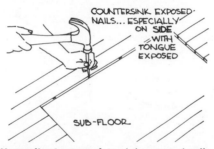

Hammer and chisel through saw cut to the sub-floor. Keep beveled face of chisel facing area to be removed. Take special care to make clean cuts in each corner, or strips may splinter into good area.

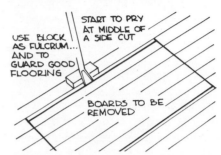

Lift boards with pry bar, starting at mid-point of a side cut. Use a small wood block to gain leverage and avoid marring any part of floor. The trimmed edges of the outside boards will remain.

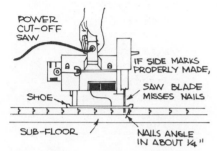

Chip away the edges left outside the saw cuts, using hammer and chisel or pry bar as needed. Work slowly to avoid damaging adjacent boards that are to be retained. They must fit new boards.

Use nail set or punch to sink exposed nail heads on side strip with its groove exposed, and any other nails that protrude into work space. Sub-floor and edges must be level, straight.

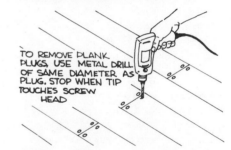

Special step: If you are working with plugged plank floor, use a metal drill to cut away the wood plugs until drill tip touches screw head. Clean slot, then use screwdriver to free plank.

VARIATIONS FOR OTHER FLOORS

Square-edge and plank floors may vary in several ways from the steps illustrated above.

Square-edge: Square-edge needs only end cuts, since no tongues secure one board to the next, which simplifies Step 1 and eliminates Step 3.

Set the saw blade at ⅜ inch deep, which assures that the blade will not cut into and weaken the sub-floor, and also assures that only a very shallow chisel cut is needed to complete the cut through the finished floor.

Next comes the step that differs most from the technique for tongue-and-groove. Using a nailset, punch down *all* of the nails in the section to be removed until they have gone clear through the finished floor and are well sunk into the sub-floor.

Start using the pry bar at one end of the end cuts, proceeding

gently so as not to mar the boards still in place. If strips do not come free, check to make sure all nails are punched down far enough. If it still binds, toe-nail a block to the end of one strip, leaving nail heads exposed. Use pry bar to pull up on nail heads in the block.

Plugged plank: Most plank floors are tongue-and-groove so are blind-nailed *and* held down by screws hidden beneath plugs.

As the second step, after marking out the work area, remove the plugs and screws as illustrated in the extra step above. There may also be face nails in plank; look for the tell-tale dots of plastic wood. If you find some, drive them into the sub-floor as described above.

Proceed next to saw the four sides, setting the saw depth at ¾ inch rather than ⅜ inch. Thereafter, the steps are as illustrated.

REPLACING TONGUE-AND-GROOVE

You will need:

• Replacement strips of the same kind, grade, and dimensions used in the original floor, cut 6 inches longer than the space they are to fill. (Have the tongue ripped off one strip at the suppliers).

• Hammer, nailset, supply of 6d floor finishing nails, some plastic wood, and a sheet of fine sandpaper.

• Crosscut saw, preferably set into miter box (to assure accurate end cuts).

• Carpenter's square, steel measuring tape, and soft-lead pencil.

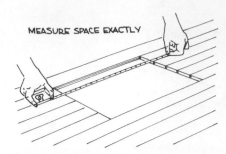

MEASURE SPACE EXACTLY

Measure the length of each strip with a steel tape marked in 1/32's or 1/100's of an inch. Start from the 2 inch mark if tape end does not give a clear mark to start the first inch. Hold tape taut.

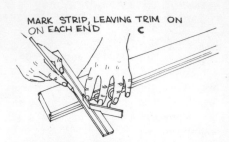

MARK STRIP, LEAVING TRIM ON ON EACH END

Mark length on down side of each strip with pencil. Put marks to allow 3-inch waste at each end. Use a square aligned on the edge so marks are precisely at right angles to the edges.

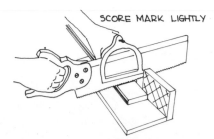

SCORE MARK LIGHTLY

Score each pencil mark lightly with saw at 90° miter. Saw cuts should be just outside each pencil mark (toward the closest end of the strip) or the saw kerf may cause the strip to be short.

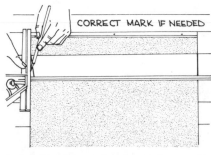

CORRECT MARK IF NEEDED

Lay strip, with scoring faced up, over the work area. Align one mark accurately, then check other mark for tight fit. Make any adjustment required for the strip to fit precisely and tightly.

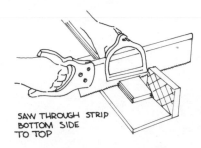

SAW THROUGH STRIP BOTTOM SIDE TO TOP

Saw completely through each end of the strip to its measured length using the miter box. Saw from the down side toward the top side. Sand burrs smooth, then check strip for accuracy of fit.

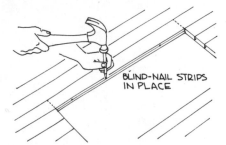

BLIND-NAIL STRIPS IN PLACE

Blind-nail new board as shown, after setting groove of first new board over tongue of in-place board at edge of original flooring. Work steadily toward opposite edge, where your tongueless board will fit.

LAST BOARD BUTT-JOINTED HAMMER INTO PLACE

Place final strip square-edge to square-edge of in-place strip. This final strip should fit tightly enough to resist placement. Tap it down using hammer and 2x4 block. Face-nail.

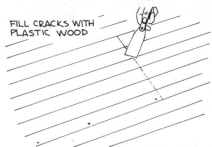

FILL CRACKS WITH PLASTIC WOOD

Fill any nail holes and conspicuous end-joint mis-matches with plastic wood. The patch is ready for seal, stain, and finish coat of varnish to match original floor. Sealer can match sample.

VARIATIONS FOR OTHER FLOORS

Techniques for replacing square-edged strips and planks vary.

Square-edged strips: Techniques are the same as above up to the point at which the strips have been cut to fine finish length. Then: (1) Starting at either edge of the work space, lay all strips in place without beginning to nail. Tap the last one into place with a hammer and 2x4 block. (2) Once all strips are in place, face-nail, matching the nail pattern in adjacent original flooring. Begin using the nailset well before nail heads are flush with flooring in order to avoid hammer mars in surface. (3) Countersink nails far enough so hole will hold plastic wood filler. Sand the filler after it dries, before sealing the floor.

Planks: Because of the extra width of the boards, planks are blind-nailed, then face-nailed as well. The sketches plus the preceding text explain both steps. If the planks are fastened with screws covered by plugs, the following are additional steps. (1) After marking the lines for fine finish cuts, use these lines as guides to measure plug locations. (2) Measure location of plugs in original flooring with bisecting lines that meet at the center of the plug. Use a square to keep the lines perpendicular to each other. (3) Use the measurements to mark plug centers on the new planks. (4) Center punch the holes, then, using a drill of the same diameter as plugs in the original flooring, drill plug holes ½ inch deep. A drill press gives the most accurate holes. Or, you may be able to take the boards back to the supplier and have him do the drilling. (5) Lay plank, and nail to match original flooring. (6) Drill guide holes for screws with a small diameter drill. (7) Use screws of same size and type as those in original floors. (8) Daub glue in plug holes and seat plugs.

• Patching Concrete

Concrete can break—leaving anything from hairline cracks to several large loose chunks. A profusion of chemically sophisticated patching materials has made repair relatively simple.

Emulsified-epoxy concrete. This is a two-part epoxy that mixes with water (an advantage most other concrete epoxies do not have). As a bond for ordinary Portland cement and sand (plus gravel for concrete), it adheres extremely well to concrete, steel, wood, and other building materials. It can be spread in thin sheets without later flaking or cracking. As a result, the material is well-suited to patching wide cracks or building up low spots in a floor.

Epoxy concrete. There are several types of epoxy concrete. One clear type can be spread as an adhesive. Within an hour of spreading it, shovel or trowel in ordinary concrete to match the surrounding surface. This will build up a low spot.

This same type can be mixed with sand to form a sort of plastic mortar for filling narrow cracks.

Another type forms a heavy gray paste that blends well with the color of regular concrete. It is especially good for gluing together chunks of concrete that have suffered a "shatter" break.

Vinyl patching compounds. These can be mixed with Portland cement and sand and used as a mortar to fill in cracks. Full strength, they act as a glue to bond new cement to old. Since vinyl compounds remain flexible, they tend to move with the crack if it is a result of settling. This flexibility can be enhanced by using the compounds with a special, fine-mesh fiberglass cloth (see also page 61 for a similar indoor patch).

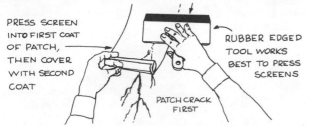

PRESS SCREEN INTO FIRST COAT OF PATCH, THEN COVER WITH SECOND COAT

RUBBER EDGED TOOL WORKS BEST TO PRESS SCREENS

PATCH CRACK FIRST

When used as a cement over and under the cloth screen, vinyl patching serves especially well in concrete walls.

Latex patch. Concrete latexes are milky white formulations of polymers in water. Most come in gallon jugs for use on sizeable patching projects. The latex, mixed in with regular concrete in place of part of the water, works best at thicknesses of ½ inch or more.

HANDLING EPOXY PATCHES

Clean the concrete surface well. Wire brushing is usually adequate. For oil stains, or waxed or crumbly concrete, clean with a solvent, or etch the surface with a 5 to 15 per cent muriatic acid.

Mix the epoxy thoroughly, following the manufacturer's instructions precisely. Then move fast. Most epoxies have a pot life of about an hour at 70°, less in hot weather, more in cool. You can extend hot weather time by placing the can that holds the epoxy in a pan of cold water or ice. If a bonding coat hardens before you make the patch, let it dry and make a second coat.

The concrete must be dry before the epoxy is applied.

Epoxies should *not* be thinned with solvents. A rough patch can be trowelled smooth with a lubricating coat of warm water and detergent.

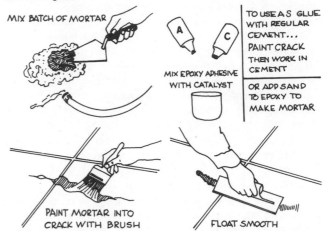

MIX BATCH OF MORTAR

MIX EPOXY ADHESIVE WITH CATALYST

TO USE AS GLUE WITH REGULAR CEMENT... PAINT CRACK THEN WORK IN CEMENT

OR ADD SAND TO EPOXY TO MAKE MORTAR

PAINT MORTAR INTO CRACK WITH BRUSH

FLOAT SMOOTH

Any thin patch should be covered and kept damp until the concrete has set to keep it from cracking.

Repairs of narrow cracks made with an epoxy mortar do not require covering.

Clean tools immediately with acetone or lacquer thinner.

HANDLING LATEX

Clean the concrete well, as for epoxy, but wet it for a few hours before beginning instead of keeping it dry.

Mix concrete in the usual way, but use latex instead of water as directed.

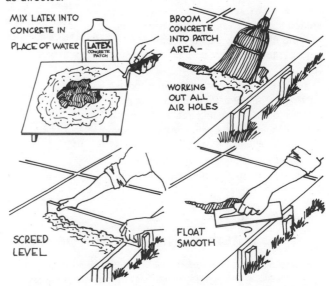

MIX LATEX INTO CONCRETE IN PLACE OF WATER

LATEX CONCRETE PATCH

BROOM CONCRETE INTO PATCH AREA—

WORKING OUT ALL AIR HOLES

SCREED LEVEL

FLOAT SMOOTH

Pour some of the new mix over the old concrete and work it down with a stiff broom. Then pour on the rest of the latex mix, screed, and trowel.

Alternately, dampen the old concrete and apply a thin bonding coat of latex (50-50 mix with water) with a brush. When this coat becomes tacky—in about 30 minutes—pour the latex-mix and finish.

Latex has a short working time, so screed and trowel almost immediately after pouring. Keep the surface damp and covered for 48 hours if it is exposed to warm and sunny weather.

Clean tools immediately with water.

• Removing or Replacing Ceramic Tile

One or a few ceramic tiles in a floor, wall, or counter top occasionally are damaged by cracking, breakage, loosening, or heavy staining. Replacement is a fairly easy job. However, if many tiles must be removed (i.e. the floor of a leaky shower), it is a time consuming job even for experts.

Ceramic tile is a thick clay product with a glazed surface on the finish side and a ridged surface on the bonding side. In place, thin plastic or metal tiles may look similar to ceramic tile. However, the methods of bonding ceramic tile and plastic or metal tiles to the work surface are different. Ceramic tile is set in mortar or attached by one of a number of different types of adhesive. The cracks between tiles are filled with grout. Non-ceramic tiles are set in a bonding agent that combines an adhesive with the appearance of grout.

If you are doubtful whether your repair job involves ceramic or non-ceramic tiles, there's an easy way to find out. Check thickness and edge appearance of the tile by lifting trim plates (around plumbing, at door thresholds, counter edges, etc.), or check the depth of the curves of the bull-nose tiles making the transitions between tiled areas and surfaces of other materials. The curved edge of ceramic bull-nose tile has a radius of nearly an inch, non-ceramic bull-nose tile less than one-half inch.

MATCHING REPLACEMENT TILES

Except in the case of undamaged loose tiles, you will need new tile for replacements. If you do not have spare tiles from the original installation, obtaining exact matches may be difficult. Here are some alternatives to try if they fit the decor:

- Match as closely as possible short of an exact match.
- Replace with a tile in a contrasting or complementary color.
- Use a deliberately ornate or decorative tile readily available in many different designs from most tile retailers.

Tile designs and color tend to become obsolete with time. If you do find an exact match for your job, it is wise to buy a supply of spares for future repairs.

REMOVING CERAMIC TILE

Removing an in-place ceramic tile takes patience and care. If it was originally set in mortar (instead of adhesive), there is a welding effect. Therefore, if you strike the tile a hard blow with a hammer and cold chisel, you may chip not only the tile to be removed but also crack adjacent ones. Even though there is no welding effect with tile set in adhesive, it is safest to assume that all tile is mortar-set.

If the tiles are very small, they probably come in sheet form glued to paper, with the downside facing out. This simplifies laying the tile. In removing damaged tile, you can widen the work area to undamaged adjacent tile for convenience and not worry about complicating the replacement.

To remove ceramic tile, you will need the following tools: A "chipping" hammer with a pointed head (usually available on a rental basis from tile specialty retailers); a common center punch, or nailset; a heavy screwdriver; an inexpensive glass cutter; and a metal carpenter's square.

Proceed as follows:

(1) Using hammer and nailset, deeply center punch the glaze of each tile to be

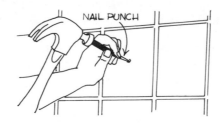

removed. Caution: on tile walls possibly backed by sheet rock, avoid center punching completely through the tile and damaging the sheet rock.

(2) Using glass cutter and carpenter's square as guide, heavily score grout (filled cracks between tiles) at all edges of each tile to be removed; then heavily

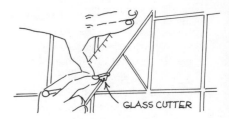

score the face of each tile with an "X" from edges to edges through the center punch hole.

(3) Using the pointed head of the chipping hammer, start chipping out the tile at the center punch hole working

around the hole to enlarge it. Caution: Make small chips with light, rapid blows. *Do not strike hard.*

REPLACING PLASTIC OR METAL TILE

Loosening is the commonest problem with thin plastic or metal tiles. Usually the remaining bond holding the tile in place can be broken with a putty knife. Start by working under a loose edge and gently pry out the tile.

Then reset the original tile with an adhesive or epoxy recommended by your materials supplier. Spread the bonding agent on the back of the tile evenly following instructions on the adhesive or epoxy container; leave about ⅛ inch dry at all edges to prevent excess bonding agent from oozing over edges.

If tile does not set flush, remove and rotate it 90° at a time until it fits flush in its original position. This eliminates the need to clean off the old bonding agent completely before resetting the tile.

On a wall or vertical surface use a quick drying adhesive or epoxy and press the tile in place tightly until the bonding agent begins to set, usually in a few minutes.

Complete the job the next day by grouting as necessary, using the method described for ceramic tile.

(4) Using the screwdriver in the enlarged center hole, try prying a scored piece of tile loose. If the tile is set in adhesive, one or more of its scored pieces may come out if the scoring in Step #2 is deep enough.

Don't force this step if the pieces will not come out relatively easily; the tile is probably welded in mortar and prying won't work without damaging adjacent tile. Go to the next step.

(5) Using chipping hammer as in Step #3, continue enlarging center hole until all tile is removed and mortar underneath is roughly chipped out to a depth of ¼ inch to ½ inch. Also chip out grout at the edges, taking special care to avoid damaging adjacent tile.

With the completion of these steps, you are now ready to put in the replacement.

PUTTING IN NEW TILE

In addition to the new tile, you will need the following basic materials and tools: (A) Patching plaster and primer to seal it, tile adhesive or an epoxy, and grout. For the proper type of each of these, consult your materials supplier (preferably a tile specialty retailer). (B) Hammer, block of scrap wood, putty knife, a spreader with serrated blade, and a small paint brush.

If cutting, shaping, or making a hole in the tile is required, you will also need pliers or tile nippers; glass cutter; metal straightedge and a large nail; nailset and a screwdriver; and a carborundum stone or emery paper. For methods see "Hints on Handling Ceramic Tile" below.

To place the new tile in the prepared area, proceed as follows:

(1) Using putty knife, patching plaster, and following manufacturer's directions, fill prepared area with patching material

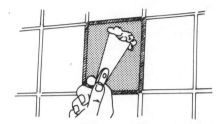

to level with bottoms of adjacent in-place tiles. Surface should be smooth at finish.

(2) After patching plaster has dried per manufacturer's instructions, paint it with the primer and again let it dry as directed.

(3) After primer is thoroughly dry, and using serrated spreader, apply adhesive

COVER PATCHING PLASTER WITH ADHESIVE

or epoxy as directed by manufacturer's instructions on the container.

(4) Place tile and tap new tile level using hammer and scrap wood overlapping original in-place tile. Immediately remove any surplus bonding agent that may have oozed over edges on to tile

finish surface, using method recommended by manufacturer.

If new tile is in sheet form and still glued to paper, wait 24 hours before pulling off paper.

GROUT

Grout is a plaster-like paste that is used basically to fill spaces between tiles. It may or may not have a variety of additives to make it waterproof, stain resistant, tinted, etc. There are also various types of grout requiring different methods of preparation and application. To choose the right grout for your job, consult your materials supplier and follow manufacturer's instructions.

Wait 24 hours after setting tile before grouting.

Regardless of type, grout is usually applied by mixing grout powder with water to a consistency of heavy cream or paste. It is wiped into the space between tiles with a damp rag, sponge, or squeegee. The cracks and corners are finished smooth by finger, the eraser

FINGER IS BEST TOOL FOR SMOOTHING GROUT

end of a pencil, a clothespin, or a piece of doweling. After grout dries (20-30 minutes), the tile surface is washed clean with a rag and polished with a dry cloth.

Grouting is a messy job and rubber gloves are recommended.

Grouting completes your repairs. However, the *area should not be walked on or exposed to water for another 24 hours.*

HINTS ON HANDLING CERAMIC TILE

Cutting Straight Edges. To cut large tiles approximately in half: (1) Using glass cutter guided by metal straightedge, heavily score glazed surface of tile parallel to ridges on back of tile. (2) Place tile scored side up on floor with large nail directly under scoring. Straddle scoring with your feet and full weight. Tile should snap in two.

Cutting Narrow Strips. (1) Score as above with glass cutter and metal straightedge parallel to ridges on back of tile. (2) Clamp

the narrow strip at scoring in a vise and snap off the exposed large portion by hand.

Punching Small Holes. (1) Using hammer and center punch, or nailset, start by center punching through glaze deeply into tile. (2) Using screwdriver only, enlarge hole gradually by bearing down and twisting in jerks to drill.

Cutting Curves. To cut a curved section of tile, a food can of appropriate diameter makes a good glass cutter guide for scoring. For nipping out the tile, ordinary pliers

work almost as well as tile nippers. To finish cut edges, emery cloth wrapped around a block of wood is a good substitute for carborundum stone. Goggles will protect your eyes from flying tile chips during nipping. Proceed as follows: (1) Using food can as guide and glass cutter, heavily score glazed side of tile. (2) Using pliers or tile nippers and starting at an edge, nip tile away with many small bites until scoring is reached. (3) At scoring, finish edge clean with carborundum stone or emery cloth.

Stairs

During the past few years, there has been a rapid growth in the variations of stair designs. Most of the new designs are executed in steel, concrete, or a blend of both. When a joint in one of these loosens, weakens or breaks, the best an average handyman can do is tighten the loosened bolt and hope that such a repair is sufficient. Sometimes there will be an obvious way to shim or wedge a joint that has warped. In general, however, repairs should be entrusted to a professional.

The old stringer-tread stairway made of wood is far more likely to develop squeaks or a broken tread, but it is also easier to repair. The following material explains repairs for wooden stairs.

CURING SQUEAKS IN STAIRS

Squeaks in a stairway are usually caused by a loose tread that rubs against a riser or the stringers when someone steps on it. All remedies are attempts to tighten or brace the joints and piece that are loose. The best remedy will depend mostly upon your judgment of what will work, although the source of the squeak may help limit the choice.

The following general points should help produce an accurate diagnosis of where the squeak originates.

If the noise is accompanied by noticeable sagging or give in the step when you put weight on it, the problem Is either in a joint that has opened because of warping; where wedges or nails have worked loose; in a broken rabbet or dado joint; or in a tread or riser that has split.

Noise with slight or imperceptible movement in the tread may be caused by a loose nail or a joint or nail head that loosened as the wood dried. These noises are hardest to find and fix.

Another cause of noise is a tread or riser that has lost its original strength and is unable to bear weight without flexing.

If the wood has weakened or broken in any way, replacement of the defective piece is the best cure. Re-nailing, gluing, and wedging will probably quiet a squeaky joint.

The location of the noise is a good indication of where to begin. If the noise comes from the same place you step, concentrate your efforts there. If the noise comes from a different place than you step—such as one side when you step in the center, or toward the rear of the tread when you step at the front—try first to secure the place where you step, then move to the apparent source of the noise.

If you get behind the stairs, this is the most effective place to hunt down the source of a squeak. Look especially for warping, loosened wedges, or loosely fitting joints. Also check for split wood, especially around joints and nail holes. Have a helper tread on the squeaking steps as you hunt.

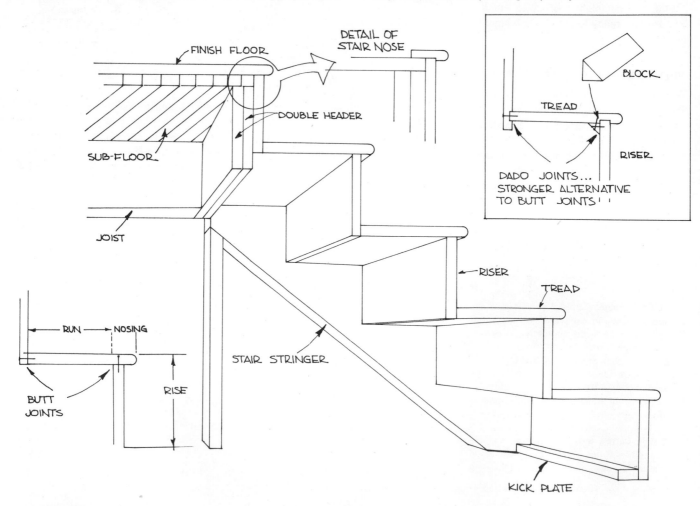

Working behind the stairs: If the loosened gap is narrow, glue wood blocks to either the riser or stringer—or both. The blocks should be at least half an inch wide on the bearing surface and should be several inches long. Butt each block tightly against the tread when the tread is in its normal position. Secure with woodworking glue. Keep the blocks firmly in place while the glue dries by driving two finishing nails through each.

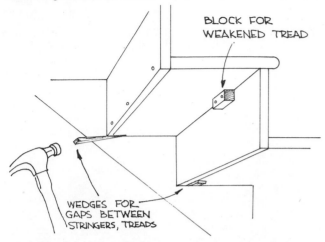

BLOCK FOR WEAKENED TREAD

WEDGES FOR GAPS BETWEEN STRINGERS, TREADS

This is usually the best solution when no obvious source of a squeak reveals itself.

Wider gaps are best stabilized by driving wedges. The gap between a tread and stringer takes a long, narrow wedge. Gaps between treads and risers are more effectively silenced by short, wide wedges. The shapes are shown in the sketches.

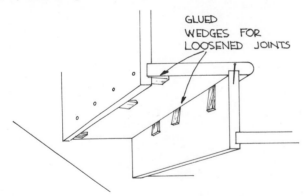

GLUED WEDGES FOR LOOSENED JOINTS

Both can be cut from shingles. The wedges between treads and stringers need not be glued, but others should. All wedges should be driven as tightly as possible with a hammer, and all should be nailed in place.

Both when blocking and wedging stairs, a few added nails will help strengthen joints away from the added or renovated supports.

Working in front of the stairs: If getting behind the stairs is impractical, lubrication and re-nailing are the principal cures for squeaks. Powdered graphite and talcum powder work about equally well. Forcefully blow the powder into joints, especially where the backs of treads meet risers.

Re-nailing can tighten joints between treads and stringers and between the front edge of a tread and the riser below. Drive 8-penny finishing nails in pairs, angled so they form a V. If the wood is not too old and dry, screws may work better than new nails. Drill pilot holes through the tread, but not into the stringer or riser. A pilot hole minimizes the chance of splitting

the tread; the absence of it in the stringer or riser assures the best chance of a firm grip by the screw in old wood that has lost resiliency. Countersink the screw heads.

REPLACING TREADS AND RISERS

If a tread or riser is broken, or if you must repair an extremely poor fit between two parts, remove one or more treads. If you can get below the stairs you can easily hammer the tread up to free it. If you can't, the problem is more difficult. Whether you reset the old part, or replace a broken one, the sequence of steps is about the same. To get the old piece out: (1) Take up any edge trim, using a chisel to pry it up. (2) Begin prying up the tread, working with a chisel at the edges. As soon as you have the leading edge of a salvageable tread lifted a bit, push

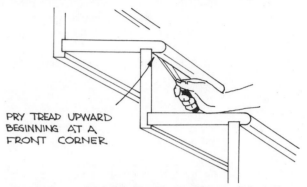

PRY TREAD UPWARD BEGINNING AT A FRONT CORNER

it back down. The heads of the nails should pop up enough for you to pull them out. (It is difficult to pull the tread up enough to get all the nails out without splitting the tread.) There may be nails securing the front of the tread to the riser beneath; watch for these and pry between tread and riser if they appear, in order to keep progress about even all the way across the tread. (3) The rear edge of the tread will be secured to the riser above it by a rabbet or dado joint, or by nails driven horizontally into the tread, or both. Once the sides and front are free, pull the tread outward as evenly and smoothly as possible.

Removing a tread may be complicated by the presence of a baluster (the vertical member in a hand rail). If you are faced with one of these, saw it off flush with the tread. If you encounter a nail, saw through it with a hacksaw. Trying to lift a baluster out almost always results in its being split. One that is sawn off flush can be toe-nailed to the new tread once that piece is in place.

Once the ill-fitting or broken tread is removed, check all the bearing surfaces of the stringers and risers with a straightedge and level. Plane or sand down any high spots, or glue blocks in place to raise any low spots until the tread has a perfectly level support.

Check the risers above and below to make sure that both of them are in good condition. Once satisfied that the supporting members are in good shape, place the new tread in position. Secure it with finishing 8d nails.

LOOSE BOTTOM SUPPORTS

If a whole stairway seems to flex, check the anchor points at the bottom. Usually there are wood plates set into concrete beneath the stringers for basement stairs, or the stringers are toe-nailed directly to wood floors. If the nails have loosened, drive 6d common or larger nails to resecure the stringers.

Drawers

Drawers suffer so much heavy use that they frequently develop irritating ailments. Most of the troubles are caused by over-worn surfaces that allow drawers to slide crookedly until they bind and stick.

Two other common troubles are drawers that fit so loosely they fall out of their cabinets, and drawers that have loosened with use and age until they are no longer rigid.

Softwood cabinetry is the greatest source of all these woes, both because the wood wears more rapidly than hardwood and because these inexpensive cabinets—often built-ins—are expected to take heavy duty abuse in kitchens, work rooms, and children's rooms. Problems caused by wear are easy to correct in such cabinets, because refined woodworking is of little or no importance. This section explains several basic approaches to these repairs.

The underlying principles are valid when applied to fine cabinets although mastercraftsmen add many thoughtful extras to assure good performance and durability. Some of these refinements will be hard to duplicate.

Before resorting to carpentry on a balky drawer, try a lubricating coat of paraffin on all of the sliding surfaces. Also, hunt for small stray objects in the drawer's space. A small bead of pitch or one lost bobby pin can cause remarkable resistance to orderly operation.

When you do sand or plane a sticking drawer, look first to the side guides. They are much more likely to be the source of a tight fit than the top or bottom rails.

If possible, remove an adjoining drawer and use its space as access while you push and probe to find any problem spot in a drawer. Also, remove the problem drawer and look for any unusually burnished wood (a symptom of tight fit), or split or broken pieces.

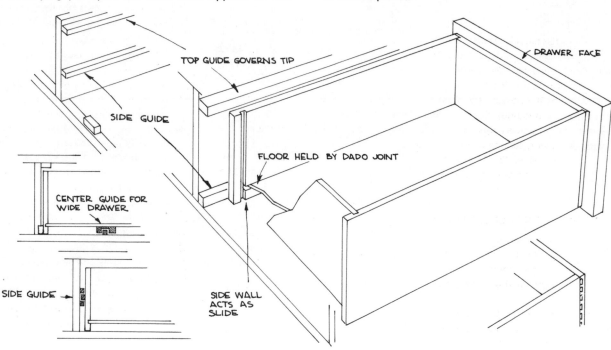

DRAWERS THAT FALL OUT

The drawer that pulls clear out of its cabinet and dumps its contents on the floor usually has broken stops or was originally built without them. The cure in either case is simple.

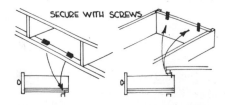

Stops are small wood or metal "ears" that catch the back of the drawer before it comes out of the cabinet. The sketch shows two basic locations for stops, and alternate ways to anchor them.

Bottom-fastened stops function only if the drawer is designed to stay nearly level even pulled all the way out. The top-fastened stops can scrape against a solid surface above.

Stops must be shallow enough so the drawer can be removed by tipping it to its maximum angle when it is wide open.

DRAWERS THAT TIP TOO MUCH

The degree of tip in a drawer is governed by a guide or guides secured above the side rail or rails.

The greater the distance between rail and guide, the sharper the drawer's tilt. If this degree of tip is too great for your purposes, the cure is a thicker guide (or one that is reset closer to the drawer).

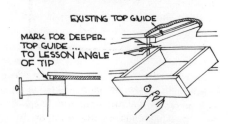

To determine where the guide should be: (1) Pull the drawer out to its maximum, then let it tip down to the desired angle. (2) Holding it in that position, use a pencil to mark each side of the drawer space even with the highest point of the back corner. (3) Measure the distance from the guide to the mark on each side.

At this point, your next step will depend on how the guides are engineered. If they are nailed to the sides of the drawer space, remove them and reseat them at the new marks. If they are secured to the top of the drawer space, you will have to cut new pieces or laminate new wood to the old guide to achieve a deeper guide.

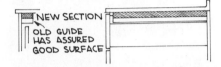

NEW SECTION
OLD GUIDE HAS ASSURED GOOD SURFACE

To cut new pieces: (1) Measure the length and width of the old guide, plus the total depth desired. (2) Choose a durable piece of wood with one straight, knot-free edge for the new guide. If you are keeping the old guide, dismount it and use the old surface as the one that will catch the drawer; laminate the new piece to the other side. (3) Secure the new guide in the same way as the old one.

DRAWERS THAT DO NOT CLOSE FULLY

The sides provide the surfaces on which the drawers slide. When a drawer does not close properly, the cause is almost always uneven wear on the sliding surfaces.

If a drawer appears to be canted in its space, one rail probably has worn down or split off. The cure is a new slide for the drawer.

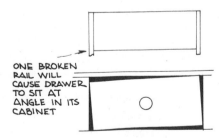

ONE BROKEN RAIL WILL CAUSE DRAWER TO SIT AT ANGLE IN ITS CABINET

If a drawer slides most of the way closed, but stops an inch short, both rails have worn down until the face of the drawer catches on the front of the cabinet. (If this is the cause, the drawer will close if it is lifted up, then pushed the last inch.)

Pull the drawer out and lay a straight edge along the bottom of each rail. If you can see a definite curve or notch, the problem is to straighten it.

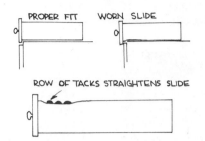

PROPER FIT   WORN SLIDE

ROW OF TACKS STRAIGHTENS SLIDE

A small dip can be cured by sticking a row of thumbtacks into the rail. Long-shanked, round-headed brass brads will correct a slightly deeper notch.

DRAWERS THAT STICK

All drawers have a guide rail on each side. Extra wide drawers may have an added guide centered under the bottom. The purposes are to keep the drawer aligned in its space to minimize friction and to allow adjustment when a drawer gives trouble.

A drawer that has swollen tight against its guides (or vice versa) can almost always be cured by sanding. This does not require dismantling any part of the assembly, but only careful observation to see where the tight spot is. Use a sanding block for accuracy.

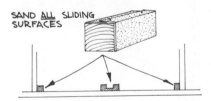

SAND ALL SLIDING SURFACES

A drawer that fits so loosely it strays off course needs its guides adjusted to fit more tightly. Any time a guide is dismounted, it should be re-positioned using a square.

If guides appear to be in good condition and a drawer will slide part way in or out freely before it sticks, either the drawer or its cabinet is likely to be out of square. A loose or crooked drawer should be re-built. If a built-in cabinet is to blame, settling in the house is probably the true cause. Adjusting the guides to compensate is the only cure. A piece of furniture sometimes can be coaxed back into square by putting shims under

the legs that rest on low spots in the flooring.

Checking guide alignments: (1) Fit a carpenter's square into a back corner of the drawer space, flush against the back wall and touching the side wall at whichever point is square. (2) Measure and note the widest gap between guide and

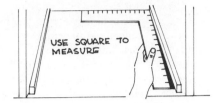

USE SQUARE TO MEASURE

square, and where it occurs (front or back corner). (3) While you have the square in place, measure the length of the guide and note. (4) Perform the same tasks on the other side of the drawer space.

Re-positioning guides: (1) Pry up old guide, chiseling out any splinters. (2) Measure the width of the drawer; mark the width on the front cross-piece of the cabinet so the drawer will be centered when it is closed. (3) On the side where the front of the new guide will be narrower than the rear, mark the corrected position of the guide on the floor of the drawer space (or on the front and rear cross-pieces if there is no floor). Use a square to align the mark. (4) Mark the corrected position for the opposite guide, which will be widest at the front. (5) Be sure that neither guide dwindles to nothing at any point; if one threatens to do so, move the drawer slightly off center and make new marks. (6) Cut guides. Or, if you prefer, use regular milled pieces and glue shims in the spaces where the guides do not butt up against the sides of the drawer space.

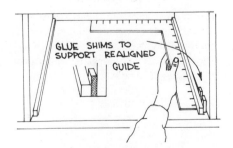

GLUE SHIMS TO SUPPORT REALIGNED GUIDE

The working surface of the guide should be absolutely straight, free of pitch pockets or knots, and sanded smooth. Once installed it should be lubricated with a coat of paraffin.

Roofs

Abandoned buildings are always conclusive proof that roofs are not permanent structures. The gaping holes that develop when a roof is left untended for a few years are dramatic evidence of the daily and seasonal weathering forces at work.

Roofs must withstand extremes of temperature without expanding or contracting enough to leak, buckle, or pull apart. They must withstand the strain of winds. And, in many areas, they must bear heavy loads of snow.

The sketches below show the major types of framing for roofs, and the basic sequence of materials used in the assembly.

For the average handyman, patching up the finished surface is his only area of concern, or competence.

Four principal roofing materials are in current use: Wood shingle (or the thicker, rougher shakes), composition shingle, asphalt, and clay tile. Each of these can be maintained by an average homeowner and can be repaired by him if the trouble is a small one. The subsequent pages explain how these roofing materials are put together, and how they may be repaired.

Also, there are some brief explanations of underlayments and patching materials on page 87, and some details about flashings on pages 82-83.

However, it cannot be stressed enough that roof repairs are difficult to make. A small obvious leak that can be caulked is one thing. Any repair that calls for removing some of the existing roofing material should be approached warily, if at all. Any repair that calls for replacement of flashing is purely in the province of a professional, because the flashing is an extra safeguard built into an area that tends to leak.

The principal problem is that roofing materials tend to be layered in such a way that you must begin at one edge and work up to the roof peak (or the opposite side of a flat roof). The overlapping with many materials is what does most of the work in shedding water. A repair, of necessity, eliminates the overlapping in some way. The patch must take up the slack.

A second source of complications is that most roofs last for no more than 40 years. Most endure only half as long. An older house, then, may have two or more layers of finished roofing on it. How these layers interact with each other can be very difficult to understand when you have to start at the surface.

Finally, the material is not always what it appears to be. For example, one manufacturer now has a very durable mineral material that is molded and colored to look like ordinary wood shingles. It is, however, secured quite differently and should be repaired by a professional. Many of the modern composition materials for roofing have to be studied for pliability and chemical compatibility with cements.

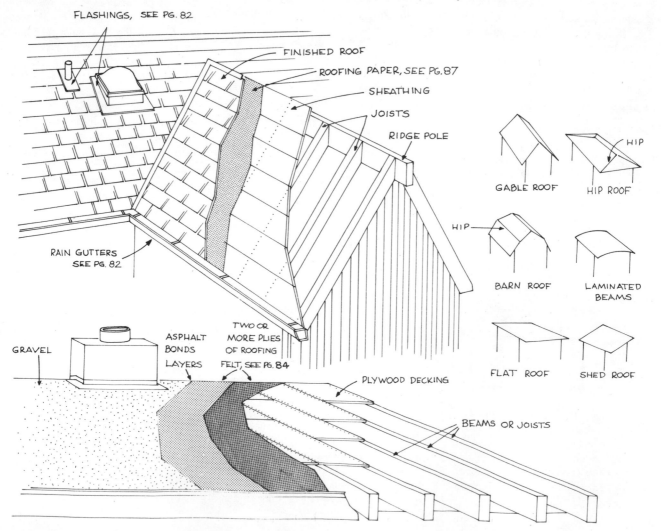

FLASHINGS, SEE PG. 82

FINISHED ROOF

ROOFING PAPER, SEE PG. 87

SHEATHING

JOISTS

RIDGE POLE

RAIN GUTTERS SEE PG. 82

GRAVEL

ASPHALT BONDS LAYERS

TWO OR MORE PLIES OF ROOFING FELT, SEE PG. 84

PLYWOOD DECKING

BEAMS OR JOISTS

GABLE ROOF

HIP ROOF

HIP

HIP

BARN ROOF

LAMINATED BEAMS

FLAT ROOF

SHED ROOF

• Tracking Down Leaks

There is one nearly sure thing about a leak in the roof—it does not originate directly above the spot where the puddle forms. Water can, and usually does, run an amazing distance along a sloping piece of sheathing or joist before it finally drops off and begins to gather on the top surface of a ceiling or on the floor. (The most frequent exception is a flat roof with its sheathing doubling as the finish ceiling.)

The prime source of leaks are flashings around vents, skylights, or chimneys. The sheet metal corrodes or warps so that its seal with the roof breaks. Also, the roofing compound that forms the seal may dry and crack.

The next most likely source of a leak is a peak or valley—both are subject to extra weathering. A peak—which may be either the ridge or a hip—has a row of special shingles designed to cover the framing joints beneath—where the underlayment is likely to be weakest. Valleys, the troughs between one gable and another, have metal flashings to collect runoff water from rain. These flashings corrode or warp just as others do.

Finally, there may be some sort of break in the general expanse of surfacing material or in its underlayment. This is especially true of tar and gravel on a flat roof.

When a leak does spring up, you may be fortunate enough to have an unfinished attic or ceiling crawl space. These afford the best means of searching for the source. Whatever access you have, the following are techniques for looking for leaks.

In the attic. Locate the point at which the water puddles. From there, work up the roof slope, following watermarks. If it is raining or dark so that you cannot get onto the roof to make a patch, tack up a piece of wire to guide water from the leak into a pail or pan.

If the source is a flashing, locate it by measuring the distances from it to the ridge pole and some other landmark visible from the outside. If the leak is in the roofing material or underlayment, push or drive a nail up through the hole so you will be able to see it once on the roof. Try to hunt for such leaks during daylight hours, when they often reveal themselves as pinholes of light.

On the roof. Having narrowed down the area as much as possible by indoor observation, get on the roof and look for broken seals in the flashings, then for broken spots in the roofing material. Loose, cracked, or warped shingles are symptoms. Composition roofs reveal leaks through cracks and blisters.

Sometimes leaks will be caused by breaks in the underlayment. These can be extremely hard to locate on the weather side of the house, since wind can push water a distance back up under shingles or tiles.

If possible, wait for warm weather before getting on the roof. The materials are more flexible then; you are not as likely to add new cracks to the original ones. On flat roofs, lay down a long plank to help distribute your weight. On pitched roofs, lay a ladder on the roof. Attach a rope to it, and to a solid support (a tree, for example) on the opposite side of the ridge pole. The ladder spreads weight and provides safe footing. It is unwise to get on a roof that is wet or to get on one during a high wind.

The best time to make a complete repair of any roofing leak is during good weather. As a temporary expedient, tack down a piece of waterproof canvas with four pieces of lath and coat the edges with roofing compound.

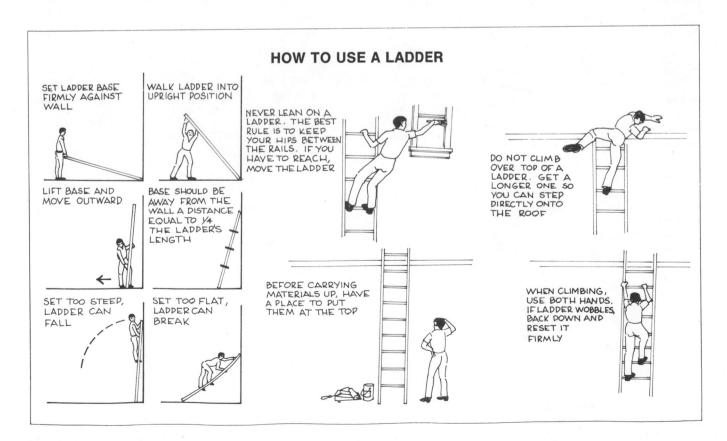

HOW TO USE A LADDER

SET LADDER BASE FIRMLY AGAINST WALL

WALK LADDER INTO UPRIGHT POSITION

NEVER LEAN ON A LADDER. THE BEST RULE IS TO KEEP YOUR HIPS BETWEEN THE RAILS. IF YOU HAVE TO REACH, MOVE THE LADDER

DO NOT CLIMB OVER TOP OF A LADDER. GET A LONGER ONE SO YOU CAN STEP DIRECTLY ONTO THE ROOF

LIFT BASE AND MOVE OUTWARD

BASE SHOULD BE AWAY FROM THE WALL A DISTANCE EQUAL TO ¼ THE LADDER'S LENGTH

SET TOO STEEP, LADDER CAN FALL

SET TOO FLAT, LADDER CAN BREAK

BEFORE CARRYING MATERIALS UP, HAVE A PLACE TO PUT THEM AT THE TOP

WHEN CLIMBING, USE BOTH HANDS. IF LADDER WOBBLES, BACK DOWN AND RESET IT FIRMLY

• Fixing Flashings

Flashings are the devices—usually metal, sometimes plastic —that carry water away from joints between gables of a roof, or between the roof and vents or chimneys.

Sometimes flashings corrode until they require replacement. More frequently, the adhesive that seals their edges to the roofing dries out and cracks.

Vents and soil stacks are the simplest kind of flashing and the easiest to repair. Leaks may occur at the joint between

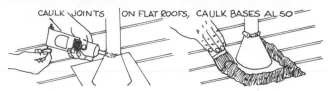

the vent pipe and the flared skirt that is part of the flashing or may occur where the flat shield part of the flashing adjoins the roofing material. If the leak is between two metal surfaces, use an aluminized caulk to seal it. If it is between metal and asphalt, wood, or tile, use a caulk with asphalt in it. Both caulks come in small squeeze tubes or small caulking guns.

Sometimes, the flared skirt of a vent flashing will be of plastic. Aluminized caulk or plain butyl caulk will adhere properly to this material.

Valley flashings are far more extensive in size. Leaks are correspondingly harder to pin down. Search first for corrosion in the visible metal suface. If none is present, water may be seeping back under the adjacent roofing material to a leak in the underlayment. If this is the case, sealing the entire run of the valley flashing may be a temporary solution. (The permanent one is to take up the finish roofing, patch the under-

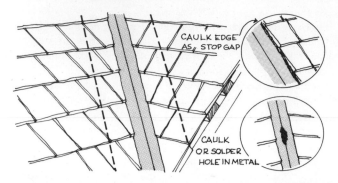

layment, and replace the roofing—all in the province of a professional roofer.)

If you wish to try sealing the edges of the valley, use asphalt roofing cement painted onto the joints between the metal and the roofing surface. If the roofing material itself is sound, the seal should last for a year or more.

• Repairing Chimney Leaks

Chimneys can leak in several ways: Through cracks between the flue and bricks, through loosened mortar between bricks, or through flashing that has corroded or loosened.

Cracks around the flue. The cap of mortar that seals the top of the chimney against weather becomes the source of a leak as it crumbles with age. The seeping water may run down into the fireplace or may evaporate before it gets that far. In either case, damage to the chimney is progressive.

If cracks are minor, use an exterior caulk (a non-drying one is best) to seal the joint between the flue and the mortar cap, any cracks in the surface of the cap, and the joint between the cap and the top course of bricks.

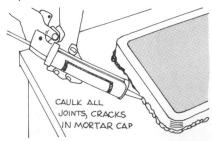

If the mortar cap is badly decomposed, remove it entirely and form a new cap.

The formula for mortar is given below.

Crumbled mortar. Weathering sometimes breaks down the mortar between bricks, allowing water to seep down along the flue from the point of the leak. Close visual inspection will reveal the cracks; a prodding finger will usually dislodge some sizeable pieces of mortar.

Clean out all the broken and loose mortar. A cold chisel or a sturdy screwdriver will do the heavy work. Brush out the hole so no loose material remains. If the cracks are old, you may find two or three bricks completely unseated, but this is relatively rare.

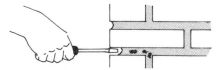

Mix a small batch of mortar (1 part cement; 4½ parts clean, fine sand; ½ part dehydrated lime; enough water to make the mortar slip cleanly off the mixing trowel) if you have the materials on hand. Otherwise, buy a small bag of pre-mixed mortar and add water per the manufacturer's instructions.

Trowel this into the cracks. (More detailed instructions on laying brick and making finish cuts are in the section on exterior walls, page 88.)

Leaking flashing. A double layer of flashing metal seals the joint where a chimney comes through the roof framing. The cement that bonds the flashing to the bricks of the chimney will dry out and crack from time to time.

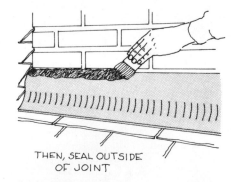

The repair is best made with non-drying roofing cement liberally smeared on the back side of the flashing, then across the face of the joint. Bend the flashing slightly away from the chimney and use a wide-bladed putty knife to spread the cement on the back side of the flashing. Press the flashing back into place and hold it or brace it tight long enough for the cement to set. Then brush a narrow strip of cement along the face of the joint to cover it.

• Skylight Leaks

There are skylights that cover enormous areas, and there are tiny ones. There are skylights that are wood frames set into the roof and skylights that are pre-fabricated metal. The well-manufactured ones are as leakproof as the general roof. However, some of the home-made ones can be somewhat more troublesome.

Flashing leaks. Some skylights are self-flashing; that is, the formed metal unit has flanges. Others are without their own flashing—so-called "curb-mounted" units. These are flashed in the same way chimneys and other protusions are. If the flashing has separated from the roofing, asphalt cement or an asphaltic caulking can be used as cement. If the flashing has corroded or otherwise developed a hole, solder (rosin-flux) the hole or seal it with an aluminized caulking compound. If the flashing is damaged beyond easy repair, it should be replaced by a professional.

Weather seal leaks. Some skylights can open for ventilation or for access to the roof. The joints are sealed with a foam rubber or similar material. Most weather seals are glued in place.

If these dry out or peel off, they can be replaced with an identical strip, plus the recommended glue.

Glass or plastic leaks. Some home-made units have glass panes. These should be replaced—or re-puttied—exactly as any other window. If the frame is metal, and the glass is clinched between metal panels, seal the joints of the metal with butyl caulk.

If a plastic or plexiglass dome is cracked, and you do not wish to replace it, the leak can be sealed with a clear butyl caulk meant expressly for use with the assorted clear plastics. If possible, patch from both inside and outside. The outside patch should overlap at least ½ inch on all sides of the crack.

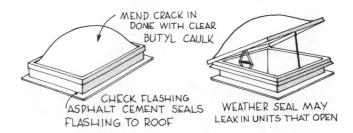

MEND CRACK IN DOME WITH CLEAR BUTYL CAULK

CHECK FLASHING ASPHALT CEMENT SEALS FLASHING TO ROOF

WEATHER SEAL MAY LEAK IN UNITS THAT OPEN

• Gutters and Downspouts

Gutters and downspouts are made of metal and plastic. Most of the troubles with these stem from long accumulations of debris in the gutters. Under the circumstances, the hanger straps of metal gutters may loosen through corrosion. The gutter itself will develop leaks whether it is of metal or plastic.

Small holes can be patched. Hanger straps can be replaced to cure sagging gutters. Completely worn-out gutters can be replaced rather easily.

In general, it is best to work from below, standing on a ladder. Although this may necessitate some juggling, it puts you in the best position to secure the gutter and to look into it for leaks.

Patching leaks. Metal gutters can be patched with epoxy cement, or solder, or—if you are just buying a little more time for an old gutter—with aluminized roof caulking.

The epoxy cement should be of a type formulated to bond with metal and must be applied under the manufacturer's directions. Galvanized or tin plate gutters should be soldered using rosin flux. Aluminized caulking is applied directly from a squeeze tube or caulking gun.

In every case, the metal must be scraped free of corrosion and rust before the patch is applied. Before begin-

ning, check along the entire gutter in question. Frequently, one leak is only the first of many to come. You may find that the repair is not worth making.

Plastic gutter leaks can be repaired with the appropriate epoxy glue, or with butyl caulking. (There is a clear butyl especially meant for use with plastic.)

Adjusting gutters. The straps that hang metal gutters will sag with time, especially in snow country. During every general clean out of accumulated debris, finish by pouring a pail of water into each gutter. If the water does not run out directly, adjust the bend of the hanger straps to lower the gutter at its downspout end and raise it at the opposite end. This will appreciably improve the longevity of metal gutters.

Broken straps should be replaced slightly to one side of the original to avoid weakened nail or screw holes. For techniques, see the section below on replacing gutter.

Replacing gutter. Metal gutters hang just below the edge of the roof, supported by a series of metal straps. In most designs, the straps are nailed or screwed to the roof sheathing, then looped down under the gutter and back up to clinch its outer lip. Some designs loop all the way around the gutter. In either case, to secure the strap, the edge course of shingles or

other roofing material must be lifted as shown in the sketch.

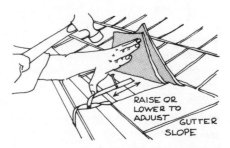

RAISE OR LOWER TO ADJUST GUTTER SLOPE

Nail the straps in place before raising the gutter into place. In nailing the straps, plan to give the gutter a slight downward run so water will not stand.

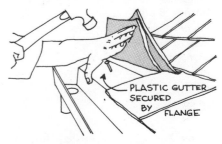

PLASTIC GUTTER SECURED BY FLANGE

A plastic gutter is designed with a continuous flange that is nailed to the roof edge. As in the case of metal straps, the nailing is to sheathing just beneath the edge course of roofing material.

Both metal and plastic gutters come in kits with installation details included. The instructions specify which cutting tools to use.

• Asphalt Roofs

Asphalt roofs, also known as built-up roofs, are used on dead-level roofs and on slopes to 5 in 12.

The true built-up roof consists of layers of asphalt-saturated felt. Hot asphalt is mopped over each layer for lamination. The final application of asphalt is covered with fine gravel or mineral chips to protect the asphalt from drying in the sun.

A more recent layering material is a glass-fiber mat that is porous. One layer of mat soaks up the mopping of asphalt to form a single, solid roofing material. (The technique is much similar to that used to make "glass" boats.)

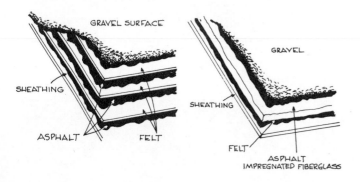

GRAVEL SURFACE

GRAVEL

SHEATHING

SHEATHING

ASPHALT   FELT

FELT

ASPHALT IMPREGNATED FIBERGLASS

The built-up roof is prone to blisters and cracks that result in leaks. Whatever leak develops, asphalt cement alone or in combination with a patch is the cure.

Patching simple cracks. If there is a visible crack in built-up roofing, the repair is simple and straightforward: (1) With a brush, clean all loose gravel and dust out of the crack, and clean three or four inches around all sides of it. (2) With a trowel or putty knife, spread a layer of asphalt cement about ⅛ inch thick over the cleaned area. (3) Place a strip of roofing

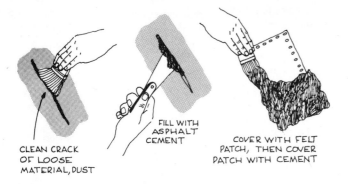

CLEAN CRACK OF LOOSE MATERIAL, DUST

FILL WITH ASPHALT CEMENT

COVER WITH FELT PATCH, THEN COVER PATCH WITH CEMENT

felt big enough to cover the crack into the wet cement and press it down firmly. (4) Spread a second layer of cement over the strip of felt and well past its edges. (5) Brush gravel back over patch.

Patching blisters. The repair is much the same as for simple cracks: (1) Cut the blister with a sharp knife and force asphalt cement into the blister area with a putty knife or trowel. (2) Press the blistered tar down until it bonds firmly with the cement beneath. (3) Paint a coat of cement on top of the cut.

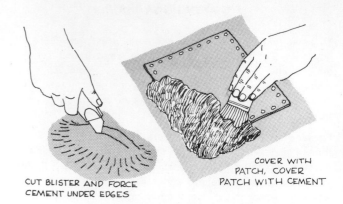

CUT BLISTER AND FORCE CEMENT UNDER EDGES

COVER WITH PATCH, COVER PATCH WITH CEMENT

(4) Place a patch of roofing felt in the cement and press it down firmly. (5) Paint a second layer of cement over the patch.

Patching large leaks. When a sizeable area of roofing deteriorates enough to allow a leak, it is best to remove as much of the broken brittle material around the leak as possible, rather than build it back up with layered patches. The steps: (1) Using a putty knife or knife, cut away as much of the original roofing as is cracked and brittle. (2) Trim the resulting hole to a neat rectangle. (3) Coat the hole with asphalt cement

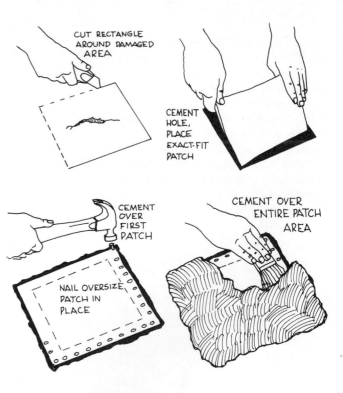

CUT RECTANGLE AROUND DAMAGED AREA

CEMENT HOLE, PLACE EXACT-FIT PATCH

CEMENT OVER FIRST PATCH

NAIL OVERSIZE PATCH IN PLACE

CEMENT OVER ENTIRE PATCH AREA

and press in a patch cut to size. (4) Coat the entire surface of the patch with cement. If you cut down into the roofing two plies, add a second patch the same size as the first. (5) Once the patch is brought up to a level flush with the original roofing, coat the surface plus an overlap of two to four inches all around with a larger patch of felt. (6) Nail the over-sized patch with several short roofing nails. (7) Paint the entire patch with cement, taking extra care with the edges and the nail heads. (8) Brush a protective layer of gravel over the surface.

• Composition Roofing

Composition roofing material is made from rag, wood, and cellulose fibers processed into a sheet of dry felt which is then saturated with asphalt to make it waterproof. The material is then finished with any of several materials ranging from sand to colored mineral chips. There are two standard forms: shingles and rolls.

ROLL MATERIAL

The roll material can blister, crack, or tear along a seam. Repair is very much like that for built-up roofing: (1) Trim the crack as neatly as possible. (2) Spread asphalt cement under the loosened roofing with a putty knife and press the roofing down to form a firm bond. (3) Nail the edges with rust-proof, wide-headed roofing nails. (4) Paint the crack and all nail

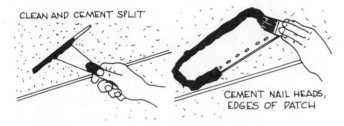

CLEAN AND CEMENT SPLIT

CEMENT NAIL HEADS, EDGES OF PATCH

heads with asphalt cement. (5) If the cracked area is extensive, add an over-layer of the composition roofing that extends at least six inches beyond the crack in all directions. Nail it around the edges, then seal the edges and nail heads with asphalt cement.

SHINGLES

Shingles are usually 12 inches wide and 36 inches long. Many designs are notched at intervals to give an appearance of smaller units. Shingles are subject to cracking, drying, and peeling. On occasion, winds can below them loose if they are already in poor repair.

Gluing loose shingles. When edges of shingles peel up from the roof, they can often be straightened and glued down with a daub of asphalt cement. Drive one nail at the cement point to keep the shingle in place. Pick a warm day when the shingle

CEMENT UNDER CURLED AREA

TACK DOWN, THEN CEMENT OVER NAIL HEAD

will be at its most pliable, or warm it with a propane torch. If the material is too brittle to bend, the shingle should be replaced.

Torn shingles. If the tear does not extend into the overlap area of the next higher course of shingles, it can be mended with cement. (1) Lift the shingle and spread cement on the

underside, then press it firmly into place. (2) Spread a liberal coat of cement on the top side of the crack. (3) Nail the shingle on either side of the split. (4) Cover the nail heads with cement.

If the tear does extend into the overlap area, insert a sheet metal plate under the tear, and drive it up until it reaches at least four inches above the split. This may require removing nails in the course in which the tear is located, and possibly

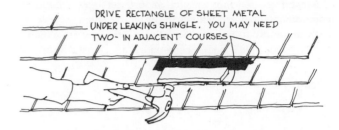

DRIVE RECTANGLE OF SHEET METAL UNDER LEAKING SHINGLE. YOU MAY NEED TWO- IN ADJACENT COURSES

the course above. Saw through the nails with a hacksaw blade if the shingles cannot be bent up enough to expose the nail heads for pulling them out with a hammer. Once the plate is in place, re-nail (through it if need be), then daub asphalt cement liberally on all exposed portions of the tear and on all nail heads.

Replacing a shingle. This begins to be touchy work. If you have doubts, call a professional to do the job. (1) Cut out as much of the damaged shingle as possible with heavy shears or tin snips (2) Pull out the nails that secure it. This involves lifting the shingles in the course above just enough to get at the nails. If they are brittle, saw off the old nails. (3) Patch any cuts or tears in the underlayment with asphalt cement once you have removed all of the damaged shingle. (4) Work the

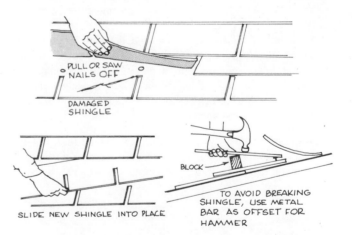

PULL OR SAW NAILS OFF

DAMAGED SHINGLE

SLIDE NEW SHINGLE INTO PLACE

BLOCK

TO AVOID BREAKING SHINGLE, USE METAL BAR AS OFFSET FOR HAMMER

new shingle into place, bending the shingles above as little as possible. (5) Nail to match pattern used on other shingles, using rust-proof, wide-headed roofing nails. (6) Daub cement on nail heads, and also use daubs of cement to secure each tab. (Some shingles have self-adhering tabs, in which case the last step is not required.)

Hip and ridge joints use specially formed shingles. These are replaced as any other shingle is, except that the underside of the shingle should be smeared liberally with cement before it is set into place. Cement all edges and nail heads after the shingle is in place.

• Repairing Wood Shingles

When a shingle or shake roof leaks, the cause is usually a splintered or cracked shingle, or one that has been lifted by the wind.

Shingles are cut in lengths of 16, 18, and 24 inches. Shakes are sometimes longer. The shingles are laid in overlapping courses, alternating with strips of rosin-sized building paper or unsaturated felt (not with the asphalt-saturated felt used in most other rooms). Depending on the degree of overlap, shingles run from three to four plies deep. They are nailed at the top edge, which is then covered by the succeeding course.

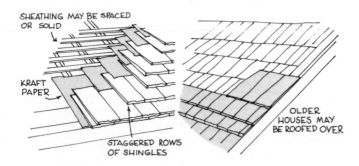

SHEATHING MAY BE SPACED OR SOLID

KRAFT PAPER

STAGGERED ROWS OF SHINGLES

OLDER HOUSES MAY BE ROOFED OVER

An original roof is laid directly on the sheathing, which may be solid, but is more likely to be spaced as shown in the sketch. It is not uncommon, however, to find that the roof of an older house is laid directly on an earlier roof of shingles or composition shingles.

Because of the light sheathing and non-continuous underlayment, shingle roofs should not be walked upon any more than necessary. The ladder-on-the-roof method for spreading weight (see page 81) is especially recommended for shingle roofs.

The simplest cause of a leak—and the simplest repair to make—is wind-lifted shingles, which need only to be pressed down flat, then secured with a nail. To avoid splitting the shingle, drill a guide hole for the nail. Daub a generous patch of asphalt roofing cement or outdoor caulking over the nail head to seal it to the shingle.

Sheet-metal patch. If you can pinpoint a small leak, but the shingles appear to be sound, an effective patch is a square of sheet metal driven up under the course of shingles where the

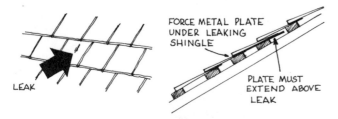

LEAK

FORCE METAL PLATE UNDER LEAKING SHINGLE

PLATE MUST EXTEND ABOVE LEAK

leak occurs, so that the top of the metal square goes beyond the leak. Whether the leak is in the shingles or the underlayment, this patch should seal it.

Cementing cracks. If the leak originates with a cracked or splintered shingle, cut or pull all splinters so that only large, solid pieces remain. Butt these tightly together and cement the

crack with asphalt roofing cement or an outdoor caulk (butyl, for example). Nail the separate halves in place to help protect

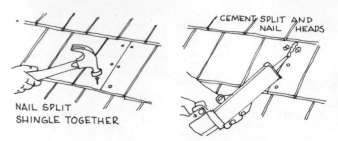

NAIL SPLIT SHINGLE TOGETHER

CEMENT SPLIT AND NAIL HEADS

the caulk. Drill guide holes for the nails and daub the heads with cement. If the crack is a wide one, it may be best to combine this repair with the sheet-metal patch.

Replacing shingles. If one or several shingles are damaged or decayed beyond repair, they should be removed and replaced. If you are not experienced at carpentry, call a roofer. This repair calls for skill and judgment. There are several steps: (1) Pull out as much damaged shingle as possible. Use a chisel to cut away the rest. (2) Remove nails that secured damaged shingle. In some cases, you will be able to pull them through the face of the shingle above. In most cases, you will have to pry the shingle above upwards enough to get a hacksaw under it, and then saw the nails off flush with the sheathing. (3) Measure the empty space, and cut a replacement shingle to fit closely. (4) Push and drive it into place, using a block of scrap wood and hammer to force the shingle into exact position. (5) Secure it with nails driven through the shingles above it. (6) Daub asphalt roofing cement or caulking over nail heads to seal them.

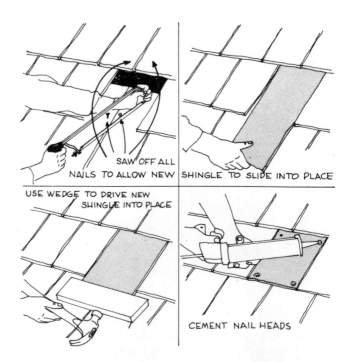

SAW OFF ALL NAILS TO ALLOW NEW SHINGLE TO SLIDE INTO PLACE

USE WEDGE TO DRIVE NEW SHINGLE INTO PLACE

CEMENT NAIL HEADS

The steps themselves are simple and logical enough, but the execution can become extremely trying when there are more nails than you expected, or the underlayment catches on the new shingle and keeps it from slipping into place.

• Ceramic Tile Roofs

There are two designs of ceramic tile used for roofing: Curved and flat. Both are laid over an asphalted felt underlayment but are secured differently.

Leaks usually are caused by one or more tiles being broken or somehow moved out of position. Sometimes there is also damage to the underlayment.

Regardless of the original roofing, replacement tiles should be hard-burned rather than soft-burned. Hard-burned tiles give a sharp ring when struck with metal; soft-burned tiles make a duller thumping sound. Harder tiles weather better.

Anytime you get on a tile roof, always step on two tiles at a time to minimize the danger of breaking tiles. Be especially cautious when walking on tile—it can be slippery and may move underfoot.

Replacing curved tiles. Also called Mission tiles, these are laid in alternate "base" and "cap" rows. The base rows are laid convex curve down and are secured to the roof sheathing

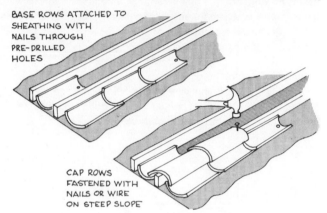

BASE ROWS ATTACHED TO SHEATHING WITH NAILS THROUGH PRE-DRILLED HOLES

CAP ROWS FASTENED WITH NAILS OR WIRE ON STEEP SLOPE

with nails (through pre-drilled holes). The cap rows are laid convex curve up. On a gentle slope, they are held in place only by their own weight. On steeper slopes, they may be secured to the roofing with wires.

In re-seating or replacing tiles, check the underlayment for cuts or tears. Seal these with asphalt cement before setting the tiles into place.

Flat tiles. Also called shingle tiles, these are usually molded so that short legs hook over strips of 1x3's nailed to the roof. Replacing them simply requires fitting them into place.

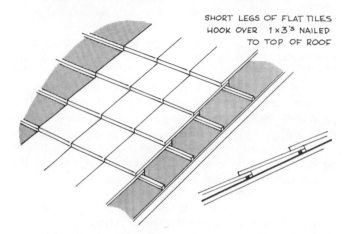

SHORT LEGS OF FLAT TILES HOOK OVER 1x3'S NAILED TO TOP OF ROOF

As with Mission tiles, check the underlayment for cuts or tears. Seal these with asphalt cement before placing tiles.

In either case, the ridge tiles are likely to be secured with mortar on all edges to prevent them from being blown off. If one of these is to be replaced, use a mason's hammer to chip away the mortar. Cement the replacement in place using the same mortar as for bricks (see page 89).

ADHESIVES AND PATCHES FOR ROOFS

Because of the variety of materials and combinations of materials used for roofing (and the objects that protrude through roofs), following is a quick summary of those adhesives or patching materials that mend particular roofs.

Asphalt cement is a cold-applied compound that is stiff enough to be ladled on with a putty knife, but soft enough to be daubed with a discarded paint brush. It is formulated from plastic—in fact, it usually is sold as "plastic asphalt cement" or "vinyl asphalt cement"—and impregnated with asphalt. The color is black. The material will bond to asphalt, metal, or wood.

Underlayments for finish roof are asphalt-saturated felt (generally called tar paper), unsaturated felt, and rosin-sized building paper (called kraft paper). Any of the three can be patched with asphalt cement.

In addition to repairing cracks in underlayment, asphalt cement is used to seal cracks in built-up roofing, to glue down asphalt shingles, to seal the edges of flashings, and to patch split shingles.

Butyl caulking compound is white or off-white—a rubberized material that stays flexible long after application. It is applied

to narrow cracks or small areas with a caulking gun. Bigger holes are easier to fill from a bulk can, using a putty knife. (A "bulk" can in this instance may be as small as a pint.)

Butyl caulking compound can be used to patch cracks in shingles, seal joints in flashings, seal cracks in mortar (such as chimney caps might develop), or seal the edges of flashings. It can be painted over.

Aluminized sealer or caulk is used principally on sheet-metal materials, such as flashings, gutters and downspouts, ducts, and skylight housings. Its color is aluminum. It can patch a fairly sizeable hole in sheet metal but is more commonly used to bond two pieces together. (One advantage is that it can be used during rain, since it bonds to wet surfaces.) It is simpler to use than the alternative, solder.

Clear butyl sealer or caulk is much like the aluminized material described above, except that the formulation is clear. It is used principally to make waterproof joints on plastic panel roofs but is a welcome patching material for cracks or broken seals in skylight domes. The sealer bonds to wood, glass, concrete, or metal.

Outside walls

Exterior walls of houses must balance a narrow line between being watertight and moisture-proof. They must repel all water, but they must also allow a minimum amount of vapor to pass in and out.

Usually windows, doors, and vents (high in the eaves and along the foundation line) accomplish this requirement. But the construction material itself must aid in the process or else the building may suffer chronically from mildew or other moisture-caused troubles of the sort.

Wood siding serves the purpose very well, and so does masonry in its commonest forms—brick, concrete block, and stucco.

The most persistent trouble with exterior walls is that the joints between the frames of doors and windows and the main framing separate, allowing water rather than vapor to pass through. These joints use metal or kraft paper flashing. The metal can corrode; both can bend. The flashing is further sealed at its edges with a caulking compound that may fail with age, even when the flashing itself remains sound.

Many inside walls have developed stains or cracks from just such a leak in an outside wall. Also, the siding itself can develop cracks that either leak or are unsightly.

Wood siding on a wood frame house is relatively easy to repair as long as the wood can be matched (some mill designs have been dropped). The specific techniques for repairing several conventional types of siding are described on pages 90-91. A shake-sided or shingle-sided wall is repaired in the same manner as a roof. See page 86 for notes on replacing shingles. Incidentally, the same warning holds true for walls as for roofs: Replacing a few shingles is fair game for an amateur, but any extensive revamping of a wall should be done by a professional.

Masonry walls are even more problematical for an amateur. Simple cracks are easy to patch with the methods outlined on page 73, in the section on floors. This holds true for either poured concrete or concrete block. The problem is in knowing if the motion which caused the crack has stopped. A simple test is to glue a thin strip of paper across the crack and watch it for about two weeks. If it twists, one part of the wall is moving, and it's time to consult a contractor to see why. If the crack is a simple result of a small pressure, a simple patch will solve the problem.

Brick walls usually crack along mortar joints; re-mortaring is tedious but within the scope of amateur skills.

Small cracks or holes in stucco walls are extremely time-consuming to patch and very expensive when done by a professional. The simple technique on the opposite page takes considerable time but is inexpensive.

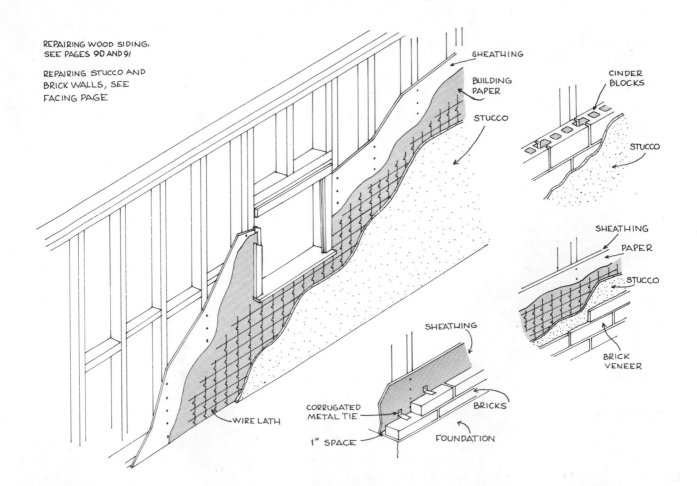

REPAIRING WOOD SIDING, SEE PAGES 90 AND 91

REPAIRING STUCCO AND BRICK WALLS, SEE FACING PAGE

SHEATHING

BUILDING PAPER

STUCCO

WIRE LATH

CINDER BLOCKS

STUCCO

SHEATHING

PAPER

STUCCO

BRICK VENEER

SHEATHING

CORRUGATED METAL TIE

1" SPACE

BRICKS

FOUNDATION

• Patching Stucco

There are two probable underlayers beneath a stucco wall. One is conventional wood framing with a layer of building paper and metal lath. The other is concrete block.

To patch stucco over wood framing. (1) Break out all loose, crumbly stucco. This will usually leave a hole in the lath as well. (2) Coat any tears in the building paper with asphalt cement. (3) "Sew" a patch into the lath. (4) Start the series of three coats of patching stucco.

The first coat fills the hole to within ¼ inch of the surface. First and second coats are made of one part Portland cement and three parts coarse sand, with enough water to make a fairly stiff paste.

As the first coat begins to set, scratch it fairly deeply with a nail point to provide a grip for the next coat.

Keep the patch damp with a fine spray while it cures for two days.

Then trowel the second coat to within ⅛ inch of the surface. Leave it fairly smooth rather than scoring it. Keep the second coat damp for two days.

The finish coat is made of one part Portland cement, 3 parts sand, and ¼-part lime. It is troweled on, then leveled with a thin straightedge.

To get a sandy finish, trowel it with a float as it begins to set up. To get a swirled or textured finish, use an old brush to scrub or jab the surface.

To patch stucco over concrete block. (1) Clean out the crumbled material. (2) Soak the blocks and adjacent stucco. (3) Proceed as with frame construction (except the first coat goes directly on the concrete block).

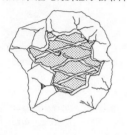

BREAK OUT ALL LOOSE STUCCO PIECES — PATCH TAR PAPER AND REWIRE BROKEN LATH

WET EDGES — SPREAD STUCCO MIX TO ¼" OF TOP — SCRATCH SURFACE BEFORE COMPLETELY DRY

AFTER DAMPENING AGAIN, SPREAD SECOND COAT TO WITHIN ⅛" OF TOP EXTERIOR

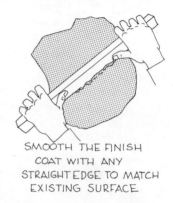

SMOOTH THE FINISH COAT WITH ANY STRAIGHTEDGE TO MATCH EXISTING SURFACE

• Repairing Brick

The mortar in brick walls, chimneys, or floors crumbles after a time, especially when subjected to hard winter freezes.

Patches can be made of vinyl cement or traditional mortar. The vinyl cement is far simpler to handle; it is applied with a caulking gun and smoothed with a putty knife.

Traditional mortar is slower and messier to handle, but it does not look like a patch.

In either case, clean out all crumbled mortar before you begin to patch. The joint should be cleaned to a depth of ¾ or 1 inch. Use a cold chisel to do most of the cleaning. Use a star drill to penetrate any hard surface area. Once the decayed mortar is removed, clean the joint thoroughly.

If you use vinyl cement, follow the manufacturer's instructions carefully.

If you use regular mortar, the following formula is a reliable one: 1 part cement, ½-part lime putty, 4 parts fine sand.

You have to mix the lime putty first. (For a typical wall job, get a 5-gallon can; fill it one-fourth full of water and add hydrated lime until the mass becomes buttery.)

To mix the mortar, stir sand and cement together until the color of the pile is uniform. Then add the lime, stirring slowly. Finally, add water slowly until

the mass becomes smooth enough to slide off a tilted trowel (but sticky enough to cling when the trowel is turned upside down).

Wet the bricks thoroughly before you begin and keep them wet as you work.

Apply the mortar with a small trowel.

Press the mortar firmly into the joint, making sure the joint is full. Slice off surplus mortar with an edge of the trowel, then strike the joint with the point.

After you have filled the joints to equal the lengths of eight to a dozen bricks, go back with a tool that will strike joints to match the rest of the wall.

Keep the work area damp for two or three days by constant wetting with a fine spray or by covering with burlap.

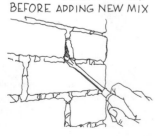

CHIP OUT LOOSE MORTAR WITH SCREWDRIVER BEFORE ADDING NEW MIX

TO PREVENT A SLOPPY JOB, KEEP FRESH MORTAR CLOSE TO WORK AREA

MATCH EXISTING JOINTS WITH SAME TYPE OF "STRIKING" TOOL

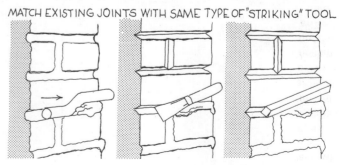

• Wood Siding

Wood siding continues to be the commonest of all exterior wall coverings for residences. It comes in literally hundreds of variations—different woods, different dimensions, different milled designs, different finished surfaces.

The greatest problem for a man who is faced with replacing a length of siding is in duplicating the original. Many designs are milled to order, then discontinued. This aside, there are three basic nailing methods as shown in the sketches. Once you know which one you have to deal with, the rest of the operation is relatively routine, even if it involves a sizeable area.

SIMPLE REPAIRS

In many cases, it is possible to repair a cracked or warped board without replacing it. Consider these possibilities carefully before you begin tearing siding off.

Warped boards. Pull the warp back into line with screws. Drill guide holes for the screws, trying for a stud if possible. If you use more than one screw keep them far enough apart to avoid splitting the board. Countersink the heads and cover them with putty before painting or staining.

Split boards. Butt the halves together as tightly as possible, then secure them with screws (following the guidelines in the paragraph on warped boards). Fill the crack with putty or an outdoor caulking (latex or butyl).

Knot holes or similar holes. Use caulking to fill a small hole. For a larger hole, plug with oakum, and then caulk.

REPLACING LENGTHS OF SIDING

Sometimes a board is so badly decayed or damaged that simple repair cannot save it. Replacement is time-consuming but rather simple.

You will need replacement boards of identical dimensions, a square, a measuring tape, a saw (preferably a backsaw), a pry-bar (and/or chisel), nails, and perhaps some small wedges and a tube of asphalt cement.

The exact approach depends upon the milled design of the siding and the method of nailing.

Bevel and bungalow. Although there are many minor variations in design as the sketches indicate, all are nailed in one of the two ways shown. (The method in which the nail passes through only one board is used most.)

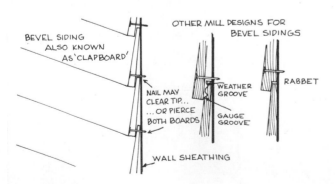

To remove old board: (1) Mark the saw cuts using a square to keep them at right angles. (2) With a pry-bar or stout chisel, pry up the bottom edge of the board to be removed. (3) Drive

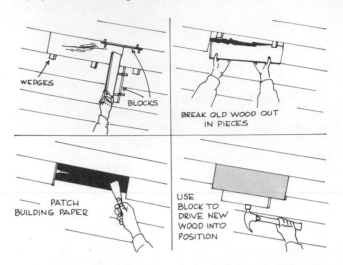

small wedges near the marks to keep the board raised slightly. (4) Cut through the board on both marks. You may want to tack small blocks to the lower edge of the board above, and to the face of the board below to avoid saw damage to them. (5) Break the damaged board out in pieces if possible, to avoid heavy pressure on the board overlapping from above. You may find it necessary to pry the board above the damaged one up enough to free the last bits and pieces. (6) Patch any cuts or tears in the building paper with asphalt cement. (7) Measure the width of the opening and trim replacement board to length. For greater accuracy, measure at both top and bottom of the opening. (8) Fit replacement board into opening. Use a block and hammer to drive it into exact position. (You may have to remove nails from the board above if the nailing method is not the recommended one.) (9) Nail to match existing pattern. (10) Caulk the end seams. (11) Seal and stain or paint to match house.

Shiplap and rustic. Because it is face-nailed flush to the sheathing, this type of siding is best sawn with a power saw set a fraction less deep than the true thickness of the siding. Once the saw cuts are made, pry up with a chisel inserted

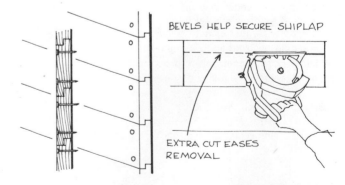

through the cuts. As soon as the nail heads can be made to pop free, pull them with a claw hammer and remove the board. Cement cuts in the underlayment. Trim the replacement to fit, face-nail it, and caulk the cuts and the nail heads. Seal and paint or stain.

Tongue-and-groove. Replacing tongue-and-groove is much like replacing shiplap, except that the boards are blind-nailed and fitted together more firmly. It may be useful to make a lengthwise cut with a power saw in addition to the end cuts. This will give prying leverage to ease the tongue out of the groove and vice versa. Cement cuts in the underlayment. Trim the replacement to fit, which in this case also involves ripping the inner lip off the groove so that the board is snug against

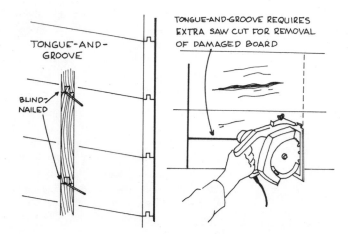

TONGUE-AND-GROOVE

BLIND NAILED

TONGUE-AND-GROOVE REQUIRES EXTRA SAW CUT FOR REMOVAL OF DAMAGED BOARD

the tongue of the board below. The replacement board will have to be face-nailed or secured with screws. In either case, countersink the heads and cover with putty or caulk. Caulk the end cuts, then seal and stain or paint. (It would be useful to read the section on removing and replacing tongue-and-groove flooring, pages 71-72, for additional information about technique.)

Board and batten. The easiest of all siding to repair, board and batten requires only the prying off of one batten, or two battens and one board. They are face-nailed and admirably designed to accept pry-bars. In most cases, it is just as well to replace the whole length rather than salvaging some fraction.

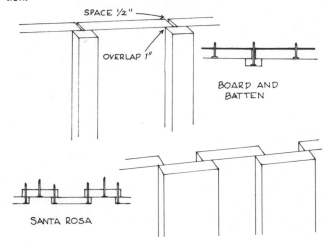

SPACE ½"

OVERLAP 1"

BOARD AND BATTEN

SANTA ROSA

Santa Rosa. In essence, this is a variation on board and batten and is just as simple to repair.

In each of the latter two cases, be sure to seal cuts or tears in the underlayment, which is especially vulnerable to moisture seeping against it.

CAULKING OUTSIDE WALLS

Builders usually use a butyl caulk during the framing of a house at points where water seal is important.

Butyl caulk's advantages are continued flexibility, ability to fill good-sized gaps, and ability to take any type of paint.

It comes in small tubes that fit caulking guns. It also comes in cans, from which it can be applied with a putty knife. This method works better than the gun where large gaps are to be filled.

A second type of caulk, somewhat simpler to apply, is rope-like. This compound comes in spool form. You simply unwind it and press it into the crack with finger pressure.

There are four places in walls that require careful caulking on a periodic basis.

First is between the frame of a window or door and the main frame of the house. The top of the header is especially vulnerable, but the sides of a frame and the lower side of the sill should be checked for cracks.

Second is within the frame of a window or door. One especially vulnerable point is between the track of a sliding door or window and the sill on which it rests (or the jamb from which it hangs).

Third is any gap between lengths of siding (see the illustration). Shrinkage and warping sometimes open relatively wide gaps between boards.

Fourth is any point at which a deck or other flat surface abuts a wall, or any framing member protrudes through a wall. The joists that support a deck are a typical example, as are ceiling joists that extend to form a patio roof.

Tint caulking compound with oil paint colors kneaded in if you must match siding.

CAULKING GUN FOR DOOR, WINDOW JOINTS

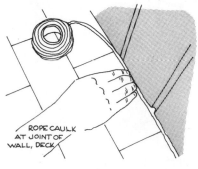

ROPE CAULK AT JOINT OF WALL, DECK

BULK CAULK FOR BIG JOBS

Terms, tools, and materials

There are literally thousands of dollars worth of tools and materials on store shelves. The following section groups tools in alphabetical categories, explains some uses, and chooses a basic supply for those who have no tools.

ABRASIVES

There are three basic uses for abrasives —trimming for fine fit, smoothing surfaces, and cleaning surfaces.

Sandpaper. Sandpaper is made of flint chips glued to a paper backing. More expensive variations are garnet paper and aluminum oxide paper. All come in sheets for hand use and in discs and belts for use with power sanders. All are graded by the size of the abrasive chips (and thus by their scouring power).

Extremely coarse paper for fast, rough work is 30 grit or 50 grit. These are used for removing old paint, for trimming down rough siding, and for trimming door edges. (When the distance involved is ¼ inch or less, sanding is a surer method than sawing and perhaps easier than planing.)

Medium, 80 grit paper is used for removing scratches in wood, for final fitting of snug joints, and for removing corrosion from metal.

Fine, 120 grit paper is used primarily as a final sanding before paint is applied to wood. This grit is also used to clean metal for painting or soldering.

There are finer grits, all the way to 600, but the use of these is limited to cabinet work and other fine carpentry.

A hand block and a range of papers are basic equipment for tool boxes. For big jobs, rent a power tool. Belt sanders are easiest for novices to control.

Steel wool. Steel wool is a tangle of steel wire that is generally more useful than sandpaper in cleaning metal—especially plumbing pipes—preparatory to fitting or soldering. It is gauged on the coarseness of the steel strand.

ADHESIVES

Adhesives are designed to make two surfaces adhere tightly together. The generic name for them is "glue," but they are also sold as "cements" and "sealers." Glue types have proliferated since plastic and epoxy. Great as the epoxies are, they should be approached with caution on one score: Be sure that you want the joint to last forever before applying epoxy. Joints that might require later dismantling or adjustment should be secured with some other adhesive.

Caulks (see below) differ from adhesives by the fact that adhesives are not designed to fill gaps. (Also see Solder, which is both a sealer and an adhesive.)

To make the best glue bond, it is important to follow manufacturer's directions exactly. For instance, when gluing porous materials, the directions will often advise you to spread a coating on each surface, let it dry, and then spread second coats before you join the pieces. If you skip this step, the material may absorb most of the glue, leaving the joint "starved." Most glues will not bond at temperatures below 70°. Life of some is shortened by high temperatures (and drying time is speeded up).

For any glue to bond properly, the surfaces to be joined must be clean, dry (except with epoxies), and as close-fitting as possible. (Wooden surfaces that do not match can be bridged to some degree by mixing sawdust with the glue.)

Animal or fish glues. The earliest of woodworking glues. Most satisfactory for use indoors where temperature and humidity do not vary widely. Can be loosened with heat and water for subsequent adjustment or re-gluing—an especially valuable quality in cabinets. Buy when needed.

White glue (also called polyvinyl glue). A generally useful glue, especially for porous surface. It sets quickly, does not stain, and gives a slightly resilient joint. Applications and limitations are about the same as for animal or fish glue. It is handier to keep in the house since it can be used on paper, plastics, and other miscellaneous materials that animal glue does not bond. Good to keep on hand.

Resorcin resin. Although expensive, it makes a very strong waterproof joint.

Resorcinal glue is often used in building boats and is one of the most durable glues for outdoor use. It will hold on oily and resinous woods. To prepare it, you mix powdered catalyst with liquid resin. You have about 10 minutes to form the joint after applying the glue. The liquid resin is flammable. It leaves a conspicuous dark line when it dries and tends to show through paint. It is generally sold as "Waterproof Glue." Buy when needed.

Epoxy Resin. This is the strongest adhesive for home repair. It comes in several forms. In the putty-like form, you get two soft sticks, knead a pinch of each together, and apply. This type has some gap-filling capacity and also can be used to repair leaks around pipe joints. Good to keep on hand. The surface glue comes in two tubes. A bead of each is mixed together on a disposable piece of board or cardboard. (A few epoxies come in tubes that allow mixing within the larger tube, thus avoiding skin contact and the mess.) Buy when needed.

Epoxy will set at lower temperatures than other glues, and in wet conditions. There is no need to clamp. Curing time ranges from 12 to 24 hours.

Epoxy will bond to almost any rigid material but is most frequently used with metal. Special formulations are used to patch concrete. See page 73.

BRACES AND BITS

The old, hand-powered approach to drilling large-diameter holes in wood may still be a useful technique, but a brace and bit is not often required for basic repairs around a house. If you do not have one, it may be just as wise to rent a power drill when the need arises.

CAULKS

Caulks combine an ability to fill gaps with adhesive qualities. There are differing formulations for use with different materials.

A supply of two or three are basic to home-repairs supplies. On page 61 is a detailed summary of the types used indoors; page 87 lists types used for roofing materials; page 91 lists types used for other outdoor repairs.

The basic three to have on hand are tub and sink caulk for use around those wet areas; asphalt cement for use on the roof; and butyl caulk for other outdoor work. Aluminized sealer for metal might also be handy.

CHISELS

Grooves, notches, and narrow cuts that cannot be finished with a saw (such as mortises) are cut with a chisel. Wood chisels have one flat side and one beveled side. Common widths are ¼-inch, ½ inch, ¾ inch, and 1 inch. A basic tool box should contain one narrow and one wide chisel for fine or fast cutting. Chisels with steel-capped handles can be driven with a hammer—saving the expense of a mallet and the risk of splitting a wooden handle.

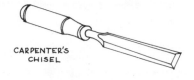
CARPENTER'S CHISEL

Cold chisels, for metal or masonry work, are infrequently needed for home repairs.

CLAMPS

Available in a variety of shapes, clamps serve several temporary purposes.

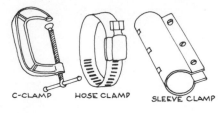
C-CLAMP   HOSE CLAMP   SLEEVE CLAMP

C-Clamp. The principal use of a C-clamp is to hold pieces of material together while glue dries, but it has many other uses. It holds materials in position for purposes such as setting or curing warped boards, holding a temporary patch over a leak in a pipe, or serving as a light vise to hold a length of board being worked upon. These clamps are measured by the width of their jaws. It is useful to have them in pairs, starting with 1 inch for tight work, and ending with a pair of 6-inch clamps for heavy duty. It might be useful to have one set between the extremes.

Hose clamps. A supply of hose clamps is useful, especially if you have plastic pipe in the garden. They can be used as a temporary patch for leaks in metal pipe as well as permanent clamps for joints in plastic pipe. They are made in several metals; the best all-purpose choice is stainless steel. Sizes are number-coded; the bigger numbers describe the smallest clamps. Diameters are adjustable, making the clamps versatile.

Sleeve clamps (or pipe clamps). Two or three sleeve clamps in the sizes of your pipes are well worth having. They are the most efficient and durable clamps for leaking pipes.

DRILLS

There are two principal types of drills—rotary and chipping. Rotary types are used on wood, metal, and—if tipped with carbide—masonry. Chipping drills are used only on masonry.

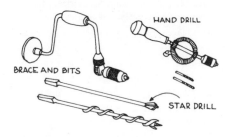
BRACE AND BITS   HAND DRILL   STAR DRILL

A small hand-powered rotary drill is a basic tool for any tool box. One or two chipping drills (called star drills) can be quite useful.

Power drills are easily available from rental shops when big jobs come up.

Hand drill. A hand drill, with bits ranging from 1/32 to ⅜-inch, will take care of most routine jobs around the house.

Brace and bit. Although not a basic tool, a brace and bit is a handy tool if you have one. Not only does it drill large-diameter holes (up to 1 inch) with hand power, it is an excellent screwdriver when fitted with bits designed for the purpose.

Star drills. Simple steel rods with star-shaped cutting tips, star drills cost so little that it is worth having two (¼ inch and ½ inch) in the tool box. (See page 65 for some hints on using them.)

FILES

Files are used principally on narrow surfaces and deep cuts rather than on the wide surfaces where sandpaper or steel wool are more effective abrasives.

There are separate types of files used for wood and metal, and several shapes. One half-round metal file is basic to a home repairman's tool kit. It can be used to smooth cuts on either flat or tubular metal.

METAL FILES   WOOD RASP

Wood files are less frequently used, but it may be useful to have at least one medium-rough file at hand, especially for shaping and smoothing cutouts in wood (such as holes for pipes, notches between irregular fitting wood members, etc.).

HAMMERS

Since the very first time a Stone Age man lashed a rock to a stick, the hammer has been the most useful tool to have around the house. The principal use today is for driving nails; the first hammer in any tool kit should be a 13-ounce claw hammer. But there are other considerations.

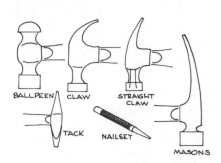
BALLPEEN   CLAW   STRAIGHT CLAW   TACK   NAILSET   MASONS

Ballpeen. A machinist's hammer meant for working metal, the ballpeen is generally not needed in a repair kit.

Claw. The essential hammer to have is the claw. For general work, a 13-ounce hammer with curved claws for nail pulling is the most versatile tool. The one-piece metal hammer has the greatest durability. A hammer with straight claws can double as a small axe for splitting boards. A light (7 ounce) hammer is useful for tacking and bradding; many women prefer it to a heavier model.

Mason's hammer. You will probably know if you need a mason's hammer. The tool is used principally to split bricks or other masonry, and also to tap bricks into place.

Tack hammer. Used principally in laying carpet or in doing fine work with small tacks, the principal advantage of a tack hammer is a magnetic head that holds small nails and tacks with ease.

KNIVES

Of the dozens of knives available for different jobs, three are essential.

Jackknife. A sharp jackknife is worth half a dozen specialty tools. It can be used to trim splintered edges of boards, whittle pegs, cut or scrape paint, free nail heads by trimming around them, pare linoleum, mark saw lines or mortises, and open stubborn packages of other tools or materials—just to name a few of its capacities.

Linoleum knife. The curved point of a linoleum knife makes it an ideal tool for deep scoring not only linoleum, but a great many pliable materials.

Putty knife. Not a cutting knife, but rather a blade for spreading any kind of paste material from putty to patching plaster, the putty knife is available in many sizes. A ½-inch or 1-inch blade and a 3-inch or 4-inch blade will cover most situations.

LADDERS

No home should be without two ladders —a short ladder for use indoors and a longer one for use on the outside walls and roof. The several choices are best guided by the architecture of your home.

STEPLADDER   EXTENSION LADDER

Ladders of all types range widely in cost, depending partly on the material of manufacture, partly on the quality of that material.

Wood ladders are weighty — to 4 pounds a running foot — and not tremendously durable. But they are far less expensive than metal ladders. In purchasing one, avoid those that are painted. Rather, look for exposed wood and check it closely for cracks, knots, or other weak spots. Also gauge the durability of rung fastenings and reinforcements, and any other hardware.

Lightweight aluminum and still lighter magnesium ladders weigh as little as one half the weight of wood but may cost three times as much. If a small woman is to use the ladder, the saving in carrying weight will repay any added cost.

Ladders of all types can be rented. This is convenient for many, especially those renting homes. Most homeowners have steady call for ladders and can save both time and money by owning at least one.

Extension ladder. The most versatile type of ladder for long reaches outdoors is the extension ladder. Most houses can use a 20-footer (it will reach only 17 feet because a 3-foot overlap is required), but the extensions range all the way to 48 feet. Choose a length that will let you step off one side of the ladder and onto the roof. (See page 81 for hints on ladder safety.)

Straight ladder. Just two long legs with rungs between, the straight ladder is cheap, light, and able to reach somewhat higher than typical stepladders (but not as far as extensions).

Stepladder. Folding ladders (or stepladders) rest quite stably on four feet. Because they do not have to lean against any supporting surface, they are highly useful for working on ceilings and working on walls that must not be marred.

They range from four to ten feet in height; when using one, keep your hips at or below the top step, or the ladder will tend to become unstable. On soft ground outdoors, two wide boards should be put under pairs of the ladder feet to spread the weight load.

Two-in-one ladder. A special locking device on some extension ladders allows the extension to pivot, forming a stepladder.

LEVELS

Levels are straightedges with small bubble tubes set into them. One good level is basic to a home repairman's tool box. It is useful in checking the slope of a floor (for drainage, or installing a washer-dryer), a gutter, a door frame, and dozens of other surfaces. Those with a check for true vertical as well as horizontal are best.

NAILSET

A nailset is a pointed metal spike that allows nails to be driven flush (or sunken) without risking hammer damage to wood surfaces. The tips are scaled to match nail heads.

PATCHING MATERIALS

These include all caulks (see page 92), patching plaster, spackle, and related paste patches. See pages 61 and 73 for detailed descriptions.

PLANES

Wood planes are handy devices for trimming door edges and other edges that must fit tight.

There are two basic designs—the block plane and the bench plane. The block plane is mostly a cabinet maker's tool. The bench plane is for rougher work.

BENCH PLANE   BLOCK PLANE

Bench planes are called jack planes when the length of the sole is 7 to 11 inches, or fore planes when longer.

A 10 or 11-inch jack plane is the most versatile tool, but is not a critical part of a home tool box. (See page 38 in the section on doors for some hints on using a plane.)

PLIERS

Pliers come in several shapes and with several different kinds of jaw action. Simple slip joint pliers with a wire-cutter at the back of the jaw will do most jobs. If you specialize, the next two types to get are a pair of needle-nose pliers for working in tight spots and for working with wire, and a pair of pliers with parallel jaws.

RULES

Exact measurement is the base of success in many repairs. Measuring devices are extremely various; to cover all of the common repair situations you will need three types: a tape, a folding rule, and a carpenter's square.

Measuring tape. Most measuring tapes now come on spring-winding spools and are made either of fabric or steel. The ideal is a 20 foot or longer steel tape clearly marked in 1/100 of an inch—or at least 1/32. This is the best measuring device for making many long measurements.

Folding rule. Many measurements do not allow the rule to lie on a flat surface, and yet depend on it remaining in a true line. The six-foot folding rule usually answers these requirements and also allows you to make fairly long measurements without a helper. This type of rule is extremely handy for measuring pipe.

Square. The square is a simple steel piece with a right angle bend in it and with measurements etched on the face. It is useful for marking square cuts across boards and also for checking the squareness of many joints.

SAWS

The maid of all work among saws is the crosscut. It and the compass saw (or keyhole saw) will get you through most home repairs. Add a hacksaw for metal work, and you have the basic saws for a home tool kit. There are a couple of more specialized saws worth consideration.

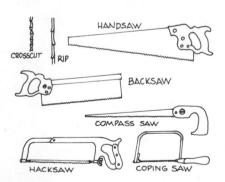

Backsaw. Named for a reinforcing strip of metal along the back, the backsaw is for fine work (the one example cited in this book of a use for it is sawing hardwood floorboards to fit). Many miter boxes are designed to fit backsaws for this reason.

Crosscut saw. The teeth are beveled—alternating left and right—so that the saw will cut efficiently across wood grain. This saws slower than a ripsaw with the grain but makes a neat cut. Blades are usually 20 to 26 inches long. There may be from 7 to 12 teeth points per inch of blade. For all-purpose use, choose a 26-inch blade with 7 or 8 points per inch.

Coping saw. The coping saw is a fine-bladed saw with a deeply arcing frame, used for cutting curves (mostly used for cabinetwork).

Compass saw. Also known as a keyhole saw, the compass saw's main use is in starting cuts in the center of a board or panel from a small drilled hole. The narrow blade also allows curving cuts (although not such scrolled cuts as a coping saw can make). Still, the compass saw can offer you an advantage in making cutouts for pipes or vents.

Ripsaw. A coarse-cutting, fast saw for making cuts along the grain, the ripsaw's teeth are not beveled and are not as sharply slanted as those of a crosscut saw. In effect, they are a long row of tiny chisels. This saw is unlikely to be of much practical use for home repairs.

Hacksaws. A hacksaw is frequently needed to cut bolts to correct length, to saw through galvanized or copper pipe, and for similar tasks. The blades run from 18 points-to-the-inch all the way to 32 points-to-the-inch and can be changed easily. In general, the coarser blades are used to cut solid materials. Fine blades are used to cut delicate tubing.

SCREWDRIVERS

The lowly screwdriver is probably the most frequently used tool a homeowner possesses. And, he probably botches more jobs with this simple tool than with any other. Here are some reasons.

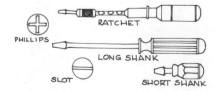

First, the screwdriver is really too handy for its own good. It's likely to be the first thing you grab when you need to scrape dried paint off a concrete floor, dig out a weed, or clean a mortar joint in masonry. A little abuse of this kind, and your screwdriver is blunted and dull. Next time it is put to its proper purpose, it may very well slip on a tight screw—burring the screw head and gouging the work.

Or a bad fit may lead to trouble. If the driver is too small or too large for the slot of the screw, it can easily burr the screw head or gouge the work. For this reason, you should try to keep at least three sizes around the house. This involves no big expense: a 49-cent, wood-handled screwdriver is as satisfactory for most work as a more expensive one.

Again, there are many situations where an ordinary driver will not work. You need a Phillips screwdriver to handle a Phillips screw. And you need at least a small selection of the other types of drivers shown on these pages to handle all the screws and small bolts you encounter at home these days.

Many jobs are bungled by screwdrivers that are simply no good. Still another source of grief may be that your screwdriver is adequate but you are not installing the screws correctly. In all but the very softest wood, you should drill lead holes for screws. In hardwood, the holes should be approximately the diameter of the screw's core (the maximum diameter of the threaded part, measured from thread to thread bottom). In softwood, the holes can be about two-thirds the core diameter, and smaller still in the end grain of the wood. When using long screws, you should also drill larger shank-sized holes in the wood to the depth of the screw's shank (the unthreaded portion), or use a screw pilot bit that cuts both hole sizes at once.

If a good screwdriver requires undue muscle and tends to burr the slot with the screw only partially in, you should remove and discard that screw and enlarge the lead hole for another. With brass screws (especially long ones going into hardwood), it is a good idea to drive in and remove a similar steel screw first, to form threads for the softer screw.

Tips for the screwdriver buyer. When you buy a large, ordinary screwdriver, choose one with a square shank. Then, when you have a stubborn screw to seat or loosen, you can easily use a wrench on the square shank and apply extra leverage.

You will find that a long screwdriver lets you apply more power than a shorter one with a tip of the same size, and the long one is less likely to be tilted in the screw slot. It's best to save the stubby one for spots where you're cramped for space.

If you need to install a number of large screws, a screwdriver bit in a carpenter's brace works easily and rapidly.

SOLDER

Whenever you need to join two pieces of metal together at home—anything from electrical wiring to joining lengths of roof gutter—soldering will give you a strong and very smooth joint. Once considered almost an art, it's easy to do with today's soldering tools and fluxes.

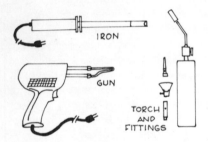

Unlike a glue or cement, solder actually alloys with the surfaces of the metals being joined—if you follow the rules. You need to clean the parts well with steel wool or sandpaper, use the proper solder and flux, and use a soldering tool that is capable of heating the parts, not just the solder. The flux further cleans the parts and prevents oxidation. The technique is to heat the joint to the point where solder and flux will melt and flow smoothly around it, continue heating a moment to vaporize the flux, and then allow the joint to cool undisturbed.

Ordinary solder is an alloy of tin and lead. A 40/60 solder (40 per cent tin) is good for most jobs; a 60/40 solder is preferable for electronic and hobby work. Resin-core solder is the most used and necessary for electrical work (it doesn't corrode). Acid-core solder holds better on sheet-metal work (wash with water after it's cooled). You can also use solid wire or bar solder with either a resin or acid flux. Buy any flux-core solder in small quantities because the flux core deteriorates.

A 175-watt soldering iron will serve to splice either electrical wiring or light sheet metal.

A propane or butane torch with necessary tips will do any typical home sheet-metal repair and is otherwise a handy tool to have.

Soldering guns, widely used for electrical and hobby work, are another possibility; they are not shaped well for use with sheet metal. The focus is too sharp.

WRENCHES

Wrenches come in all manner of shapes for all kinds of specialized uses. There

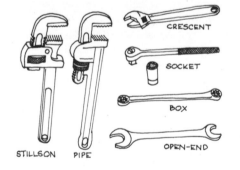

are two kinds that should be included in a home tool box. One is the pipe wrench, and the other is the crescent. Both are adjustable.

Box wrenches. These wrenches are important to machinists, but not widely useful around the house. They are mostly used on hex-headed bolts. Their advantage is precise fit.

Crescent wrenches. Crescents have some of the advantages of both open-end and box wrenches. Their technical weakness and practical strength is that they adjust. A good tool box should have two—a small one for tight spots and a big one for heavy duty.

Open-end wrenches. Much like box wrenches, the open-end wrench is better adapted to square-headed bolts and less suited for hexagonal ones.

Pipe wrenches. The adjustable jaws of a pipe wrench are mounted on the handle in such a way that pressure increases the grip (not true of Crescents or Stillsons). This design is meant to grip round pipes. A home tool box should have one 12-inch and one 10-inch (or longer) for plumbing repairs.

Socket wrenches. The advantages of socket wrenches are that they have ratchet handles (so they can work well with a limited arc), and they have snug-fitting heads of varying sizes. They are, however, expensive — especially when you need a whole range of heads.

Stillson wrenches. The jaws of a Stillson operate in the same way as Crescent wrench jaws do, but the handle is set straight rather than at an angle. As a result, you can exert more pressure on work out in the open, but less than a Crescent will allow in cramped quarters.

PHOTOGRAPHERS

Paul Aller: page 10, 11. Eastman Chemical Products: page 13 (top left). V. Lee Oertle: page 63. Ells Marugg: page 5 (bottom center, bottom right). Tom Riley: page 14. Darrow M. Watt: cover, page 5 (top, bottom left), 6, 13 (top right, bottom).